Religiosity, Secularity and Pluralism in the Global East

Religiosity, Secularity and Pluralism in the Global East

Special Issue Editors

Fenggang YANG
Francis Jae-ryong Song
SAKURAI Yoshihide

MDPI • Basel • Beijing • Wuhan • Barcelona • Belgrade

MDPI

Special Issue Editors

Fenggang YANG
Purdue University
USA

Francis Jae-ryong Song
Kyung Hee University
Korea

SAKURAI Yoshihide
Hokkaido University
Japan

Editorial Office
MDPI
St. Alban-Anlage 66
4052 Basel, Switzerland

This is a reprint of articles from the Special Issue published online in the open access journal *Religions* (ISSN 2077-1444) from 2018 to 2019 (available at: https://www.mdpi.com/journal/religions/special_issues/east)

For citation purposes, cite each article independently as indicated on the article page online and as indicated below:

LastName, A.A.; LastName, B.B.; LastName, C.C. Article Title. *Journal Name* **Year**, *Article Number, Page Range.*

ISBN 978-3-03897-808-4 (Pbk)
ISBN 978-3-03897-809-1 (PDF)

Contents

Jens Reinke
Sacred Secularities: Ritual and Social Engagement in a Global Buddhist China

About the Special Issue Editors

Fenggang YANG is Professor of Sociology, the founding Director of the Center on Religion and Chinese Society at Purdue University, West Lafayette, Indiana. He is the founding Editor of the *Review of Religion and Chinese Society*. He has been elected and served as the President of the Society for the Scientific Study of Religion (2014-15) and the first President of the East Asian Society for the Scientific Study of Religion (2018-2020). His research focuses on the sociology of religion, religious change in China and immigrant religion in the United States. He is the author of *Atlas of Religion in China: Social and Geographical Contexts* (2018), *Religion in China: Survival and Revival under Communist Rule* (2012), and *Chinese Christians in America: Conversion, Assimilation, and Adhesive Identities* (1999), and the co-editor of more than ten books. Among his numerous journal articles, two won distinguished article awards. He has given many invited lectures and keynote presentations at major universities and professional associations in the US, Asia and Europe. His media interviews have appeared on National Public Radio, *New York Times, Washington Post, Los Angeles Times, USA Today, Time, Economist, CNN, BBC,* etc.

Francis Jae-ryong Song is Professor of Sociology Department and former Dean of Graduate School, Kyung Hee University. He is Director of the Institute for Religion and Civic Culture at Kyung Hee University. He is past Chairman of the Korean Association for Sociology of Religion. Dr. Song received his Msc and Ph.D. from the Department of Sociology, University of Bristol, UK. His research interests lie with a liberal communitarian view in such areas as culture, religion, ethics and knowledge. He is the author of *Religion and Social Progress* (co-authored in Korean); *Communitarianism in the Postmodern Culture* (sole-authored in Korean). He has recently published translations of books including *Religion in China* (Fenggang Yang), *Varieties of Religion Today* (Charles Taylor) and *On Secularization* (David Martin). His recent presentations include, "The Cultural Habits of the Heart of Confucianism and Christianity: Focused on 'Transcendental Horizon' of Zuo Guangdou's and Thomas More's Religious Life" (2017 EASSSR Conference, Hong Kong Baptist University); "Development of a Korean model of religiosity measurement based on Korean religious experiences and values", (2017 ISSR Conference, University of Lausanne, Switzerland).

SAKURAI Yoshihide is a professor of sociology at the Graduate School of Letters, Hokkaido University, Japan. He obtained his Ph.D. in Development Studies of Thailand at Hokkaido University and has published more than twenty books (in Japanese) about contemporary religion in Korea, China and Japan. One of his English papers is included in the Hokkaido University Collection of Academic Papers : http://eprints.lib.hokudai.ac.jp/dspace/index.jsp?locale=en. He has been executive board members of several academic associations such as the Japanese Association for the Study of Religion and Society (President from June 2009 to 2011; Chief Editor, Religion and Society from 2014 to 2016), the Hokkaido Sociological Association (President from July 2011 to June 2013), Japanese Association for Religious Studies, The Japanese Society for Thai Studies, The Japanese and Chinese Society for Sociology, RC22 of ISA, ISSR, and EASSSR.

Preface to "Religiosity, Secularity and Pluralism in the Global East"

This special issue of Religions is part of the fruits of the Inaugural Conference of the East Asian Society for the Scientific Study of Religion (EASSSR), which was held at the Singapore Management University on July 3–5, 2018. The theme, "Religiosity, Secularity and Pluralism in the Global East," is well articulated in these two paragraphs of the Call for Papers:

East Asia is felt throughout the world. Whilst the region's economic and political power has been a reason for both global integration and resistance in recent decades, its presence within the rest of the world has been forged over centuries of migration and the establishment and strengthening of diasporic communities. Such communities have helped to shape the societies and cultures of their host countries, of their home countries, and, through such interplay, of the diasporas themselves. To unify these constituent parts (host country, home country, diasporic community), and to represent both the expansion of East Asian influence around the world, and its reflexive relationship with the places in which it has taken root, Yang Fenggang's concept of the "Global East" has been most helpful. The Global East encompasses not just the countries of East Asia—China, Korea and Japan—but these countries' diasporic communities, and the transnational linkages that serve to connect and shape both country and community as well. Additionally, East Asia is also host to diasporic communities of its own, which adds another layer of connectivity and influence to the framing of the Global East.

The effects of the Global East are felt in many walks of life, but one of the most transformative has to be religion. The religious landscapes of China, Korea, and Japan (including but not limited to state-sponsored atheism, shamanism, Shintoism, resurgent Buddhism/Christianity) are replicated and challenged in their diasporic communities, which, over time, have been shaped by the religious traditions of Southeast Asia, Europe, North America, and beyond. For the diasporic communities located within East Asia, the reverse is also true. These linkages between home country and diasporic community, and between community and host country have led to the circulation and sharing of religion and religious idea(l)s, and to the sharpening or dilution of (anti-)religious sensibilities. Greater religious diversity is an invariable outcome of such processes, yet the extent to which such diversity leads to religious co-operation, competition or conflict within and between individuals, families, communities, organisations and territories still deserves much more research attention. Accordingly, there is a need for more focused consideration of the topics of religiosity, secularity and pluralism in the Global East.

This special issue includes 11 articles, which is only a very small number of papers presented at the conference. However, the articles cover various religions in various East Asian societies and diasporic communities. The Presidential Address by Fenggang Yang and the Keynote-turned articles by Grace Davie and Jose Casanova offer important theoretical and methodological suggestions for research on religion in East Asia. Indeed, the nature and complexity of East Asia's religions merit the adoption of a new concept—the Global East, a view shared by scholars at the inaugural East Asian Society for the Scientific Study of Religion conference.

The Inaugural Conference of EASSSR was made possible by the host institution, Singapore Management University, especially Professor Lily Kong, and the local program committee led by Dr. Orlando Woods. We wish to thank these cosponsors: Brill Academic Publishers, Fetzer Institute, Nanyang Technological University's School of Humanities and School of Social Sciences, Kyung Hee University's Institute for Religion and Civic Culture, Purdue University's Center on Religion and

Chinese Society (through a grant from the John Templeton Foundation), and Singapore Management University's Wee Kim Wee Centre. This special issue of Religions was made possible in part with the financial support of the Fetzer Institute. As the guest editors, we would like to express our appreciation to Ms. Jie Gu and other editors of *Religions* who provided excellent service in the process of review and publishing.

Fenggang YANG, Francis Jae-ryong Song, SAKURAI Yoshihide
Special Issue Editors

religions

MDPI

Article

Religion in the Global East: Challenges and Opportunities for the Social Scientific Study of Religion

Fenggang Yang(iD)

Center on Religion and Chinese Society, Purdue University, West Lafayette, IN 47907, USA; fyang@purdue.edu

Received: 25 September 2018; Accepted: 9 October 2018; Published: 10 October 2018

Abstract: This essay is based on the Presidential Address at the East Asian Society for the Scientific Study of Religion Inaugural Conference on 3–5 July 2018 in Singapore. It discusses some aspects of the key concepts, some of the distinct characteristics of religion in East Asia, and some implications for the social scientific study of religion in general.

Keywords: Global East; religion; religiosity; atheism; Sheilaism; spiritual but not religious

1. The Notion of the Global East

The Inaugural Conference of the East Asian Society for the Scientific Study of Religion set the theme as "Religiosity, Secularity, and Pluralism in the Global East". The terms "religion", "religiosity", "secularity", and "pluralism" all need careful examination and reexamination in the context of the Global East. But first of all, what is the Global East?

The Global East is a cultural and social concept that includes East Asian societies and ethnic communities of East Asians around the world that maintain East Asian cultural traditions, are closely connected with East Asia, and play important roles in East Asian developments. These societies, communities, and individuals share distinct social and cultural characteristics. The Global East, as a new concept, is necessary primarily because the existing groupings of countries in the world are either Euro-centric or North-Atlantic-centric and may lead to improper understanding or misunderstanding of East Asian societies, communities, and individuals. Moreover, this concept may help in the effort to reconceptualize and improve measurements of "religion", "religiosity", "secularity", and other key terms in the social scientific study of religion in general.

When we take a broad view of the contemporary world, there have been two widely-used ways of grouping countries in some sort of geographical sense: East versus West, which was commonly used during the Cold War, and North versus South, which has become popular since the 1970s. While the East-West dichotomy was based on the ideological conflict between the Communist-ruled countries and the so-called "free world" (Buchholz 1961; Loth 1994),[1] the North-South division is primarily about the economic divide between developed countries and underdeveloped or developing countries (Horowitz 1966; Erb 1977; Eckl and Weber 2007; Reuveny and Thompson 2007). However, it is difficult to fit East Asia into either of these constructs.

Ideologically, some of the major East Asian countries, such as Japan, South Korea, or the Republic of China on Taiwan, belonged to the so-called West during the Cold War. Although ideological conflicts

---

[1] Loth summarizes it well: "The conflict between East and West had its origins in diverging views of how society should be organized, which emerged in the course of nineteenth- and early twentieth-century industrialization: The contrast between the pluralism of 'Western' civilization, which in principle permitted a multiplicity of ways of life and patterns of power, and the centralized all-powerful state with its 'Asiatic' imprint; the contrast between capitalist means of production and socialist planning; the contrast between a parliamentary state under the rule of law and a totalitarian state" (Loth 1994, p. 193).

have waned in the contemporary world, Communist ideology has notably persisted in three major Asian countries: China, North Korea, and Vietnam (with the only other Communist nation being Cuba in Central America). The ideological persistence in these Asian countries cannot be brushed off because it has significant social, political, and cultural consequences for the residents of those societies and beyond.[2]

Economically, some East Asian countries are said to belong to the so-called South, even though they all lie in the northern hemisphere. More importantly, in terms of the economy, things have been changing dramatically in the last few decades. Japan was the first developed country in the Far East. Since the 1960s, we have witnessed the rapid rise of the four little tigers or dragons: South Korea, Taiwan, Hong Kong, and Singapore (Midgley 1986; Vogel 1992; Morris 1996; Hamilton 2007). This was followed by the so-called tiger cubs of Indonesia, Malaysia, the Philippines, and Thailand (Heng and Niblock 2014), and the big dragon of China (Burstein and De Keijzer 1999). In recent years, Vietnam has also experienced an economic upsurge (Hayton 2010). In contrast, some of the Eastern European countries in the so-called global North have struggled economically in recent decades (Tlostanova 2011).

It was Max Weber who first brought scholarly attention to the relationship between religion and the economy. He tried to explain why modern rational capitalism first emerged in the Protestant West, but not elsewhere, and he made careful examination of the religions of China (i.e., Confucianism and Daoism) and India (i.e., Hinduism and Buddhism) in addition to Christianity, Judaism, and Islam (Weber [1904] 1930, Weber [1920] 1951, Weber [1917] 1952 and Weber [1916] 1958). I would acknowledge that these books by Weber are full of insights and should be read by all students and scholars who study religion in East Asia, but I must also say that many parts of these writings, even some of Weber's main conceptualizations, are off the mark. One of the most obvious problems is that Weber grouped Buddhism into the religion of India. In fact, by the time that Weber was writing on these in the 1910s and 1920s, Buddhism had been a major religion in East Asia for nearly two thousand years, but was negligible in India proper. More importantly, throughout East Asia, shamanism and folk religions were much more prevalent in society than institutionalized religions (see, e.g., Yang 1961). Furthermore, for much of the last two millennia, several institutionalized religions have coexisted without a religious monopoly in most parts of East Asia, a situation radically different from the West where one of the multiple forms of Christianity dominated for centuries.

In short, both of these commonly used groupings are Euro-centric or North-Atlantic-centric notions. That is, both of these groupings are from the vantage point of Western Europe and North America. Additionally, that presents a problem for properly understanding a large segment of the world population. The North-Atlantic world has a combined population of about 1.1 billion, whereas East and Southeast Asia have a combined population of 2.3 billion people, or 30 percent of the world population. When 30 percent of the world population cannot easily be fitted into the conceptual constructs, we must find an alternative way to work. This is especially true when we study culture, religion, and society. Culturally, East Asian societies are distinct from the rest of the world; in East Asia, the predominant religious traditions have been a mixture of Confucianism, Buddhism, some indigenous traditions, such as Daoism or Shintoism, and local folk religions. Moreover, post-Weberian phenomena, especially the economic rise of East Asia and the spread of Christianity in East Asia, are very important for scholars who want to understand religion and the changing dynamics in East Asia today.

---

2 Edward Said's *Orientalism* (Said 1978) has been very popular in the West. However, its applicability to the Far East needs to be reexamined from the Global East perspective. Unlike the Near East, which is predominantly Islamic, East Asia sustains distinct religious and cultural traditions. Moreover, European colonialism failed to colonize most of East Asia. Both of these historical factors are important when we try to understand and explain religion in contemporary East Asia.

2. Christianity, Confucianism, Atheism, and Folk Religion in the Global East

Contemporary Western scholars have paid great attention to the phenomenon of Christianity moving to the "Global South". For example, the historian, Philip Jenkins, published a book in 2002 with the title, *The Next Christendom: The Coming of Global Christianity* (Jenkins 2002), which highlights the rapid growth of Christianity in the Global South, especially in Africa. By 2011, it had been updated and expanded into a third edition and translated into multiple languages (Jenkins 2011). In 2006, he published a further book, *The New Faces of Christianity: Believing the Bible in the Global South*, that highlighted even more prominently the imagery of the Global South. Continuing this popular trend, an *Encyclopedia of Christianity in the Global South* (Lamport 2018) was published just a few months ago. The editor, Mark A. Lamport, invited me to participate in the project. I told him that I did not like the notion of the Global South because Christians in East Asia would be obscured in this kind of generalization. Conceptualizing the project as describing Christians in the Global South makes it difficult to understand Christians in East Asia in their own place. As the Pew Research Center's reports suggest (Pew Research Center 2011, 2012), Christians in East Asia and among diasporic communities of ethnic East Asians comprise a significant segment of the Christian population in the world today. Geographically speaking, how can it be appropriate to group South Korea and China into the Global South? Both are obviously in the northern hemisphere. Culturally, their religious traditions are radically different from Africa and Latin America. It is against these cultural backgrounds that Christianity has swelled in a post-World War II context. Socially and economically, these countries are developed or are fast-developing. Despite my misgivings about the notion of the Global South, Mark Lamport encouraged me to write down my thoughts about Christianity in the Global South vs. the Global East, and eventually included my observations as an "afterword" in the Encyclopedia (Yang 2018). I was pleased by his inclusiveness and openness toward critical reflections, but we need to do much more to change the narrative that renders East Asia both invisible and incomprehensible. We know that about 90 percent of Filipinos are Christian. Some surveys show that about 30 percent of South Koreans are Christian (Pew Research Center 2011). The Singapore Census reports 18 percent Christian in 2010 (SDS 2011). Christianity has been growing rapidly in China in the last few decades (Yang 2016a). The growth of Christianity in East Asian societies is having a profound impact on the religious landscape of the world.

Another issue needing to be addressed is the supposed prevalence of Confucianism. Max Weber said that Confucianism was the major religion of China and, by expanding this line of thought, we could say that Confucianism was a major religion of East Asia, as many scholars do (e.g., Tu 1996). However, in social surveys, very few Chinese, Koreans, or Japanese self-identify as followers of Confucianism (Yang and Tamney 2011). The Pew Research Center conducted a survey of Asian Americans in 2012. It reports that Christianity is a major religion among several Asian ethnic groups: Chinese Americans, Filipino Americans, Korean Americans, Japanese Americans, and Vietnamese Americans. The only exception is Indian Americans, of whom a majority are Hindus. Buddhism is a major religion among the Vietnamese, Japanese, Chinese, and Koreans, but not Indians. Again, where are the adherents of Confucianism? Extremely few Asians or Asian Americans self-identify with Confucianism.

These problems in surveys raise questions about the measurement of religiosity, but also the conceptualization of religion itself. In East Asia, people may admit to being Buddhist, Confucian, or Daoist, but would not admit to being religious, or belong to any religion, as they honestly do not regard Buddhism, Confucianism, Daoism, or Shintoism as religions. As one may infer, there is a language problem. In Chinese, *zongjiao* 宗教 is a modern term, borrowed from Japanese, which was a *kanji* translation from European languages (Beyer 2013). During this translation and importation, the exact meaning was altered and it takes time for the populace to accept the translated concept. For many Asians today, religion is still not a concept in their everyday language, even though the political and cultural elites have adopted it into public institutions. For those who have received a secularist education that is heavily influenced by the French Enlightenment, religion is often a sabotaged concept in their normative, progressive thinking. Therefore, scholars in the social scientific study of religion have to find ways to learn and use the spiritual language of ordinary people.

In fact, even the cultural and political elites in Asia are confused and confusing. In China, Confucianism is not classified as a religion, but Daoism is. However, not many people self-identify with Daoism as a religion either. In real life, Daoism and the so-called folk religions share many of the same beliefs and practices. Some scholars want to include all folk religions in greater Daoism 大道教 or the religion of China (Freedman 1974; Lagerwey 2010). Others have argued to make Confucianism a religion, even the national religion of China (see Billioud and Thoraval 2008; Ownby 2009; Sun 2013). These advocates often refer to the model of Hinduism as the religion of Indians or Shintoism as the state religion of Japan prior to 1945. They posit that if Indians and Japanese have their own named religions, why should the Chinese be treated differently? Indeed, Confucianism has been classified as one of the major religions in Indonesia. However, a scholarly question must be posed: Under what social and political conditions can you construct a religion (Sun 2013)? In thinking about this question, we must also examine how successful the elite campaigns are in constructing the religions of Hinduism, Shintoism, Daoism, and Confucianism. What are their relationships with folk religions and other world religions? Additionally, how are things changing in the contemporary globalization era? These difficult questions lead to further questions worth pondering: Can non-Japanese convert to Shintoism, non-Indians convert to Hinduism, and non-Chinese convert to Daoism or Confucianism? In fact, Confucianism and Daoism have transcended Chinese boundaries and are shared by the Japanese, Koreans, and Vietnamese (see Ivanhoe and Kim 2017), but we must ask a further question: Is this in a religious sense, in a philosophical sense, or in some other sense? These questions all need to be answered with care and nuance, and more importantly, with systematically collected data, objective analysis, and appropriate theoretical concepts in the social scientific study of religion.

A further problem is atheism. Religion is a universal phenomenon of human society. According to Bellah (2011), religion emerged along with the human race in the process of evolution. Of course, in any given society, be it a primitive society or modernized society, there are always some individuals who do not believe in any supernatural being or supernatural force. In other words, atheists are not a modern phenomenon; they have existed in all societies (Stark and Finke 2000). However, atheism as a secularist ideology is a modern phenomenon, and it has a twisted understanding in an Asia that has been striving to modernize. By some measures, East Asian societies have the highest proportions of people claiming to be atheists. For example, according to the World Values Surveys (WVS), about five percent of Europeans (N = 62,545) and Americans (N = 2232) are "convinced atheists", but there are nearly 30 percent of "convinced atheists" among South Koreans (N = 1200), 27 percent among the Chinese (N = 2300), 17 percent among the Taiwanese (N = 1238), and 11 percent among the Japanese (N = 2443). Hong Kong was first included in the WVS in 2005, which revealed five percent of atheists in the city. In the 2013 sample of 1000 Hong Kongers, however, 55 percent reported to be atheists. Obviously, something must be wrong with these surveys, even though the World Values Surveys are considered one of the best cross-national surveys.

Returning to Robert Bellah, in 1985, he and his colleagues (Bellah et al. 1985) coined a new term, Sheilaism, for a new phenomenon in American religion: Individualized eclecticism—taking some elements from various religious or spiritual traditions to form one's own religion. Sheila is a good hearted and spiritually conscious person, but very individualized in terms of religion. Can we find Sheila in East Asia? Probably, the majority of people in these societies can be called "Asian Sheilas". It is common for East Asians to take something from Confucianism, Daoism, Buddhism, and other sources to form their own individualized spirituality. Instead of converting to one particular religion, they move around different religions without dedication to or even identification with any one in particular. For example, many Japanese may be said to be "Asian Sheilas", in that they use the birth rites of Shinto, the marriage rites of Christianity, and the funeral rites of Buddhism, yet they may also say that they are atheist.

In the same train of thought, scholars of religion in the United States have noticed several new phenomena: The rise of Sheilaism and New Age spiritualties in the 1980s, the rise of people who claim to be "spiritual but not religious" since the 1990s (Tong and Yang 2018), and the rapid rise of religious "nones", or those who claim no religion at all even though most hold some religious beliefs and engage in selected religious practices. These may be new phenomena in the new world, but I would say, "Hello, America! Welcome to East Asia". In East Asia, these are traditional patterns of being religious or spiritual. In modern scholarship of Chinese studies, we often refer to these phenomena as folk religious expressions. Can we refer to these new phenomena in the United States as new folk religion in America? I think so, but the writers of the Pew Research Center's report, *The Future of World Religions* (Pew Research Center 2015), did not. This report includes folk religion among Asians, Africans, Native Americans, and aboriginal Australians, but not among Europeans or European Americans. This is another sign of Euro-centrism in the conceptualization of religion and religiosity, even though it probably happened unconsciously. Regardless, we need to study these widespread or universal phenomena as part of the postmodern or late modern world, both in East Asia and North America (Yang 2016b).

3. Secularization in the Global East?

Secularization theories have dominated the world, especially the intelligentsia, for a long time. For several decades following the 1960s, Peter Berger was one of the most important theorists who argued that modernization will necessarily lead to religious decline (Berger 1967, 1969). Both of the keynote speakers at the inaugural EASSSR conference, Casanova (1994) and Davie (1994, 2000), have played important roles in questioning these assumptions. Facing a myriad of empirical evidence as well as theoretical development, Peter Berger himself rescinded his secularization theory in the 1990s (Berger 1999; Berger et al. 2008). Warner (1993, 1997), Stark and Finke (2000), Yang (2006, 2011), and many others have argued that there has been a paradigm shift: The social scientific study of religion has shifted focus from explaining religious decline to explaining religious vitality in modern societies. Recently, however, Voas and Chaves (2016) have revived the debate again, arguing that secularization is finally taking effect in the United States as well as Europe.

What about East Asia? In China, secularization was a state-engineered program, but since the 1970s, religions have been reviving and becoming increasingly important in society (Yang 2014a). How about other East Asian societies? Recently, my students and I began to explore some survey data. Unfortunately, survey data are very limited and less reliable for this part of the world. The best available cross-national survey data is probably the World Values Surveys, which began in 1990 and included some Asian societies in various years. Based on these limited surveys and our preliminary analysis, we do not see a pattern of religious decline. Take the question of religious affiliation as an example (see Figure 1), we see certain fluctuations in Japan, South Korea, and Taiwan, but no clear indication of decline. In other societies, there is even an increase. Take another question as an example, the importance of religion in the lives of the respondents (see Figure 2). Again, there is no decline and perhaps some slight increase in all of these Asian societies.

We have also explored other datasets. In the Japan General Social Survey, the proportion of people who claim to have a religion or a family religion has remained about the same since the year, 2000. The proportion of people who claim to be Buddhists fluctuated a lot, but there is no clear pattern of decline. In the Korea General Social Survey, there are noticeable fluctuations of the self-identified Protestant Christians and Buddhists, but no clear decline of religion in general. The same is true of religious attendance. Similarly, the Taiwan Social Change Surveys, which began in the 1980s, show no clear signs of religious decline, although there have been changes. Of course, all of these surveys were done within a relatively short period of time and may not fully capture the historical trajectories. We need more and better surveys as well as other types of empirical data.

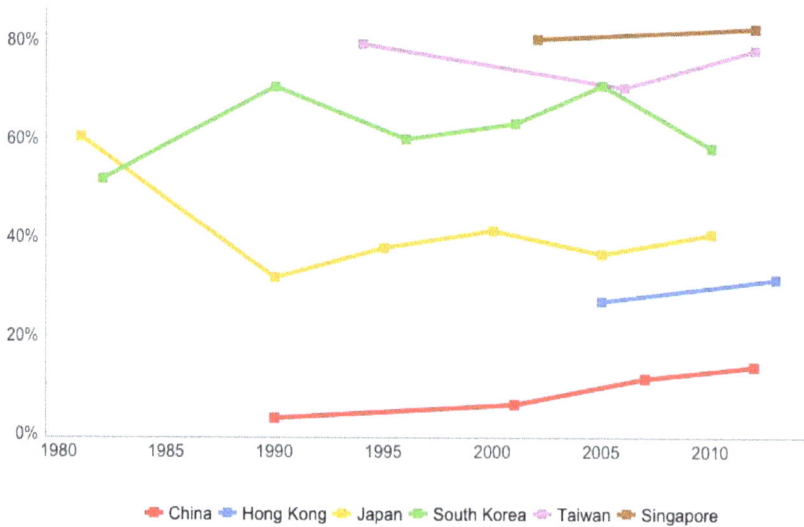

Figure 1. Percentage of respondents with religious affiliation in East Asian societies (World Values Surveys, weighted).

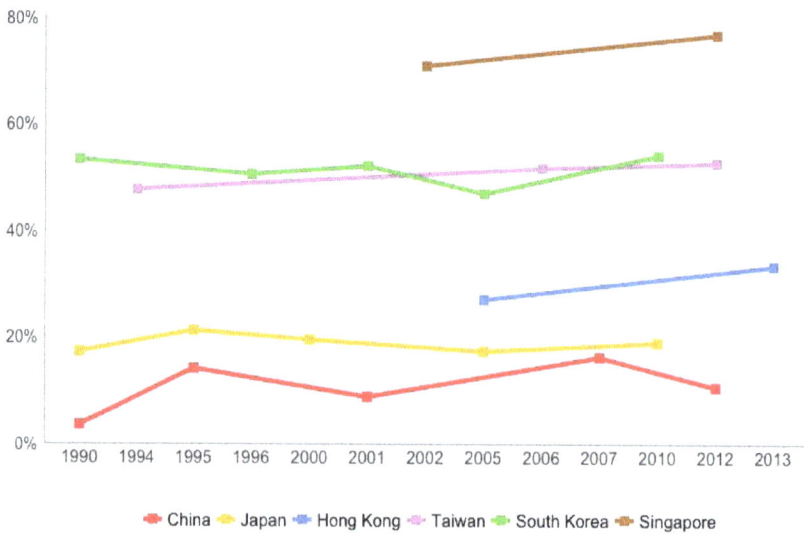

Figure 2. Percentage of respondents in East Asian societies who say religion is important (World Values Surveys, weighted).

In the social scientific study of religion and spirituality in the Global East, a key problem is how to measure religion and religiosity. The existing measures commonly used in the West and around the world are primarily based on Judeo-Christian understandings of identity, membership, and attendance. To be more precise, in the Judeo-Christian context, it is assumed that religious identity is exclusive, that every religious person is a member of a local congregation that is part of a denomination or a distinct religion, and that regular activities include weekly attendance at a corporate worship service. However, East Asian religions have distinct characteristics: Religious identity is not necessarily exclusive, religious practice is not based on a weekly rhythm, individual devotion or practice is at least as important as corporate rituals, and the boundaries of religiosity and secularity are ambiguous or blurred. Moreover, these societies are characterized by a lack of religious monopolies. Instead, the situation is more akin to a religious oligopoly, where several religions are considered acceptable while many others are suppressed by the state and the public (see Yang 2014b).

4. Conclusions

In sum, the cultural and social differences of East Asian societies from the rest of the world make it necessary to adopt a new concept—the Global East. Global East societies, communities, and individuals share some common cultural and religious traditions, including Confucianism, Buddhism, Daoism/Shintoism/Shamanism, and other local or folk religions. Christianity has grown rapidly in some of these societies and communities, but not others. This is not to gloss over internal differences of East Asian societies. Good scholarship should examine both particularities and commonalities, but the commonalities in East Asia deserve to be examined carefully. The Global East is a cultural and social concept enabling such studies together with cross-national comparisons in that part of the world.

It is important to point out that, given their distinct cultural and community characteristics in the globalizing world, the Global East not only includes East Asian societies, but also includes diasporic communities of ethnic East Asians in other countries around the world, as they tend to share more similarities with East Asian societies than with others. Furthermore, in this era of globalization, selected westerners have adopted traditional religions or spiritualties of the Global East. Recently, I reviewed *Dream Trippers: Global Daoism and the Predicament of Modern Spirituality* (Palmer and Siegler 2017), which describes Americans and other Westerners who have become Daoists and have taken trips to sacred mountains in China to meditate in caves (Yang forthcoming). These are all part of the Global East.

Religion in the Global East presents theoretical and methodological challenges for the social scientific study of religion. First, there are language problems, as discussed above. Second, religion-state relations in the Global East have been very different from Europe and America. Religious monopolies have been rare throughout the history of societies in the Global East, as multiple religions have coexisted for long periods of time. Third, at the micro level, religious identity may not be exclusive or salient. A majority of people are open to beliefs and practices of multiple religions, yet may or may not self-identify with any particular religion, or when they do, may identify with multiple religions. Simply identifying these characteristics should be sufficient to emphasize not only the distinctiveness, but the importance of the concept of the Global East.

Religion in the Global East presents great opportunities for the social scientific study of religion in the globalizing world as well. First, if we can develop good measures of religiosity in the Global East, it should substantially improve the measurement of religiosity around the globe (Chao and Yang 2018). Second, cross-referencing and comparative studies of religions in the Global East are likely to shed new light on many theoretical issues in the general social science of religion, including the debate on secularization. Third, a better, scholarly understanding of the religion-state relations in the Global East may help to present meaningful alternatives to the existing models of modern religion-state relations.

There are numerous scholarly associations for the study of religion based in North America and Europe. Religions in East Asia are quite distinct from other parts of the world, and religious change in this part of the world has been rapid and dramatic. I very much hope that the East Asian Society for the Scientific Study of Religion will become an important platform for scholars of religions in East Asia and elsewhere to regularly engage with each other. Together, we can make a significant contribution to better understandings of religion in the modern world, and to the methodology and theory necessary for the social scientific study of religion both in East Asia and in general.

Funding: This research is supported in part by a grant from the John Templeton Foundation (#56480) for the project "Chinese Religious Markets and Spiritual Capital: A Research and Field Development Initiative".

Acknowledgments: The author would like to express thanks to many scholars for their comments and feedbacks during and after the Inaugural Conference of EASSSR, to Brian McPhail for research assistance, and to the editors of *Religions* for their professionalism.

Conflicts of Interest: There is no conflict of interest.

References

Bellah, Robert Needly. 2011. *Religion in Human Evolution: From the Paleolithic to the Axial Age*. Cambridge: Belknap Press.

Bellah, Robert N., Richard Madsen, William M. Sullivan, Ann Swidler, and Steven M. Tipton. 1985. *Habits of the Heart: Individualism and Commitment in American Life*. Berkeley and Los Angeles: University of California Press.

Berger, Peter L. 1967. *The Sacred Canopy: Elements of a Sociological Theory*. New York: Random House.

Berger, Peter L. 1969. *A Rumor of Angels: Modern Society and the Rediscovery of the Supernatural*. Garden City: Doubleday.

Berger, Peter L., ed. 1999. *The Desecularization of the World: Resurgent Religion and World Politics*. Washington and Grand Rapids: Eerdmans Publishing Co.

Berger, Peter L., Grace Davie, and Effie Fokas. 2008. *Religious America, secular Europe? A Theme and Variations*. Hampshire: Ashgate.

Beyer, Peter. 2013. *Religion in the Context of Globalization*. London: Routledge.

Billioud, Sebastien, and Joel Thoraval. 2008. The Contemporary Revival of Confucianism: Anshen Liming or the Religious Dimension of Confucianism. *China Perspectives* 75: 88–106.

Buchholz, Armin. 1961. Problems of the Ideological East-West Conflict. *Studies in Soviet Thought* 1: 120–31. [CrossRef]

Burstein, Daniel, and Arne De Keijzer. 1999. *Big Dragon: The Future of China: What It Means for Business, the Economy, and the Global Order*. New York: Free Press.

Casanova, José. 1994. *Public Religions in the Modern World*. Chicago: University of Chicago Press.

Chao, L. Luke, and Fenggang Yang. 2018. Measuring Religiosity in a Religiously Diverse Society: The China Case. *Social Science Research* 74: 187–95. [CrossRef] [PubMed]

Davie, Grace. 1994. *Religion in Britain since 1945: Believing without Belonging*. Oxford and Cambridge: Wiley-Blackwell.

Davie, Grace. 2000. *Religion in Modern Europe: A Memory Mutates*. Oxford: Oxford University Press.

Eckl, Julian, and Ralph Weber. 2007. North—South? Pitfalls of Dividing the World by Words. *Third World Quarterly* 28: 3–23. [CrossRef]

Erb, Guy F. 1977. 'North-South' Negotiations. *Proceedings of the Academy of Political Science* 32: 106–19. [CrossRef]

Freedman, Maurice. 1974. On the sociological study of Chinese religion. In *Religion and Ritual in Chinese Society*. Edited by Arthur P. Wolf. Stanford: Stanford University Press, pp. 19–41.

Hamilton, Clive. 2007. Capitalist Industrialization in East Asia's Four Little Tigers. *Journal of Contemporary Asia* 13: 35–73. [CrossRef]

Hayton, Bill. 2010. *Vietnam: Rising Dragon*. New Haven: Yale University Press.

Heng, Panha, and Scott J. Niblock. 2014. Rise of the 'tiger cub' economies: An empirical investigation of Southeast Asian stock market efficiency. *International Journal of Economics and Business Research* 8: 474–89. [CrossRef]

Horowitz, David. 1966. *Hemispheres North & South: Economic Disparity among Nations*. Baltimore: Johns Hopkins Press.

Ivanhoe, Philip J., and Sungmoon Kim, eds. 2017. *Confucianism, a Habit of the Heart: Bellah, Civil Religion, and East Asia*. Albany: SUNY Press.

Jenkins, Philip. 2002. *The Next Christendom: The Coming of Global Christianity*. New York: Oxford University Press.

Jenkins, Philip. 2011. *The Next Christendom: The Coming of Global Christianity*, 3rd ed. New York: Oxford University Press.

Lagerwey, John. 2010. *China: A Religious State*. Hong Kong: Hong Kong University Press.

Lamport, Mark A., ed. 2018. *Encyclopedia of Christianity in the Global South*. Lanham: Rowman & Littlefield.

Loth, Wilfried. 1994. The East-West Conflict in Historical Perspective: An Attempt at a Balanced View. *Contemporary European History* 3: 193–202. [CrossRef]

Midgley, James. 1986. Industrialization and Welfare: The Case of the Four Little Tigers. *Social Policy and Administration* 20: 225–38. [CrossRef]

Morris, Paul. 1996. Asia's Four Little Tigers: A Comparison of the Role of Education in their Development. *Journal of Comparative Education* 32: 95–110. [CrossRef]

Ownby, David. 2009. Kang Xiaoguang: Social Science, Civil Society, and Confucian Religion. *China Perspectives* 80: 101–11.

Palmer, David A., and Elijah Siegler. 2017. *Dream Trippers: Global Daoism and the Predicament of Modern Spirituality.* Chicago: The University of Chicago Press.

Pew Research Center. 2011. Global Christianity: A Report on the Size and Distribution of the World's Christian Population. Available online: http://www.pewforum.org/files/2011/12/Christianity-fullreport-web.pdf (accessed on 30 December 2015).

Pew Research Center. 2012. Asian Americans: A Mosaic of Faiths. Available online: http://assets.pewresearch.org/wp-content/uploads/sites/11/2012/07/Asian-Americans-religion-full-report.pdf (accessed on 4 September 2018).

Pew Research Center. 2015. The Future of World Religions: Population Growth Projections, 2010–2050. Available online: http://www.pewforum.org/files/2015/03/PF_15.04.02_ProjectionsFullReport.pdf (accessed on 30 December 2015).

Reuveny, Rafel X., and William R. Thompson. 2007. The North-South Divide and International Studies: A Symposium. *International Studies Review* 9: 556–64. [CrossRef]

Said, Edward W. 1978. *Orientalism.* New York: Pantheon Books.

SDS (Singapore Department of Statistics). 2011. Census of Population 2010 Statistical Release 1: Demographic Characteristics, Education, Language and Religion. Available online: https://web.archive.org/web/20110303155259/http://www.singstat.gov.sg/pubn/popn/C2010sr1/cop2010sr1.pdf (accessed on 5 September 2018).

Stark, Rodney, and Roger Finke. 2000. *Acts of Faith: Explaining the Human Side of Religion.* Berkeley and Los Angeles: University of California Press.

Sun, Anna. 2013. *Confucianism as a World Religion: Contested Histories and Contemporary Realities.* Princeton: Princeton University Press.

Tlostanova, Madina. 2011. The South of the Poor North: Caucasus Subjectivity and the Complex of Secondary 'Australism'. *The Global South* 5: 66–84. [CrossRef]

Tong, Yunping, and Fenggang Yang. 2018. Internal Diversity Among 'Spiritual But Not Religious' Adolescents in the United States: A Person-Centered Examination Using Latent Class Analysis. *Review of Religious Research.* [CrossRef]

Tu, Weiming, ed. 1996. *Confucian Traditions in East Asian Modernity.* Cambridge: Harvard University Press.

Voas, David, and Mark Chaves. 2016. Is the United States a Counterexample to the Secularization Thesis? *American Journal of Sociology* 121: 1517–56. [CrossRef]

Vogel, Ezra F. 1992. *The Four Little Dragons: The Spread of Industrialization in East Asia.* Cambridge: Harvard University Press.

Warner, R. Stephen. 1993. Work in progress toward a new paradigm for the sociological study of religion in the United States. *American Journal of Sociology* 98: 1044–93. [CrossRef]

Warner, R. Stephen. 1997. A paradigm is not a theory: Reply to Lechner. *American Journal of Sociology* 103: 192–99. [CrossRef]

Weber, Max. 1930. *The Protestant Ethic and the Spirit of Capitalism.* Translated by Talcott Parsons, and Anthony Giddens. London and Boston: Unwin Hyman. First published 1904.

Weber, Max. 1951. *The Religion of China: Confucianism and Taoism.* Translated by Hans H. Gerth. New York: Free Press. First published 1920.

Weber, Max. 1952. *Ancient Judaism.* New York: Free Press. First published 1917.

Weber, Max. 1958. *The Religion of India: The Sociology of Hinduism and Buddhism.* New York: Free Press. First published 1916.

Yang, Ching Kun. 1961. *Religion in Chinese society: A Study of Contemporary Social Functions of Religion and Some of Their Historical Factors.* Berkeley: University of California Press.

Yang, Fenggang. 2006. The Red, Black, and Gray Markets of Religion in China. *Sociological Quarterly* 47: 93–122. [CrossRef]

Yang, Fenggang. 2011. *Religion in China: Survival and Revival under Communist Rule*. New York: Oxford University Press.

Yang, Fenggang. 2014a. Agency-Driven Secularization and Chinese Experiments in Multiple Modernities. In *The Many Altars of Modernity: Toward a Paradigm for Religion in a Pluralist Age*. Written by Peter L. Berger. Berlin: De Gruyter, pp. 123–40.

Yang, Fenggang. 2014b. Oligopoly is Not Pluralism. In *Religious Pluralism: Framing Religious Diversity in the Contemporary World*. Edited by Giuseppe Giordan and Enzo Pace. Berlin: Springer, pp. 59–69.

Yang, Fenggang. 2016a. The growth and dynamism of Chinese Christianity. In *Christianity and Freedom*. Volume 2: Contemporary Perspectives. Edited by Allen D. Hertzke and Timothy Samuel Shah. Cambridge: Cambridge University Press, pp. 161–90.

Yang, Fenggang. 2016b. Exceptionalism or Chinamerica? Measuring Religious Change in the Globalizing World Today. *Journal of the Scientific Study of Religion* 55: 7–22. [CrossRef]

Yang, Fenggang. 2018. Afterword (on the notion of Global East). In *Encyclopedia of Christianity in the Global South*. Edited by Mark A. Lamport. Lanham: Rowman & Littlefield, pp. 957–58.

Yang, Fenggang. Forthcoming. A Review of Dream Trippers: Global Daoism and the Predicament of Modern Spirituality. *American Journal of Sociology*.

Yang, Fenggang, and Joseph Tamney, eds. 2011. *Confucianism and Spiritual Traditions in Modern China and Beyond*. Leiden and Boston: Brill.

religions

MDPI

Article

Thinking Theoretically about Religiosity, Secularity and Pluralism in the Global East

Grace Davie

Department of Sociology, Philosophy and Anthropology, College of Social Sciences and International Studies, University of Exeter, Amory Building, Rennes Drive Exeter EX4 4RJ, UK; G.R.C.Davie@exeter.ac.uk

Received: 25 September 2018; Accepted: 23 October 2018; Published: 31 October 2018

Abstract: This paper addresses the religiosity, secularity and pluralism of the Global East from a theoretical perspective. To do so it draws from work undertaken by the author within the International Panel on Social Progress (IPSP), paying particular attention to the material on religion, diversity and pluralism. The final section of the article demonstrates the rootedness of social scientific thinking in the European Enlightenment and the consequences of this heritage for the understanding of religion in other parts of the world including East Asia. There are no easy answers to the questions posed by the mismatch between theory and data; there are, however, pointers towards more constructive ways forward—ways which respond sensitively to the context under review, maintaining nonetheless a high degree of scientific rigour.

Keywords: East Asia; Global East; religion; diversity; pluralism; enlightenment thinking; sociology; sociology of religion

1. Introduction

I was delighted to be invited as a plenary speaker to the inaugural conference of the East Asian Society for the Scientific Study of Religion (EASSSR), held in Singapore in July 2018. I was asked to consider the situation regarding religion and secularity in this part of the world from a theoretical perspective. I found this a challenging assignment: whilst I was relatively familiar with social scientific theories regarding religion and secularity, as far as these apply to the European or Western cases, I was painfully aware that my knowledge of East Asia was limited. Experience had shown me however that applying theoretical approaches honed and developed in the West to almost any other context is likely to be at best ambiguous and at worst misleading—at times seriously.

Central to that experience has been my collaboration with the International Panel on Social Progress (IPSP). This hugely important project—and the many lessons that I learnt from working within it—constituted the starting point of my plenary paper in Singapore and thus of this article; it will be covered in Section 2. Given the overall theme of the EASSSR conference—"Religiosity, Secularity and Pluralism in the Global East"—it was fitting that the chapter on religion in the IPSP report paid particular attention to diversity and pluralism. This aspect of our work will be highlighted in Section 3.[1] Taken together these sections offer a springboard for the theoretical discussion as such in Section 4, which demonstrates the rootedness of social scientific thinking in the European Enlightenment and the consequences of this for the understanding of religion in other parts of the world including East Asia. There are no easy answers to the questions posed by the mismatch of theory and data; there are,

---

[1] Earlier versions of the IPSP material summarized in Sections 2 and 3 have been published in Chapter 4 of Grace Davie, *Religion in Public Life: Levelling the Ground*. London, Theos: 2017. I am grateful to Theos for allowing me to include reworked summaries of the IPSP chapter in this article.

however, pointers towards more constructive ways forward—ways which take careful account of the context under review, maintaining nonetheless the highest standards of scientific rigour.

2. The International Panel on Social Progress

The International Panel on Social Progress brought together more than two hundred scholars, from a wide range of disciplines and from many different parts of the world, in order to assess and to synthesize the state-of-the-art knowledge that bears on social progress across a wide range of economic, political and cultural questions.[2] The immediate goal was to provide the target audience (individuals, movements, organizations, politicians, decision-makers and practitioners) with the best expertise that social science can offer on whatever aspect of social progress was under review.

The process—to a significant extent modelled on the Intergovernmental Panel on Climate Change (IPCC)—was a long one, leading to publication in 2018.[3] In the final, three volume report, there are two introductory and two concluding chapters. The remaining eighteen are divided into three sections: economic, political and cultural. Unsurprisingly the chapter on religion falls into the last of these categories, along with the material on cultural change, the pluralization of families, global health and the parameters of human living, education and belonging and solidarity. Social progress—the key to the whole enterprise—is defined in Chapter 2. Setting aside Enlightenment assumptions that progress is somehow built into history, the chapter constructs what its authors take to be the most important normative dimensions for making comparisons in this multifaceted arena (over time and between places). These are conceptualized as values (against which to measure progress) and principles (which guide action), mindful that what is considered progress in one context may be differently assessed in another. The notion of a compass is deployed as a metaphor: the map in question is complex and the destination elusive; it is possible nonetheless to set the line of travel.

Early in 2015, I was invited to become a Co-ordinating Lead Author (CLA) for the chapter on religion in the IPSP report. My partner was Nancy Ammerman—a distinguished sociologist of religion from Boston University in the US. Our first task was to build the team, bearing in mind that we needed expertise from different disciplines, different world faiths and different global regions (including East Asia) in order to cover the necessary literature.[4] Above all however we needed hands-on experience in empirical work, in order that our text might be fully grounded in the realities of religion as they exist in different parts of the world. At the same time, we had to find a discourse that related these realities to the concept of social progress as this was understood by the project as a whole. We had moreover to find ways of making this speak to a diverse readership both inside and outside the academy. Every member of the chapter team contributed to this task.[5]

The first meeting of the IPSP authors (including ourselves) took place in Istanbul in August 2015. It was a learning experience in every sense of the term. Not only was this the first time that the chapter team had come together (some of them travelling many thousands of miles), it was also the moment when we appreciated that significant sections of the social-scientific community were hesitant about the relationship between religion and social progress as we were learning to understand this. This hesitancy took two forms: either religion was irrelevant (i.e., no longer of significance), or it was negatively perceived—in other words necessarily inimical to social progress. The fact that

---

[2]   The published version of the IPSP report is listed in the bibliography—see International Panel on Social Progress (2018). See also the project website, available online: https://www.ipsp.org. Individual chapters can be downloaded from https://www.ipsp.org/downloads. There are two online versions of Chapter 16 on "Religions and social progress: Critical assessments and creative partnerships", one which replicates the published version and one which contains additional case studies (in the form of sidebars). Both websites accessed on 17 August 2018.

[3]   Following IPCC practice an initial draft of the chapters was posted on line for several months in the latter part of 2016 in order to collect comments from the widest possible audience and to allow all authors to read and respond to each other's work.

[4]   The team included Fenggang Yang (the first President of the EASSSR) and Vineeta Sinha, a sociologist from the National University of Singapore.

[5]   The full team (together with institutional affiliations) is listed in the published versions of the chapter (see note 2).

religion was—or more accurately was deemed to be—"back" as a factor in global affairs, was therefore a problem.[6]

In the 48 h that we spent together, we worked hard on finding ways to counter these at best partial and at worst inaccurate, views starting with a clear definition of religion itself. Escaping the limitations of a purely Western perspective was the first step. We argue that religion is more—much more—than the broad range of institutions and beliefs traditionally recognized by social science; it is rather a very much larger cultural domain that encompasses the beliefs and practice of the vast majority (over 80%) of the world's population (Johnson et al. 2016). Religion is a lived, situated and constantly changing reality and has as much to do with navigating everyday life, as it does with the supernatural. It follows that the secular, or secularity, should be considered an equally fluid entity, whose distinction from religion will vary from place to place—a division decided more by the context in question than by pre-determined categories. That said, we recognized that what we term humanity's "limiting conditions"—death, suffering, injustice—are likely to be confronted and explained in religious terms across a wide range of societies.

From this starting point, we developed our approach to the relationship between religion and social progress. Our task was to scour the available literature in order to document our case. Importantly we began from the belief that neither good nor ill could be assumed from the outset. We had rather to look case by case at different social and cultural domains and in different parts of the world, to see what was happening on the ground. We were well aware that particular forms of religion were perceived negatively, sometimes rightly so. Without doubt religion can take forms which are destructive of people and places. Elsewhere, however, religious individuals and religious communities are manifestly associated with the health and wellbeing of their respective societies—an entirely positive feature.

In order to get a grip on the agenda, we worked "upwards" from the micro to the macro. Specifically, we began with the most intimate of human relationships (i.e., those that relate to gender, sexuality and the family), appreciating that these have been moulded from time immemorial by religious rules, rituals and prohibitions. But here as elsewhere, it is important to set aside an over-simple binary between secular progress and religious reaction—the reality is infinitely more complex. The focus on everyday lived religion was a valuable corrective in this respect. It pointed us to a multi-disciplinary literature which documents the ways in which men, women and young people negotiate their very personal lives. It is clear that they accept some of the limitations that derive from religion but question others and extract from these complex negotiations the means to confront the vicissitudes of life.

The subsequent sections of the IPSP chapter deal with political issues. The first of these addressed the question of diversity—looking: (a) at its shape and forms in the late modern world and (b) at its governance. Both questions were central to the Singapore conference and will be expanded in more detail in the following section of this article.

The second political theme concerned the much talked-of connections between religion and conflict. The core argument is easily stated. To ask whether religion—or certain forms of religion—cause conflict or violence is not the most helpful approach. Much more constructive are enquiries which deploy a social scientific lens to look systematically at the circumstances in which a violent outcome is likely. Contestation over physical spaces is one such, as is an excess of regulation which leads all too often to negative attitudes towards minorities. Even more important is the considerable evidence that weak or failed states (and the fragile economies associated with them) encourage—by default—violent and authoritarian attempts to restore order. Some of these are religiously inspired.

---

[6] The shorthand of "God is Back" is taken from the title of a widely read book; see Micklethwait and Wooldridge (2010).

There is however another side to this coin. Clearly there are situations in which religion becomes entangled with violence but it is equally a resource for peace-making. This can be seen in the attention to values (those associated with justice or righteousness) promulgated by all the world faiths; it can also be expressed organizationally. Both dimensions are illustrated in the local and concrete—in for example the sensitive management of particular sacred spaces—and in the expertise of global movements such as the Sant'Egidio Community, the World Council of Churches and (to give but one American example) the Interfaith Dialogue and Peacebuilding Program at the US Institute of Peace. It is equally clear that religious actors are often critical players in post-conflict situations: good examples can be found in South Africa or Northern Ireland.

The relationship between religion and human rights offers a linking theme in this respect. The concept of human rights has become a defining discourse in the management of diversity, in the resolution of conflict and in the fair distribution of resources. Across all of these domains, however, the relationship between religion and human rights is differently regarded: from active advocacy at one end of the spectrum to open hostility at the other. There are those who draw from Article 18 of the United Nations Declaration on Human Rights to uphold the freedom of religion and belief as a fundamental and universally applicable human right; there are others who see the demands of religion and religious people as inimical to an alternative range of freedoms (those, for instance, of free speech, of women and of LGBTi communities). The existence of a UN Special Rapporteur on Freedom of Religion and Belief is indicative of a determination to find a way forward not only in places where diverse religious and secular norms are valued but also in places where they are likely to come into conflict—gender-specific abuses being a case in point.

There are two further substantive sections in the IPSP chapter. The first reflects an additional theme in the EASSSR conference in that it deals with the place of religion in the wellbeing of individuals and communities. Particular attention is paid to welfare, education and healthcare. A striking example will be taken to illustrate the approach. Faced with the seeming impasse between secular health professionals and faith-based initiatives in parts of the developing world, a series of contributions in *The Lancet* offers an evidenced-based way forward.[7] The emphasis is on partnership, arguing that secular and faith-based organizations can work together even when there are areas of disagreement regarding policy and practice. The crucial point is to ascertain exactly what these are—and thus to establish not only what cannot be done in partnership but the (normally much greater) areas of work that can be shared. The need is such that it is unwise to rule out significant resources on principle. Not all partnerships with religious organizations are advisable but many are.

One further area requires attention—that is the role of faith-based organizations in caring for the earth itself (the final step in our ascending scale). Unsurprisingly given its genesis, a number of chapters in the IPSP report engage growing concerns about the environment and the role of social science—as well as natural science—in understanding these better. Our task was more specific: namely to draw attention to the place of religious groups in this enterprise. Again, a single example captures the potential. *Laudato Si'*—the second encyclical of Pope Francis—was published in 2015. It is regarded as a landmark moment in the debate surrounding ecological issues. It is not only the size of the Pope's constituency that counts (though that most certainly matters) but the fact that he draws on established research to deliver a powerful ethical message: that deprived communities will suffer most from climate change. Taking both these points together, there can be no doubt that the Pope has vastly extended not only the reach but the impact of the debate—a fact recognised as much by scientists as by theologians.[8]

---

[7] See *The Lancet*, Vol. 386, No. 10005. The articles in question are available online: http://thelancet.com/series/faith-based-health-care (accessed on 17 August 2018).

[8] See, for example, the editorial in *Nature*, 23 June 2015, entitled "Hope from the Pope", available online: https://www.nature.com/news/hope-from-the-pope-1.17824 (accessed on 17 August 2018).

The final part of the chapter is constructed differently. It takes the form of an action toolkit deriving from a set of cross-cutting themes that run right through our material. These include: the *persistence* of religion in the modern world, in the sense that it is neither vanishing nor resurgent; the importance of context in discerning outcomes (both positive and negative); the urgent need to enhance cultural competence (not least religious literacy) in different parts of the world; the significance of religion in initiating change; and the gains that accrue from effective partnerships. In short: " … researchers and policy-makers pursuing social progress will benefit from careful attention to the power of religious ideas to motivate, of religious practices to shape ways of life, of religious communities to mobilize and extend the reach of social changes and of religious leaders and symbols to legitimate calls to action" (International Panel on Social Progress 2018, p. 643).

3. Managing Global Diversity

Rightly the inaugural conference of the EASSSR paid particular attention to the presence of religious diversity in East Asia, seeing this as the result of two things: first, population movements both within and the beyond the region; and second, shifts in government policies. Both causes and consequences were explored in a wide variety of papers. It was, moreover, significant that the conference was held in Singapore—one of the most religiously diverse places in the modern world.[9]

Religious diversity was an equally central theme in our IPSP work, as we sought both to document and to explain the capacities (or not) of diverse populations to live alongside one another in different parts of the world. Our first task, however, was to untangle a tricky vocabulary and to underline the difference between diversity (which is a descriptive term) and pluralism (which is normative and implies judgments about diversity)—a distinction which is not always recognized in the literature (Beckford 2003). We also needed to establish the facts and figures in different global regions, mindful that it is not necessarily the case that diversity is increasing in the modern world. Establishing whether or not this is happening is an empirical rather than an a priori question.

For example, it is most certainly the case that religious diversity is growing in Western Europe (Figure 1),[10] a fact with huge implications both for religion as such and for the theories that we deploy to understand this (see Section 4). This is much less the case further East, that is, in post-communist Europe (Figure 2), where the historic churches are becoming noticeably more assertive, often at the expense of religious minorities, both Christian and other. In this part of Europe, the fall of communism (in 1989) marked a watershed, bringing to an end a prolonged period of politically enforced secularization. To an extent a similar shift has taken place in China following the Cultural Revolution (1966–1976) but here there has been a marked growth both in religion per se and in religious diversity (Figure 3), prompting a key theme in the EASSSR conference program and an excellent IPSP case study.[11] The future, however, remains uncertain.

Religious diversity can also flat line as is the case in South East Asia (Figure 4), a region where diversities of all kinds should be seen as "constitutive." Singapore offers an excellent example, providing the IPSP chapter team with a further instructive case study.[12] Such flat-lining can also be found in the US (Figure 5), though here the never-ending choices lie almost entirely *within* Christianity

---

[9] In the course of the conference, delegates were invited to attend the Institute of Policy Studies Forum on "Understanding Religious Harmony in Singapore." See https://lkyspp.nus.edu.sg/news-events/events/details/ips-forum-on-religious-harmonyforfurtherdetails (accessed on 17 August 2018).

[10] Figures 1–7 in this section are reprinted from the on-line version of "Religions and social progress: Critical assessments and creative partnerships", which is Chapter 16 in (International Panel on Social Progress 2018). See note 2 for further details. I am grateful to Cambridge University Press for permission to re-use this material.

[11] See Fenggang Yang, "Accommodating new forms of religion: Chinese dilemmas", sidebar 16.2 in Chapter 16 "Religions and social progress: Critical assessments and creative partnership" (long version). Available online: https://www.ipsp.org/downloads (accessed on 17 August 2018).

[12] See Vineeta Sinha, "'Religious Education' in a Southeast Asian Context: Insights from Singapore", sidebar 16.3 in Chapter 16 "Religions and social progress: Critical assessments and creative partnership" (long version). Available online: https://www.ipsp.org/downloads (accessed on 17 August 2018).

rather than beyond it. Diversity, finally, can and does diminish but for different reasons in different places. One reason, sadly, is conflict, as in the seemingly unresolvable situation in the Middle East where large numbers of both Jews and Christians see no alternative but to leave, after centuries of continuous presence (Figure 6).[13] In parts of Africa an entirely different process is taking place in countries where the gradual ascendancy of world faiths, notably Christianity and Islam, has emerged at the expense of multiple indigenous religions (Figure 7).

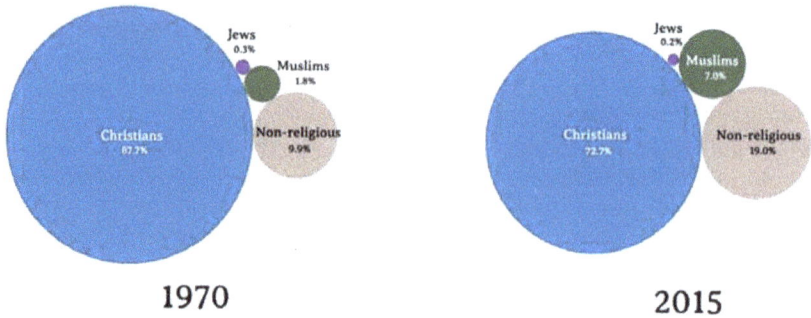

Historically Europe (39 countries) has been the most Christian continent in the world. However, the region experienced a sharp decline in its Christian affiliation between 1970 and 2015, resulting in a rise of non-religious self-identification (atheist and/or agnostic). That said, large numbers of Europeans still identify with their churches despite the fact that they neither believe nor practice their religion. There has also been a significant growth in the Muslim population due to immigration. The Jewish population continues to decline.

Data source: Todd M. Johnson, Brian J. Grim, & Gina A. Zurlo, eds. World Religion Database. Leiden/Boston: Brill, accessed April 2017.

Figure 1. Religious diversity in Southern, Western and Northern Europe, 1970 and 2015.

Patterns of religious affiliation in Eastern Europe (Belarus, Bulgaria, Czech Republic, Hungary, Moldova, Poland, Romania, Russia, Slovakia, Ukraine) differ markedly from the rest of the continent. The year 1970 marked the height of identification as non-religious, as large sections of Eastern Europe were then dominated by state-imposed atheism. In the early 1990s, non-religion began a gradual decline as Christianity, primarily Orthodoxy, grew, offsetting secularizing trends in other parts of the continent. Judaism has also declined partly as a result of anti-Semitism.

Data source: Todd M. Johnson, Brian J. Grim, & Gina A. Zurlo, eds. World Religion Database. Leiden/Boston: Brill, accessed April 2017.

Figure 2. Religious diversity in Russia and Eastern Europe, 1970 and 2015.

---

[13] The data in Figure 6 extends to 2015. The trend is likely to continue.

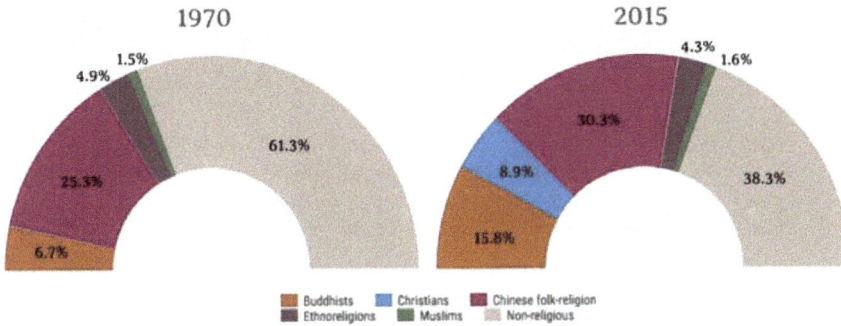

Religious adherence of all kinds in China has been steadily increasing since 1970. The practice of more "traditional" Chinese religions like Buddhism, Chinese folk-religion, and Confucianism has increased. Christianity grew dramatically in China from 1970 to 2015, from under 1% of the population (876,000) to nearly 9% (123 million). The Chinese constitution states that citizens have "freedom of religious belief" but limits protections for religious practice to "normal religious activities." Religious groups must register with the government and belong to one of five state-sanctioned "patriotic religious associations": Buddhist, Taoist, Muslim, Catholic, or Protestant.

Data source: Todd M. Johnson, Brian J. Grim, & Gina A. Zurlo, eds. World Religion Database. Leiden/Boston: Brill, accessed April 2017.

Figure 3. The growth of religion in China, 1970 and 2015.

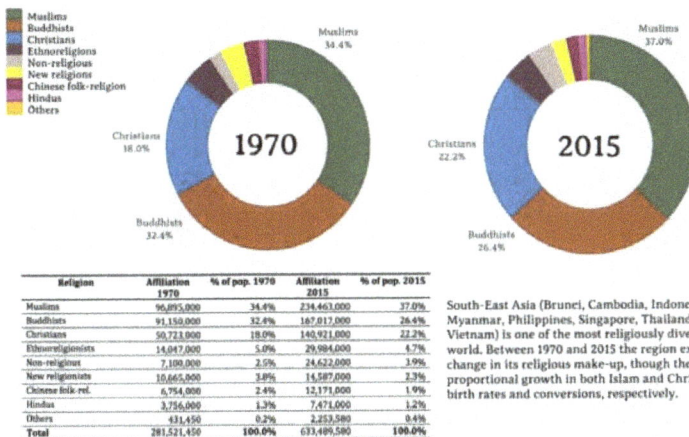

Religion	Affiliation 1970	% of pop. 1970	Affiliation 2015	% of pop. 2015
Muslims	96,895,000	34.4%	234,463,000	37.0%
Buddhists	91,150,000	32.4%	167,017,000	26.4%
Christians	50,723,000	18.0%	140,921,000	22.2%
Ethnoreligionists	14,047,000	5.0%	29,984,000	4.7%
Non-religious	7,100,000	2.5%	24,622,000	3.9%
New religionists	10,665,000	3.8%	14,587,000	2.3%
Chinese folk-rel.	6,754,000	2.4%	12,171,000	1.9%
Hindus	3,756,000	1.3%	7,471,000	1.2%
Others	431,450	0.2%	2,253,580	0.4%
Total	281,521,450	100.0%	633,489,580	100.0%

South-East Asia (Brunei, Cambodia, Indonesia, Laos, Malaysia, Myanmar, Philippines, Singapore, Thailand, Timor-Leste, Vietnam) is one of the most religiously diverse regions in the world. Between 1970 and 2015 the region experienced little change in its religious make-up, though there has been proportional growth in both Islam and Christianity due to high birth rates and conversions, respectively.

Data source: Todd M. Johnson, Brian J. Grim, & Gina A. Zurlo, eds. World Religion Database. Leiden/Boston: Brill, accessed April 2017.

Figure 4. Religious diversity in Southeast Asia, 1970 and 2015.

In short, the picture is complex; so also are the questions that follow. A constructive starting point lies in the recognition that *religious* diversity is part and parcel of a broader agenda but that it has particular characteristics. Religious differences, for example, are likely to strike more foundational chords than variations in taste or style—quite simply there is more at stake. Equally central is an awareness that diversities exist, largely (if not exclusively) because of the movement of people, both forced and unforced. The interrelationships of religion and migration become therefore a central theme. They run, moreover, in different directions. On the one hand, religions inspire, manage and benefit from the migration process but on the other, they are shaped and moulded by the dislocations of populations that inevitably ensue. You cannot have one without the other.

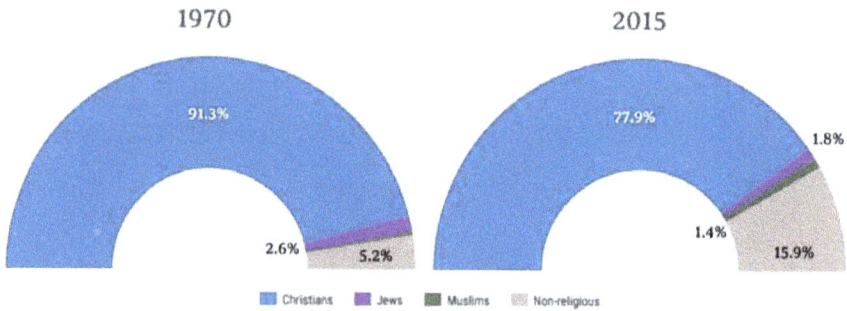

Despite a gradual decline of its Christian population, the United States remained the country with the most Christians in 2015 at nearly 251 million. Many mainline denominations (Methodists, Baptists, Lutherans, etc.) are losing members, while Pentecostal/charismatic and Evangelical denominations are growing, such as the Assemblies of God and smaller, Independent churches. Losses from Christianity resulted in gains for atheists and agnostics, who in 2015 represented nearly 16% of the population. The United States has also experienced an increase of its Buddhist, Hindu, Sikh, Baha'i, and Jain populations, though these each represents 1% or less of the population.

Data source: Todd M. Johnson, Brian J. Grim, & Gina A. Zurlo, eds. World Religion Database. Leiden/Boston: Brill, accessed April 2017.

Figure 5. The changing diversity of the United States, 1970 and 2015.

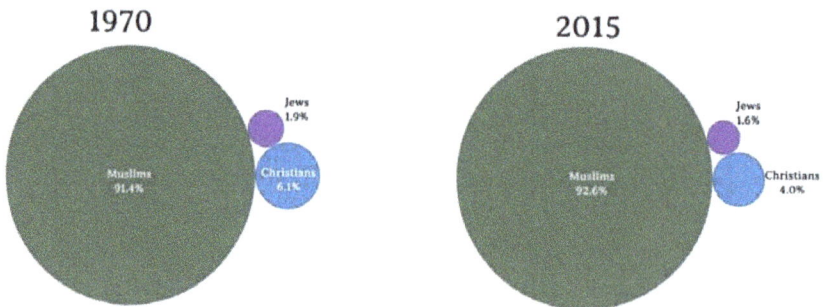

The political situation of the Middle East (Bahrain, Cyprus, Egypt, Iran, Iraq, Israel, Jordan, Kuwait, Lebanon, Oman, Palestine, Qatar, Saudi Arabia, Syria, Turkey, United Arab Emirates, Yemen) has significantly influenced its religious composition. Historic communities of religious minorities—particularly Christians, Jews, and Baha'is—have emigrated from the region in large numbers after centuries of relative stability. It is likely that the Middle East will continue to become less religiously diverse over time.

Data source: Todd M. Johnson, Brian J. Grim, & Gina A. Zurlo, eds. World Religion Database. Leiden/Boston: Brill, accessed April 2017.

Figure 6. Religious diversity in the Middle East, 1970 and 2015.

The consequences require careful management: migration is a hot political issue. For which reason we reflected carefully on the various forms of governance discovered in this field and the debates that surround them. These include the pros and cons of multiculturalism, of diverse forms of secularism and of democracy itself. We recognized, however, that there are deeper questions to address: those that probe the ways in which religiously diverse people do not simply co-exist but flourish in each other's company. We discovered, for example, that "street level ecumenism" (working side by side) is often more effective than a dialogue between elites.[14] Such an approach drives us back once again to the realities of lived religion in addition to its official formulations.

---

[14] Beaman (2017) addresses this point. She asks a very pertinent question: what might we discover if we turned our attention to the success stories of diverse living rather than dwelling disproportionately on points of conflict?

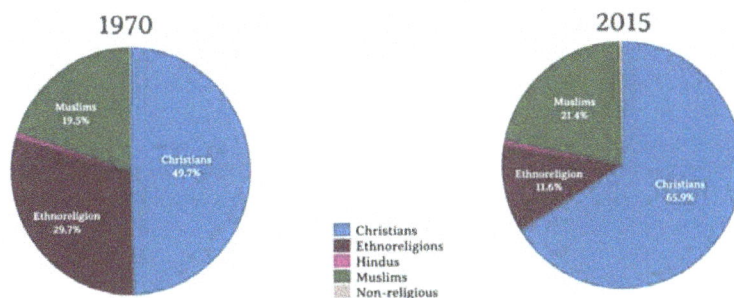

Eastern Africa (Burundi, Comoros, Djibouti, Eritrea, Ethiopia, Kenya, Madagascar, Malawi, Mauritius, Mayotte, Mozambique, Reunion, Rwanda, Seychelles, Somalia, South Sudan, Tanzania, Uganda, Zambia, Zimbabwe) has experienced a decrease in religious diversity through the continued growth of Christianity and Islam, each of which have received converts from traditional religionists (ethnoreligionists). However, the range of diversity varies within the region, as some countries are Muslim-majority (Somalia, Comoros), some are Christian-majority (Burundi, Kenya), and some have large populations of both (Eritrea).

Data source: Todd M. Johnson, Brian J. Grim, & Gina A. Zurlo, eds. World Religion Database. Leiden/Boston: Brill, accessed April 2017.

Figure 7. Religious diversity in East Africa, 1970 and 2015.

One final point concludes this section: that is to appreciate that the concept of diversity as such is far from uniform and means different things in different places. The significance of this fact for the understanding of religious life is nicely captured in the following paragraphs, taken from a relatively recent essay by Martin (2013). The focus of the essay is the global spread of Pentecostalism (an example of transnational voluntarism); the implications, however, are far-reaching:

"The big contrast on the global scale is between transnational voluntarism and those forms of religion based on a closed market, which regard certain territories as their peculiar and sacred preserve and assume an isomorphic relation between kin, ethnicity and faith. The principle of the transnational voluntary organisation competes globally with the religions of place and ethnicity ... The global variations run along a scale from North America, where it [the exercise of choice] is normal, to Western Europe and Australasia, where it is accepted but not all that frequent, to the Arabian Peninsula, which is by definition Islamic territory where even foreigners cannot establish their own sacred buildings" (Martin 2013, p.185).

In short, diversity is taken for granted in the US and is becoming more so in Western Europe. In East Europe—where ethnicity and religion significantly overlap—a different pattern has emerged (see above). What Martin terms "Islamic territory" lies at the opposite extreme to the US. Here diversity is barely permitted and acquires therefore an entirely different meaning. Not all Muslims, however, live in Muslim territories: in the Global East, for example, they constitute one minority among others, as they do in Western Europe. The evolving situation in Europe provides the link to the following section.

4. Thinking Theoretically about Global Religious Diversity

Two points come together in this discussion: the first describes the origins of the social sciences (specifically sociology) in the European Enlightenment; the second reflects on the consequences of this situation for the understanding of religion in the modern world, starting with the changing situation in Europe itself before returning—step by step—to the Global East.

Correctly sociology has been described as the "epistemological child of the Enlightenment" and like the Enlightenment thinkers themselves, "early sociologists saw rationality and empirical observation as the ultimate source of knowledge" (Spickard 2017, p. 48). For this reason, sociology finds its disciplinary identity in its opposition to religion. And once religion and still more theology, is cast as sociology's "other", it follows that the notion of secularization, as the concomitant of modernization (and thus progress), is built into the DNA of the discipline. The story is a French one, in which the Enlightenment takes a markedly anti-religious turn, squaring off against an equally intransigent Catholic Church. This—it should be noted—is much less the case in Protestant Europe and by the time that Enlightenment ideas cross the Atlantic, the core notion of a "freedom from belief" (meaning freedom from the dominance of the Catholic Church), mutates into a "freedom to believe"—a noticeably different formulation (Himmelfarb 2004).

These variations on the theme are important but the crucial point endures. Sociology and the social sciences more generally, developed their disciplinary self-understanding in a specific intellectual environment—one, moreover, which has been formative in European culture.

Does this matter? Does it matter, in other words, that these disciplines emerge from a distinctive environment and are necessarily coloured by this? We must answer this question in stages, looking first at the situation in Europe. The starting point is clear: in most parts of the continent, the relatively good fit between what might be termed "traditional" understandings of sociological theory and empirical realities remains intact, keeping in mind regional variations, growing complexities and unexpected developments. Undeniably, the dominant trend towards greater secularity continues, noting that the *process* of secularization takes place very differently in different European societies.[15]

That however is not the whole story. In my own work (Davie 2006, 2015) I have discerned five very different factors that must be taken into account if we are to understand fully the present situation in Western Europe. These are: the centrality of the Judaeo-Christian tradition in Europe's cultural heritage; the continuing—if diminished—significance of Europe's historic churches which work on the principle of a public utility (i.e., they are there at the point of need for anyone who lives in a designated place); a growing number of alternatives to these churches which, taken together, look more like a market than a public utility; a marked influx of new arrivals since 1945 who come from many parts of the world and bring with them a wide variety of world faiths (among them are Christians, Muslims, Hindus, Sikhs and Buddhists); and finally a noticeable growth in the numbers of people who describe themselves as "nones"—that is, as having no religion.

More—much more—could be said about all of these factors but the crucial point to note is that they push and pull in different directions to produce the following, largely unexpected, paradox. At one and the same time European populations are becoming both more secular and more religiously diverse. The former is closely associated with the privatization of belief, a trend in line with classic understandings of secularization. The latter does the reverse: it enhances the *public* profile of religion not least in public debate. Put succinctly: Europeans talk more about something that they do less. The consequence, all too often, is an ill-informed and ill-mannered conversation about matters of extreme importance to the functioning of a healthy democracy. The catalysts for these debates vary depending on the country under review. In France for example they are dominated by (mostly Muslim) dress codes; in Britain or Denmark, freedom of speech—including the freedom to insult a religious minority—is more prominent. That said, the underlying question remains the same: how do Europeans, who have shared up to two millennia of Christian history, learn to accommodate minorities whose religious aspirations are coloured by very different cultural backgrounds and are likely to manifest themselves in unexpected ways—in public and well as private life.

A second, rather more searching, question cannot be avoided. It is easily articulated: is Europe secular because it is modern, or is Europe secular because it is European? Expressed thus, the question opens up the relationship between modernization and secularization. Is it the case that modernization necessarily brings about secularization, or does this only happen in particular—i.e., European—circumstances? One way of responding is to reverse the line of argument: in other words, to ask not what Europe is but what Europe is not. Following the examples that I used in a book which explored this theme is some

---

[15] That the process of secularization takes place differently in different places is a key insight in sociological thinking (Martin 1978). Martin's theory is applicable within Europe and between Europe and other global regions.

detail (Davie 2002), the answer is clear. Europe is not (yet) a vibrant religious market such as that found in the United States; it is not a part of the world where Christianity is growing exponentially, very often in Pentecostal forms, as is the case in the Global South; it is not a part of the world dominated by faiths other than Christian but is increasingly penetrated by these; and it is not for the most part subject to the violence often associated with religion and religious differences in other parts of the globe—the more so if religion becomes entangled in political conflict. Hence the inevitable, if at times disturbing (for some) conclusion: that the patterns of religion in modern Europe, including its relative secularity, might be an exceptional case in global terms. A rather similar conclusion emerges from a second publication, which developed the comparison between Europe and the US in more detail (Berger et al. 2008).

The corollary in terms of the argument of this article is clear. The theoretical corpus of mainstream social science has been honed, in what has turned out to be the atypical case with respect to global patterns of religiousness, for which reason universalizing the theory really does cause trouble. That was so in our initial encounters with the IPSP project, where our colleagues had considerable difficulty in seeing the significance of religion for the topic under review; it is equally likely to be the case in East Asia.

A book that not only captures the significance of this statement but relates it at least in part to the East Asian situation was published in the spring of 2013. Christian Caryl's *Strange Rebels* weaves together a complex narrative which involves four protagonists and five countries and finds its focus in a series of changes that take place in 1979. The protagonists are Mrs. Thatcher, Deng Xiaoping, the Ayatollah Homeini and Pope John Paul II. The five countries are the United Kingdom, China, Iran, its neighbour Afghanistan and Poland, then part of the Eastern bloc. Mrs. Thatcher and Deng initiated market reforms challenging deeply held assumptions about the way to manage the economy. The Ayatollah and John Paul II, conversely, were motivated by their respective religions to challenge the hegemony of the secular (socialist) state. In Afghanistan, Islamism became a major factor in the resistance to the Soviet Union, as did Catholicism in Poland.

The imaginative leap in Caryl's analysis is to draw these factors together:

> "The forces unleashed in 1979 marked the beginning of the end of the great socialist utopias that had dominated so much of the twentieth century. These five stories—the Iranian Revolution, the start of the Afghan jihad, Thatcher's election victory, the pope's first Polish pilgrimage and the launch of China's economic reforms—deflected the course of history in a radically new direction. It was in 1979 that the twin forces of the markets and religion, discounted for so long, came back with a vengeance" (Caryl 2013, p. 13).

The "victims" in this particular scenario were the dominant ideologies of the twentieth century embodied in the secular state, in either its socialist or communist forms. Both adjective (secular) and noun (state) are important in a formulation which was seen as the lynch pin of modernization. To be modern meant to be secular and the accepted form of political organization was the state. The "new" combination of market and religion not only erodes both elements but reveals the connections between 1979 and 1989 and in the fullness of time 2001. By 1989 the market had proved itself more effective than the command economy of the Soviet Union and religion—whether in its Muslim or Christian forms—was clearly more durable than its secular equivalent, in this case communism. Forces set in motion in 1979 led inexorably to the fall of the Berlin wall just over ten years later and the collapse of the Soviet Union overall led in turn to a radical realignment of the global order which—to an extent—is still in train.[16] The attack on the Twin Towers in 2001 is not covered in Caryl's account but the connections are clear enough. Quite clearly Islamism is one factor among others behind this epochal moment, to the evident bewilderment of the West.

---

[16] It should not be assumed that the ascendancy of either the market, or indeed religion, will necessarily continue. The global recession of 2008, itself unexpected, has undermined confidence in this respect.

It is important to remember that Caryl is writing some thirty years after the event and can make connections that were not at all clear at the time. Indeed, for those involved the principal feature that linked these three world-changing events was their unexpectedness. Manifestly, both policy-makers and pundits were caught unawares—in every case. Why was it that the Shah of Iran, a western figurehead, was obliged to flee before an Ayatollah motivated by conservative readings of Islam? And why did observers of all kinds fail to anticipate the concatenation of events that led to the fall of the Berlin wall and the collapse of communism as a credible narrative? And why finally did the events of 9/11 come like a bolt from the blue? By this stage there was a growing awareness of events in the Muslim world and their significance for Western policy,[17] but nobody—nobody at all—expected hi-jacked planes to fly into iconic buildings in New York. Hence the abruptness of the wake-up call: religion was undeniably important in that it was clearly able to motivate widely different groups of people to act in dramatic and unforeseen ways—a realization that prompted renewed attention to an aspect of society that had been ignored for too long.

All too often, however, the wrong inference was drawn. Commentators were rather too ready to assume that religion was resurgent or back, reasoning that we are now in a post-secular, rather than a post-religious, situation. To argue thus, however, is to conflate two rather different things. Was it really the case that religion (or God) was back? Or was it simply that the disciplines of social science in the west, along with a wide variety of politicians and policy-makers, had become aware (or re-aware) of something that had been there all the time? Was it, in other words, perceptions that had altered rather than reality? It is, I think, a complex mixture of both. New forms of religion have asserted themselves in different parts of the world; that is beyond doubt. It is incorrect to assume, however, that the new manifestations emerged from a vacuum. What is—or has been—lacking, however, is a social-scientific narrative that is fit for purpose: one in other words that is sensitive to the religious factor in all its manifest diversity but which sees this not as an aberration but as an entirely "normal" element in late modern, twenty-first century life.

5. Conclusions

What might this factor look like in the Global East in the coming decades? I had a glimpse of the possibilities in the papers that I listened to in Singapore. I am well aware, however, that a more informed answer must come from scholars who are specialists in the field. That said, I will conclude with the following suggestions. I have argued in this article that social scientific theories concerning religion have emerged from a very specific—some would say exceptional—case and (rather like French wine) they do not travel well. Keeping this in mind, I would suggest that scholars of East Asia should use these theories sparingly and be ready to adapt them where necessary.[18] Much more positively, they should have confidence in their own modes of explanation, encouraging approaches that are sensitive to aspects of religion unfamiliar to Western scholars but which demand social-scientific interpretation. It is important that such explanations are able to accommodate change: in this part of the world, as in any other, the unexpected can and does happen. Clearly the East Asian situation will continue to evolve and differently in its constituent nations. Graduate students—the next generation of scholars—should be trained accordingly.

In inviting a certain distance from the social-scientific literature that has developed in the West, I do not wish to imply that there should be a diminution in scientific rigour. There needs, however, to be a developed awareness that a scientific intentionality that is appropriate to the social sciences is quite different from a scientific intentionality appropriate to the natural sciences. Or—as David Martin puts this—"[t]he human world can only be understood *scientifically* if you understand means

---

[17] Samuel Huntington work can be taken as an example (Huntington 1997). His thinking on the clash of civilizations dominated debate in the 1990's, both in the United States and beyond.

[18] Yang (2012) offers an excellent example of how Western theories—in this case rational choice theory—must be adapted if they are to be used effectively in the Chinese case.

and ends, meanings, motives and intentions as these are variably realised in widely different contexts." (Martin 2014, p. 38). In social science, it is never the case that one size fits all.

Funding: This research received no external funding.

Conflicts of Interest: The author declares no conflict of interest.

References

Beaman, Lori. 2017. *Deep Equality in an Era of Religious Diversity*. Oxford: Oxford University Press. ISBN 978-0198803485.

Beckford, James. 2003. *Social Theory and Religion*. Cambridge: Cambridge University Press. ISBN 978-0521774314.

Berger, Peter, Grace Davie, and Effie Fokas. 2008. *Religious America, Secular Europe: A Theme and Variations*. Farnham: Ashgate. ISBN 978-0754660118.

Caryl, Christian. 2013. *Strange Rebels: 1979 and the Birth of the 21st Century*. New York: Basic Books. ISBN 978-0465018383.

Davie, Grace. 2002. *Europe: The Exceptional Case. Parameters of Faith in the Modern World*. London: Darton, Longman and Todd. ISBN 978-0232524253.

Davie, Grace. 2006. Religion in Europe in the 21st century: The factors to take into account. *European Journal of Sociology* 47: 271–96. [CrossRef]

Davie, Grace. 2015. *Religion in Britain: A Persistent Paradox*. Oxford: Wiley Blackwell. ISBN 978-1405135962.

Himmelfarb, Gertrude. 2004. *The Roads to Modernity: The British, French and American Enlightenments*. New York: Knopf Publishing Group. ISBN 978-1400042364.

Huntington, Samuel. 1997. *The Clash of Civilizations: The Remaking of the World Order*. New York: Simon and Schuster. ISBN 978-0743231497.

International Panel on Social Progress, ed. 2018. *Rethinking Society for the 21st Century*. 3 vols. Cambridge: Cambridge University Press. ISBN 978-1108399579.

Johnson, Todd, Brian J. Grim, and Gina Zurlo, eds. 2016. *World Religion Database*. Leiden: Brill, Available online: https://www.worldreligiondatabase.org/ (accessed on 30 August 2018).

Martin, David. 1978. *A General Theory of Secularization*. Oxford: Blackwell. ISBN 978-0631189602.

Martin, David. 2013. Niche markets created by a fissile transnational faith. In *Religions in Movement: The Local and the Global in Contemporary Faith Traditions*. Edited by Robert W. Hefner, John Hutchinson, Sara Mels and Christianne Timmerman. New York: Routledge, pp. 180–95, ISBN 978-1138922846.

Martin, David. 2014. *Religion and Power: No Logos without Mythos*. Farnham: Ashgate. ISBN 978-1472433602.

Micklethwait, John, and Adrian Wooldridge. 2010. *God Is Back: How the Global Rise of Faith Is Changing the World*. London: Allen Lane. ISBN 978-0141024745.

Spickard, James. 2017. *Alternative Sociologies of Religion: Through Non-Western Eyes*. New York: New York University Press. ISBN 978-1479866311.

Yang, Fenggang. 2012. *Religion in China: Survival and Revival under Communist Rule*. New York: Oxford University Press. ISBN 978-0199735648.

religions

MDPI

Article

Locating Religion and Secularity in East Asia Through Global Processes: Early Modern Jesuit Religious Encounters

José Casanova

Berkley Center for Religion, Peace, and World Affairs, Georgetown University, 3007 M St, NW, Suite 200, Washington, DC 20007, USA; jvc26@georgetown.edu

Received: 25 September 2018; Accepted: 23 October 2018; Published: 7 November 2018

Abstract: The central premise of this paper is that in order to understand the social construction of religion and secularity in East Asia today we need to take a long durée historical approach, which takes into account the colonial encounters between the Christian West and East Asia during three different and distinct phases of globalization. While most of the recent scholarly work on the globalization of the categories of religion and secularity focuses on the second Western hegemonic phase of globalization, this essay focuses on the early modern phase of globalization before Western hegemony.

Keywords: globalization; East Asia; Western hegemony; Jesuits; religion; religiosity; secularity

The central premise of this paper is that in order to understand the social construction of religion and secularity in East Asia today we need to take a long *durée* historical approach, which takes into account the colonial encounters between the Christian West and East Asia during three different and distinct phases of globalization.[1] The first phase of globalization, before Western hegemony, which in East Asia lasted from the mid-sixteenth-century to the late eighteenth-century, was shaped primarily by the encounters between the Jesuits and other Catholic religious orders and the religions and cultures of East Asia. Although the categories of religion and secularity had not yet acquired a stable and identifiable form during this early modern phase, those early modern colonial encounters, which are the main focus of this paper, played a significant role in the emergence of the categories in the West in the transition from the first to the second phase of globalization.

The second phase of globalization, the phase of Western hegemony proper, lasted roughly from the end of the 18th century to the 1960s. It was during this phase that the categories of religion and secularity entered East Asian discourses, in and through the formation of secular nation states, contributing in the process to the reorganization of the pre-existing religious field in different directions.

Starting from the 1960s, we can distinguish a third phase of globalization, which initiates what we can now recognize as our contemporary global age, after Western hegemony. From the perspective of this paper, significant for this phase is the fact that the categories of religion and secularity have been subject to all kinds of critical, reflexive, post-colonial deconstruction and that the religious field in East Asia is being transformed by newly emerging global dynamics, now affecting simultaneously the entire globe.

I use the expression "religious field" to characterize the broader construct within which "religion" and "secularity" are dynamically and interactively situated. Following Van der Veer (2014), one can

---

[1] This essay is based on the Keynote Address delivered at the Inaugural Conference of East Asian Society for the Scientific Study of Religion. The text builds upon, at times literally, an earlier elaboration of the argument in Casanova (2018a).

best understand the "modern" religious field as a structural field of syntagmatic relations of which the main "modern" linguistic expressions are *religion* and *secularity*, but also *magic* (i.e., *superstition*) and *spirituality*. Each of these categories must be understood in relation to the others. Their interrelation determines the religious field in any particular context.

In organizing the religious field and in locating religion and secularity within it, diverse groups of agents play a determining role. First and most important has usually been the role of the state and political authorities. Equally significant, most of the time, is the role of competing religious authorities, religious virtuosi, and ordinary religious actors, collective as well as individual. Finally, academic experts and scholars of religion like us have also contributed to the organization of the religious field in manifold ways. But we scholars need to recognize that we are relative latecomers in our attempts to organize scientifically a field which has already been pre-organized for centuries by other agents.

Methodologically, this demands reflexive humility, on our part, to recognize that despite our high-sounding "scientific" claims, the religious field is not something which is objectively out there in nature, waiting for our scientific classifications, definitions, and general theories to replace the pre-existing classifications.

Rather, our task should be to understand and explain how the religious field is constantly being socially constructed by all the competing agents: states, political authorities, and courts; religious authorities, clerics, virtuosi, and religious people; and all the external observers and reporters like ourselves, who in the process also contribute to the continuous social reconstruction of the highly contested religious field.

1. Religiosity and Secularity

After several decades of critical deconstruction, we know that both religion and secularity are "modern" "secular" "Western Christian" categories, which have become globalized and now serve to classify and organize differently the religious field all over the globe (Asad 1993, 2003; Beyer 2006; Casanova 2008, 2011, 2012, 2018b; Mazusawa 2005; Nongbri 2013; De Vries 2008). Before becoming "modern" secular analytic categories, they had first emerged with St. Augustin as "Western Christian" theological categories that served to organize the religious field of Western Christendom and the subsequent historical process of European secularization (Casanova 2014).

Both categories, religion and secularity, have become globalized in and through global colonial encounters, beginning with the "first globalization" in the sixteenth-century. In the process, they led to the restructuration of already pre-existing very different religious fields in all non-Western cultures and civilizations. This paper is going to focus on the first phase of globalization with some brief concluding remarks on the second and third phases of globalization.

2. East Asia

Well before the first globalization, East Asia already constituted a pre-existing geographic and cultural civilizational region with its own characteristic religious field. The East Asian religious field was first shaped by the penetration of Mahayana Buddhism since the first century AD (Zürcher [1959] 2007). It was later consolidated by the diffusion of state Confucianism from the Middle Kingdom in its Neo-Confucian form, beginning in the twelfth-thirteenth centuries and peaking in the fifteenth-sixteenth centuries across East Asia (de Bary 1989; Liu 1973). As a result, East Asia shared the dynamic integration of the three teachings of Confucianism, Buddhism and Taoism as *sanjiao*.

In this respect, from a global comparative perspective, East Asia constitutes an ideal comparative unit of research, internally because of its combination of significant similarities and differences, and externally because of its radical differences with the West. At the same time, during the modern era, the entire region was transformed radically, yet very differently, through its diverse encounters with Western colonialism. In any case, examining the East Asian religious field comparatively helps to put into question the supposed universal character of modern Western processes and the historical categories derived from them.

Some of the distinguishing characteristics of the East Asian "religious field" have been:

(1) The presence of "states" much older than any and all Western states, which were first formed in the early modern era as internally competing states within the European Westphalian system and as externally competing states in their global colonial expansion. Paradoxically, one can characterize the Asian states as "quasi-religious" states with "sacred" legitimacy (Lagerwey 2010). But simultaneously, they can also be characterized as "proto-secular" states with the authority to organize the religious field through their power to define "orthodoxy" ("right way" or upright teaching) and "heterodoxy" ("crooked path" or "evil cult").

(2) A non-monopolistic context of fluid competition of multiple religious teachings (Confucianism, Buddhism, Taoism), having to vie for hegemony among themselves and with the different local versions of popular animistic folk "religions" (Shinto in Japan, shamanism in Korea, animism in Vietnam). Each of them could become at any time the state religion, or at least the officially recognized "public" religion, while trying to repress the others, pushing them underground or at least relegating them to the private sphere.

(3) The active presence of "proto-secular" observing scholars, the Confucian *literati*, who tended to look down upon other religious virtuosi and upon all forms of folk religiosity as "superstition" (i.e., magic). In this respect, Confucian scholars may be said to represent a pre-modern proto-secular form of "spiritual, not religious" identity, while one may also talk of "the secular as sacred" (Fingarette 1972).

This unstable and fluid East Asian religious field was changed dramatically by the arrival of the Jesuits and other Western colonial agents during "the first globalization" (Gunn 2003).

3. Jesuit Interreligious Encounters in East Asia in the First Globalization

The Jesuits were missionary proselytizers bringing the new "Teaching of the Lord of Heaven," which they claimed to be "the true religion." As such, they entered in competition with the representatives of East Asian teachings. But the Jesuits were simultaneously new "proto-orientalist" observing scholars from the West, who brought Western knowledge to the East and Eastern knowledge to the West. As such, they were received with enormous curiosity as they engaged in intercultural exchanges and dialogue with East Asian scholars. It was this dual identity as missionaries and scholars that made the Jesuits into pioneer globalizers during the first globalization (Casanova 2016a). It also gave them a competitive advantage over other Catholic religious orders that preceded them in South Asia, South East Asia, and East Asia.

The first organized group in history to think and to act globally were the Jesuits, following Jerome Nadal's injunction "the world is our home" (O'Malley 2013). They arrived in Asia sponsored by the Iberian colonial powers, particularly by the Portuguese *Padroado* (Aulden 1996; Boxer 1978). On the basis of the theological fiction of universal papal jurisdiction over non-Christian lands and peoples, the 1494 Treaty of Tordesillas drew an imaginary meridian line of demarcation, whereby all the lands newly "discovered" or to be discovered west of the line would belong to the Kingdom of Castile, while all the lands east of the line would belong to the Kingdom of Portugal. Naturally, neither other European powers (France, England or the Dutch Republic) nor non-Christian powers recognized the papal jurisdiction over those lands, much less the exclusive colonial claims of the Iberian empires.

In the Western Hemisphere, in the "New World," the Iberian powers were able not only to colonize the indigenous population, but also to impose their spiritual conquest through enforced Catholic confessionalization (Richard 1966). In the Eastern Hemisphere, by contrast, only in the Philippines and to a lesser extent in the Portuguese colonial enclaves of Goa and Macao could the Iberian colonizers reproduce the Latin American model. This was the era of "gunpowder empires" throughout Asia, and the Iberian powers were not in a position to subjugate any of the Asian empires (Ottoman, Persian, Mughal, or Chinese), nor any of the Kingdoms of East, South, or Southeast Asia (McNeil 1993).

In this respect it was an era of globalization and of colonial encounters before Western hegemony. But this in itself makes those encounters particularly relevant as we are entering a new age of globalization after Western hegemony. The Jesuits arrived in Goa, Macao, and Nagasaki on Portuguese ships sponsored by the *Padroado*. But they went beyond, reaching places in the interior of India, Japan, China, and Vietnam, where neither European merchants nor colonists had access. In the process, they initiated a series of intercultural encounters that transformed both East and West.

Alessandro Valignano arrived in Japan in 1579 and initiated the method of "cultural accommodation" or "inculturation" which was soon extended to other Jesuit missions in Asia (Schütte 1980–1985). His ethnographic observations on Japanese religion, culture, and society, presented in his *Sumario de las cosas de Japón* (1583) marks the beginning of Western scholarship on Japanese civilization (Valignano 1954; Tamburello et al. 2008). The arrival of Michele Ruggieri and Matteo Ricci in Zhaoqing in 1583 equally marks the beginning of the modern intercultural encounter between China and Europe. Ricci, in particular, is recognized as the foundation of modern Western Sinology (D'Elia 1942–1949; Po-chia Hsia 2010; Mungello 1989). The same can be said about the arrival of Roberto de Nobili in 1606 in Madurai and the beginning of Western scholarship on Hinduism, the arrival of Alexandre de Rhodes in Vietnam in 1619 and the beginning of Western scholarship on Vietnamese language, religion, and culture, and the arrival of Ippolito Desideri in Lhasa in 1716 and the beginning of Western Tibetan studies (de Nobili 2000; Phan 1998; Pomplun 2010).[2]

But it is important to stress that the Jesuit method of "accommodation" was not a cunning strategy devised by European missionaries. It was a practice that emerged out of the intercultural encounter. In Japan as well as in China, their local friends, the first Christians, taught the Jesuits the need to go "native" and to accommodate the local culture if they wanted to succeed. It was his friend and disciple Chü Ju-k'uei (or Chü T'ai-su) who first convinced Matteo Ricci of the need to abandon the habit of a Buddhist monk, which he had adopted at first upon entering China with Michele Ruggieri, and to assume instead the *habitus* of a Mandarin scholar (*ju*) (Rule 1986).

One may take the 1602 World Map of Matteo Ricci, *Kunyu Wanguo Quantu,* or "Map of the Ten Thousand Countries of the Earth," both as the first graphic evidence of global East Asia and as graphic illustration of the intercultural exchange initiated by the Jesuit mission (Standaert 2002). It was the first modern Chinese World Map with new Chinese names for many of the countries and cities in Europe, Africa, and the New World. It was an intercultural synthesis of Chinese and Western cartography jointly crafted by Matteo Ricci and the Chinese scholars Li Zhizao and Zhang Wentao. It was a synthesis, moreover, that decentered both Europe and the Middle Kingdom by flipping East and West and thus deconstructing both Eurocentrism and Sinocentrism.[3] In the revised form of the 1674 *Kunyu Quantu* or "Map of the Whole World," devised by the Belgian Ferdinand Verbiest, another Jesuit cartographer and astronomer in Beijing, it served for two hundred years as the basic global map used in China, Korea, Japan, and Vietnam.[4]

The Jesuit method of cultural accommodation was, moreover, grounded on a deeper theological reflection. They not only realized that they could never succeed in Europeanizing the Japanese or the Chinese, given the latter's own self-esteem and their perception of European culture as "barbarian". The Jesuits also became convinced that in order to take root in Japan, Christianity itself would have to become Japanese, in the same way as Christianity that was originally Hebrew, had to become truly Greek and Latin. If primitive Christianity could undergo such a fundamental translation and accommodation to Greek and to Roman culture, there was no reason why it could not become also Japanese, Chinese, etc. (Ücerler 2016).

---

[2] More than two thirds of the names on Urs App's list of early modern European orientalists before the establishment of Orientalism in European universities are Jesuits (App 2010). This was, however, Orientalism before the European colonization of Asia and in this respect significantly different from Edward Said (1978).
[3] https://en.wikipedia.org/wiki/Kunyu_Wanguo_Quantu.
[4] http://verbiest.asianart.org/.

The introduction of Christianity in each of the East Asian countries added a new and radically novel form of "religion," which served to de-stabilize an already fluid and pluralistic religious field. It brought new realignments and competitions but also eventually the slow emergence of the modern categories of "religion" and "secular," preparing the way for the emergence of the modern system of "world religions" in the second phase of Western hegemonic globalization.

4. The Christian Century in Japan

There are different and contrasting ways of interpreting the relevance of what has been called "the Christian Century in Japan" (Boxer 1951; Ücerler 2008). The high number of Japanese Christians, which are estimated anywhere from 300,000 to 1,000,000, from all walks of life from the highest *daimyos* to the lowest outcasts, in itself was significant. But more significant was the impact that the encounter with European Catholicism had on Japanese culture and on the determined effort of the Tokugawa regime not only to repress and to exterminate Christianity but to erase any memory of the previous encounter and to construct an authentic Japanese culture purified of any hybrid accretion from the Christian West. *Sengoku* Japan was undergoing at the time a radical transformation from a feudal "Country at War" to a centralized absolutist state and the *Kirishitan* played an important catalyst role in this transformation (Casanova 2018a).

From a comparative historical perspective, what is striking about absolutist state formation in Japan is the role played by the ethno-religious cleansing of the Christian minority, by anti-Christian state ideology, and by the confessionalization of the entire Japanese population through the Buddhist and Shinto temple registration system first introduced in 1635. The state-enforced disciplinary effort continued through the institutionalization of the "Christian *aratame*" practices through the second half of the 17th century, after Christianity had been wiped out, requiring Japanese to "prove" that they were not Christian. As Kiri Paramore points out, "the establishment of this system represented much more than just an instance of anti-Christian activity: it established an institutionalized system of social control extending to the entire population, a system of control that continued to function until the end of the Tokugawa Shogunate in the late nineteenth century" (Paramore 2009, p. 55).

Later interpretations, by Japanese as well as by Western scholars, have taken this Tokugawa Japanese ideology for granted, as an explanation for the ultimate failure of the Jesuits and of Christianity in Japan, as well as a justification for the radical isolationist policies of *Sakoku* Japan introduced by the Tokugawa, as the need to protect Japan not only from a foreign and un-Japanese religion, but from Western colonialism. Catholic Christianity was naturally rejected as a dangerous foreign body which, besides being an inferior and questionable form of Christianity, was essentially "other" and, therefore, ultimately unassimilable without undermining Japanese culture and Japanese identity (Elison 1973).

Japan represents the first non-European absolutist, secular state which developed not in imitation to the West, or consciously following the principles of Hobbes' *Leviathan*, yet following a pattern similar and parallel to the European confessional states. The Tokugawa state itself was non-confessional, and in this respect it could be characterized as "secular". Yet it introduced a policy of confessionalization of its population by enforcing the registration of every Japanese subject in Buddhist or Shinto temples, akin to the European parish registration system. Again, what was important was not that everybody had to become Buddhist, but that everybody had to become Japanese, as defined by the state. The aim of the anti-Christian state crusade was not the establishment of Buddhist "religion" per se, but the Japanization of the population. Buddhism was only a national instrument of Japanization. After the Meiji restoration, the Japanese state easily switched from Buddhism to nationalist Shintō in order to enforce an even more rigid policy of Japanization, while renewing its anti-Christian ideology (Paramore 2009).

5. Jesuit Project in Imperial Neo-Confucian China

China represented a very different type of colonial encounter. China was a huge empire, stable and relatively pacified, governed by a civil imperial bureaucracy of cultured literati. Yet, the Jesuit method of accommodation was also introduced with relative success first under the Ming dynasty and later continued under the Qing dynasty. The ultimate goal of Ricci and the Jesuits who followed him was to penetrate the imperial court of Beijing and to convert the Chinese emperor. The Constantinian model of imperial conversion from above was indeed taken for granted by European Catholics.

But Ricci soon realized that he had to become first Chinese before the Chinese could possibly become Christians. It demanded an arduous enterprise of double translation, of translation of Latin texts and of European culture into Chinese and of translation of Chinese texts and Chinese culture into Latin and into European culture. Ricci himself through his own sinicization was the key to this collective enterprise in which European Jesuits as well as Christian Confucian scholars participated. Ricci's translation of Euclid's *Elements* into Chinese, his *Treatise on Friendship* introducing famous aphorisms from Greek, Latin, and Christian authors into Chinese, his Catechism *T'ien-chu shih-i* (True Meaning of the Lord of Heaven), and his World Map "of the myriad nations of the earth" fusing Western and Chinese cartography, are the most famous illustrations of Ricci's contribution to this collective translation enterprise.

The effect of the translation of Chinese classics and culture first into Latin and then into European languages and cultures, mediated primarily by the China Jesuits, was probably even more crucial for European historical developments (Mungello 2013). Ricci and other Jesuits played a crucial role in the "manufacturing" of "Confucius" and Confucianism and in their significant reception in 17th and 18th century Europe (Jensen 1997; Mungello 1977). But it is important to stress that this dual and reciprocal process of inculturation, which crystallized in a novel form of Confucian Christianity or Christian Confucianism, was the result of synthetic collaboration and intercultural dialogue between European Jesuits and Chinese scholars such as Yang T'ing-yün, Li Chih-Tsao, and Hsü Kuang-ch'i, widely known as "the Three Pillars of Christianity in China" (Peterson 1988).

Jacques Gernet (1985) famously argued that those Chinese scholars were not truly "Christian" because they did not know the true European Christianity. Moreover, the whole encounter was based on a fundamental misunderstanding between two supposedly incommensurable cultures and conceptions of "religion." But Gernet's evaluation is based on a post-Enlightment secularist conception of Christian "religion" and on a modern essentialist conception of Western and Chinese civilizations as fixed and radically different totalities.

The encounters of early modernity show precisely that civilizational boundaries were by no means fixed and firm, but they would become so as a result of the very colonial encounters. In retrospect, re-examining the Jesuit encounters, we can certainly assume that the Christian impact on China was probably much less relevant and certainly less lasting than the Chinese impact on Christian Europe (Standaert 2008).[5] The Jesuit translation and introduction of Chinese culture into the European public sphere, particularly as it was mediated through the Chinese Rites controversy, played a crucial role in shaping what became the Enlightenment critique of religion, and in this respect affected the European process of secularization (Rubiés 2005).

The Jesuit encounter with the complex religious field they found in Asian societies forced them to rethink the classificatory categories of religion they had brought with them. In the process they contributed unintendedly to the modern differentiation of religion and culture and to the pluralist global system of world religions that became institutionalized in the 20th century (Beyer 2006; Mazusawa 2005).

Let me quote from a letter of Matteo Ricci to the Spanish colonial administrator in the Philippines, Juan Bautista Román, in which he tries to make sense of the complex Chinese religious field he has encountered. This is actually Ricci's earliest surviving letter from China, written on 13 September 1584,

---

[5] Recently, a more nuanced revisionist account of the long lasting and continuous implantation of indigenous forms of Chinese Christianity has been emerging (Mungello 2012; Standaert 1997).

almost exactly one year after he and Ruggieri arrived in Zhaoqing from Macao. I am going to translate freely from the Italian-Portuguese-Spanish "creole" frequently used by Jesuits in East Asia.

Ricci (1913, pp. 48–49) writes:

> Let me say a few words about the *religions* and *sects* of China, without being too precise, since there is no *religion* in China and the small amount of *cult* that exists is so intricate that even their own *religious people* cannot give a good account of it. Leaving aside the *Moors*, which I do not know how they got here, the Chinese are divided into *three sects*: one is called *heguia* (*Buddhists*), the other *cilitan* (*Daoists*) and the most celebrated is the one of the *literati*, who normally do not believe in the immortality of the soul, make fun of the assertions of the other two, and only give thanks to heaven and earth for the benefits they receive, but do not pray for salvation in the afterlife.

I've placed in italics the various references to the different "religious" phenomena to indicate that the terms *religion, religions, religious* at the time, at the end of the 16th century, were still unstable and did not yet have the precise meanings which they would acquire later towards the end of the 18th century (Smith 1998). The Jesuits at the time throughout their global missions used interchangeably such terms as *"faith"* (particularly in reference to the Holy Catholic Faith), *"religion"* (mostly when referring to the true Catholic religion, *de vera religione*), *teachings* (to refer to both orthodox Christian doctrines and heterodox ones, such as those of Christian heretics and sectarians, Christian schismatics, the doctrines of Jewish and Muslim infidels, and pagan and idolatrous doctrines), and *laws* (Jewish, Christian, Muslim, etc.). *Cult* refers to sacred rituals, not to the modern meaning of a dangerous "cult" that ought to be outlawed for public protection.

The assertion, "there is no *religion* in China", obviously only means there is no *true* religion. *Religiones* in the plural at the time usually referred not to "religions" in the modern sense of the term but to the multiple Catholic religious orders (Benedictines, Franciscans, Dominicans, etc.). Analogically, Ricci is going to refer to the various "religions" or monastic orders or "sects" he has found in China. The reference to "their own *religious* people" is also to the various orders of *religious virtuosi*. Besides the *Moors*, the name given to Muslims at the time in Southern Latin Europe, who Ricci clearly does not view as part of Chinese religion, he identifies the three Chinese teachings (*sanjiao*), as Buddhists, Daoists, and *literati*. The literati are not yet identified as Confucians, or followers of the teachings of Kong-fu-zi, the name which Ricci and the Jesuits would use for Kong-zi, the more common Chinese name of the Sage, which they turned into the Latin Confucius (Jensen 1997).

Already in his early encounter with Confucian teachings, Ricci realizes that they do not *believe* in the immortality of the soul or in salvation in the afterlife, look down upon Buddhist and Daoist teachings as *superstition*, and practice no *idolatrous* rituals, other than thanksgiving to heaven and earth. Clearly such teachings do not fit the category of pagan idolatrous religion. Indeed, they seem more like a proto-secular moral teaching, analogous to the moral teachings of ancient Greek and Latin classic authors, such as Socrates, Cicero, and Seneca, which Jesuits had incorporated into the Christian Humanism they were spreading in Jesuit colleges throughout the world through their *Ratio Studiorum*, the Jesuit liberal arts curriculum (O'Malley 2016; Maryks 2016).

If Cicero could be inducted as a "Saint" in Jesuit colleges, the more so, Ricci was convinced, could Kung-fu-zi be venerated as a "saint." Ricci was soon recognized by his Chinese peers as a scholar of the Chinese classics, provoking both great admiration for his erudition and virtue, but also great animosity for his relentless attacks on Buddhism and his attempt to purify the reigning Neo-Confucianism from the materialism, which Ricci viewed as a later accretion and as deviation from the ancient teachings. Towards the end of his life in a 1609 letter to Francesco Pasio, a fellow Jesuit in the Japan mission, Ricci (1913, p. 385) wrote:

> In ancient times they [i.e., Chinese] followed the natural law more faithfully than in our own countries. And 1500 years ago, this people was not inclined to the worship of idols ... On

the contrary, the books of the *literati*, which are the most ancient and authoritative among their writings, do not adore anything but heaven and earth and the Lord of both. And if we examine these books, we will find little therein against the light of reason and much that is in conformity with it [...] and we can hope in Divine mercy and that many of their ancient sages were saved by their observance of the natural law with the help that God would have given them on account of their goodness.

Leaving aside the accuracy of Ricci's interpretation of Confucianism and his negative view of Buddhism and Daoism, two things become evident from Ricci's letters. First, in their encounters with the religious other, the Jesuits are confronted with forms of religious pluralism that could not easily be fitted within the traditional taxonomies of "false" pagan or idolatrous religions. Secondly, in their recourse to natural law and the light of reason in order to account for the nature of this religious pluralism, the Jesuits initiate in fact a form of inter-cultural and interreligious encounter that takes place without reference to revelation. In a certain sense, one finds here the seeds of that which Peter Berger (2014) has identified as the two types of "modern" pluralism: multi-religious pluralism and secular-religious pluralism.

Crucial was the distinction that the Jesuits introduced in China between religion and culture; between, on the one hand, universal Christian religion, which per se is non-European, and therefore can become inculturated in any and all particular cultures, and, on the other, those components of the particular religious cultures that are idolatrous, and therefore cannot become Christianized. Those idolatrous components of culture have to be rejected. However, those components of culture that are not idolatrous, that are civil rather than religious, are neutral and therefore can become Christianized. This is the way in which Confucianism, as interpreted by the Jesuits, was understood not as an idolatrous religion, but as a humanist culture, as a natural morality, and as a civil cult. Unintentionally, once the distinction was incorporated into European debates, it signaled the beginning of the breakdown of the monotheistic distinction between "true" and "false" religion on which the entire structure of Christendom had been based (Assmann 2010).

The distinction between religion and culture was at the core of the Chinese Rites controversy (Mungello 1994). Other Catholic missionaries (Dominicans, Franciscans), and the curial officers at the *Propaganda Fide* rejected the Jesuit interpretation of the Chinese Rites as cultural, civic rites, insisting that they were idolatrous religious rituals that Chinese Christians had to reject. The European *philosophes*, however, accepted the Jesuit distinction but turned it against them and against Christianity and all revealed theist religions.

Having learned from the Jesuits that Confucianism represented a kind of deist natural religion before revelation, they gladly affirmed those elements of the Chinese rites which the Jesuits interpreted as civic customs, not as religion, to insist that this is what was needed in Europe, a deist natural religion based on civic customs, while rejecting the supernatural theist superstitious rites of revealed Christian religion. Confucian culture was indeed superior to Christian religion. This explains the Chinese craze of the European Enlightenment and deism. European deists could easily recognize the superiority of Chinese Confucian culture over European Christian culture.

John Lagerwey (2010, pp. 2–3) goes so far as to blame the Jesuits for establishing the foundation on which the entire project of secular "modernity" and "modernization" was built in the West, as well as in China. In his view, it was based on "an incomprehensible misunderstanding," fostered by the Jesuits, that has "continued to dominate Western studies of China," namely that China, at least the China of the elite, "had no religion." Lagerwey actually interprets this misunderstanding as "a profound complicity" between Jesuit Thomist rationalism and the neo-Confucian rationalism that had become hegemonic "thanks to the 'ritual revolution' of the sixteenth century."

For Lagerwey, the Jesuits appear to be accomplice in the project of the neo-Confucian elite "to transform Chinese society by ridding it of the rituals of shamans, Buddhists, and Daoists and putting Confucian rituals in their place." But accusing the Jesuits in the rites controversy of taking a "Calvinistic" view of sacramental rites as "merely symbolic" and of adopting a proto-secularist modern attitude seems to be farfetched, indeed an anachronistic misreading of a much more complex early modern attitude before the triumph of the modern "religious/secular" binary classification of reality.

Early modern Jesuits became famous not only as missionaries and court confessors but also as mathematicians, astronomers, map-makers, land-surveyors, and military engineers at the service of royal courts throughout Europe and Asia. Clearly, they had learnt not so much to compartmentalize, as Berger (2014) would say, but rather to integrate what to us appear as different religious and secular roles within society and within their minds, even if their ultimate orientation was "ad majorem Dei gloriam," to which they added for "the good of souls" and "the common good." Jesuits were to find "God in all things" and transcendence in the immanent world.

Moreover, their method of "discernment" learnt in the *Spiritual Exercises*, helped them to be attuned to the world of "the spirit" in the midst of the most profane tasks. It is not surprising that Étienne Pasquier in his *Le Catéchisme des Jésuites* (1602), one of the first works in a long list of anti-Jesuit treatises that would contribute to the Jesuit Black Legend, characterizes them as a *hermaphrodite* "religious" order actively engaged in worldly "secular" affairs. With his critique, Pasquier was offering one of the first French formulations of the strict separation between the private world of religion and the public world of *laïcité*.

Historically, with their final defeat in the "rites controversy" at the beginning of the 18th century, the Jesuit accommodating way of proceeding lost the battle within the Church and within the wider world. In retrospect, one may say that the Jesuit early modern imaginary of global humanity and their dia-praxis of cultural "accommodation" and local inculturation appears less Euro-centric, less racist, and less unilinear than later imaginaries associated with the cosmopolitan Enlightenment or with hegemonic Western modernity (Casanova 2016b).

In the 19th century with the triumph of Western colonialism, the European attitude towards China and all oriental civilizations radically changed. Now, the hegemonic military and technological superiority of industrial capitalism and political and economic liberalism proved the superiority of modern Western civilization over traditional Asian cultures and justified the imperial "White Man's Burden" and its *mission civilisatrice*.

The second phase of Western hegemonic globalization begins in global East Asia with the unequal treaties, unilaterally enforced, all of them demanding free trade, Western colonial access through foreign protectorates or outright colonization as in French Indochina, and freedom of religion for competing Protestant and Catholic missionaries. Indeed, East Asian neologisms (*shukyo*, *zongjiao*) for the modern Western secular concept of "religion" were first used in the translation of the unequal treaties and their demand for "freedom of religion." What had been originally a Buddhist term for a "particular sect" was now used to translate "Western religion", i.e., Christianity, and similar private particularist "sects" in juxtaposition to what was perceived as obligatory national "culture." The Meiji restoration, while accommodating the Western colonial demand for freedom of religion insisted that state enforced Shintō was not an established "religion" but Japanese national "culture." The particular way in which the modern categories of "religion" and "secularity" took root in modern Japan have been well studied (Jun'ichi 2014). But similar problems of translation, semantic reconfigurations of religious and secular discourses, and radical transformations of the religious field became a common phenomenon in all projects of modernization across Asian societies (Eggert and Hölscher 2013). The continuing difficulties in the semantic classification of Confucianism within the modern religious/secular binary discourse are also well known (Sun 2013).

The widespread attraction that Marxism-Leninism held as atheist scientific materialism and as an ideology of societal modernization for East Asian intellectuals may be related to some of its elective affinities with Confucian proto-secularity. Once in power, East Asian intellectuals in China, Korea, and Vietnam institutionalized radical versions of state secularism directed against all forms of traditional religion and feudal superstition.

As we are entering our contemporary post-modern, post-secular global age, which may be viewed as a third phase of globalization after Western hegemony, "the religious question" has reemerged throughout East Asia (Goossaert and Palmer 2011). The religious fields in China, Japan, Korea, and Vietnam are being transformed again rapidly and diversely under the influence of new religious global dynamics (Van der Veer 2014, 2015). There is an urgent need to deconstruct and rethink in East Asian vernacular terms the categories of religion, secularity, magic, and spirituality in order to offer a better understanding of changing East Asian religious fields. The newly created East Asian Society for the Scientific Study of Religion should be in a privileged position to contribute to this important comparative research task.

Funding: This research received no external funding.

Conflicts of Interest: The author declares no conflicts of interest.

References

App, Urs. 2010. *The Birth of Orientalism*. Philadelphia: University of Pennsylvania Press.

Asad, Talal. 1993. *Genealogies of Religion*. Baltimore: The Johns Hopkins University Press.

Asad, Talal. 2003. *Formations of the Secular*. Stanford: Stanford University Press.

Assmann, Jan. 2010. *The Price of Monotheism*. Stanford: Stanford University Press.

Aulden, Dauril. 1996. *The Making of an Enterprise: The Society of Jesus in Portugal, Its Empire, and Beyond, 1540–1750*. Stanford: Stanford University Press.

Berger, Peter. 2014. *The Many Altars of Modernity: Towards a Paradigm for Religion in a Pluralist Age*. Boston: De Gruyter.

Beyer, Peter. 2006. *Religions in Global Society*. New York: Routledge.

Boxer, Charles Ralph. 1951. *The Christian Century in Japan, 1549–1650*. Berkeley: University of California Press.

Boxer, Charles Ralph. 1978. *The Church Militant and Iberian Expansion, 1440–1770*. Baltimore: Johns Hopkins University Press.

Casanova, José. 2008. Public Religions Revisited. In *Religion: Beyond a Concept*. Edited by Hent de Vries. New York: Frodham University Press, pp. 101–19.

Casanova, José. 2011. The Secular, Secularizations, Secularisms. In *Rethinking Secularism*. Edited by Craig Calhoun, Mark Juergensmeyer and Jonathan Van Antwerpen. New York: Oxford University Press, pp. 54–74.

Casanova, José. 2012. Religion, the Axial Age, and Secular Modernity in Bellah's Theory of Religious Evolution. In *The Axial Age and Its Consequences*. Edited by Robert N. Bellah and Hans Joas. Cambridge: Harvard University Press, pp. 191–221.

Casanova, José. 2014. The Two Dimensions, Temporal and Spatial, of the Secular: Comparative Reflections on the Nordic Protestant and Southern Catholic Patterns from a Global Perspective. In *Secular and Sacred? The Scandinavian Case of Religion in Human Rights, Law and Public Space*. Edited by Rosemarie van den Breemer, José Casanova and Trygve Wyller. Göttingen: Vandenhoeck & Ruprecht, pp. 21–22.

Casanova, José. 2016a. The Jesuits through the Prism of Globalization, Globalization through a Jesuit Prism. In *Jesuits and Globalization*. Edited by Thomas Banchoff and José Casanova. Washington, DC: Georgetown University Press, pp. 261–85.

Casanova, José. 2016b. Jesuits, Connectivity, and the Uneven Development of Global Consciousness since the Sixteenth Century. In *Global Culture: Consciousness and Connectivity*. Edited by Roland Robertson and Didem Buhari-Gulmez. Burlington: Ashgate, pp. 109–26.

Casanova, José. 2018a. Asian Catholicism, Interreligious Encounters, and the Dynamics of Secularism in Asia. In *The Secular in South, East and Southeast Asia*. Edited by Kenneth Dean and Peter van der Veer. New York: Palgrave Macmillan, pp. 13–35.

Casanova, José. 2018b. The Karel Dobbelaere lecture: Divergent Global Roads to Secularization and Religious Pluralism. *Social Compass* 65: 187–98. [CrossRef]

D'Elia, Pasquale, ed. 1942–1949. *Fonti Ricciane: Storia dell'Introduzione del Cristianesimo in Cina*. 3 vols. Roma: Libreria dello Stato.

de Bary, William Theodore. 1989. *Neo-Confucian Education: The Formative Stage*. Berkley: University of California Press.

de Nobili, Roberto. 2000. *Preaching Wisdom to the Wise: Three Treatises by Roberto de Nobili, S.J., Missionary and Scholar in 17th Century India*. Translated by Anand Amalass, and Francis X. Clooney. St. Louis: Institute of Jesuit Sources.

De Vries, Hent, ed. 2008. *Religion: Beyond a Concept*. New York: Fordham University Press.

Eggert, Marion, and Lucian Hölscher, eds. 2013. *Religion and Secularity. Transformations and Transfers of Religious Discourses in Europe and Asia*. Leiden: Brill.

Elison, George. 1973. *Deus Destroyed. The Image of Christianity in Early Modern Japan*. Cambridge: Harvard University Press.

Fingarette, Herbert. 1972. *Confucius: The Secular as Sacred*. San Francisco: Harper.

Gernet, Jacques. 1985. *China and the Christian Impact: A Conflict of Cultures*. Cambridge: Cambridge University Press.

Goossaert, Vincent, and David A. Palmer. 2011. *The Religious Question in Modern China*. Chicago: University of Chicago Press.

Gunn, Geoffrey C. 2003. *First Globalization: The Eurasian Exchange, 1500–1800*. Lanham: Rowman & Littlefield.

Jensen, Lionel M. 1997. *Manufacturing Confucianism: Chinese Traditions and Universal Civilization.*. Durham: Duke University Press.

Jun'ichi, Isomae. 2014. *Religious Discourse in Modern Japan. Religion, State, and Shintō*. Leiden: Brill.

Lagerwey, John. 2010. *China: A Religious State*. Hong Kong: Hong Kong University Press.

Liu, James T. C. 1973. How Did a Neo-Confucian School Became State Orthodoxy? *Philosophy East and West* 23: 483–505. [CrossRef]

Maryks, Robert A. 2016. *Saint Cicero and the Jesuits: The Influence of the Liberal Arts on the Adoption of Moral Probabilism*. New York: Routledge.

Mazusawa, Tomoko. 2005. *The Invention of World Religions*. Chucago: University of Chicago Press.

McNeil, William H. 1993. The Age of Gunpowder Empires, 1450–1800. In *Islamic and European Expansion: The Forging of a Global Order*. Edited by Michael Adas. Philadelphia: Temple University Press, pp. 103–39.

Mungello, David Emil. 1977. *Leibniz and Confucianism: The Search for Accord*. Honolulu: University of Hawaii Press.

Mungello, David Emil. 1989. *Curious Land: Jesuit Accommodation and the Origins of Sinology*. Honolulu: University of Hawaii Press.

Mungello, David Emil, ed. 1994. *The Rites Controversy: Its History and Meaning*. Nettetal: Steyler Verlag.

Mungello, David Emil. 2012. Reinterpreting the History of Christianity in China. *The Historical Journal* 55: 533–52. [CrossRef]

Mungello, David Emil. 2013. *The Great Encounter of China and the West, 1500–1800*. Lanham: Rowman & Littlefield.

Nongbri, Brent. 2013. *Before Religion: A History of a Modern Concept*. New Haven: Yale University Press.

O'Malley, John W. 2013. *Saints or Devils Incarnate? Studies in Jesuit History*. Leiden: Brill.

O'Malley, John W. 2016. Historical Perspectives on Jesuit Education and Globalization. In *The Jesuits and Globalization*. Edited by Thomas Banchoff and José Casanova. Washington, DC: Georgetown University Press, pp. 147–66.

Paramore, Kiri. 2009. *Ideology and Christianity in Japan*. New York: Routledge.

Peterson, Willard J. 1988. Why Did They Become Christians? Yang T'ing-yün, Li Chih-tsao, and Hsü Kuang-ch'I. In *East Meets West: The Jesuits in China, 1582–1773*. Edited by Charles E. Ronan and Bonnie B. C. Oh. Chicago: Loyola University Press, pp. 129–52.

Phan, Peter C. 1998. *Mission and Catechesis: Alexandre de Rhodes and Inculturation in Seventeenth-Century Vietnam*. Maryknoll: Orbis Books.

Po-chia Hsia, Ronald. 2010. *A Jesuit in the Forbidden City: Matteo Ricci, 1552–1610*. Oxford: Oxford University Press.

Pomplun, Trent. 2010. *A Jesuit on the Roof of the World: Ippolito Desideri's Mission to Tibet*. Oxford: Oxford University Press.

Ricci, Matteo. 1913. *Opere Storiche: Vol II: Lettere dalla Cina*. Edited by Pietro Tacchi-Venturi. Macerata: Filippo Giorgetti.

Richard, Robert. 1966. *The Spiritual Conquest of Mexico: An Essay on the Apostolate and the Evangelizing Methods of the Mendicant Orders in New Spain*. Berkeley: University of California Press.

Rubiés, Joan-Pau. 2005. The Concept pf Cultural Dialogue and the Jesuit Method of Accommodation: Between Idolatry and Civilization. *Archivum Historicum Societatis Jesu* 74: 237–80.

Rule, Paul. 1986. *K'ung-tzu or Confucius? The Jesuit Interpretation of Confucianism*. Sydney: Allen & Unwin.

Said, Edward W. 1978. *Orientalism*. New York: Pantheon Books.

Schütte, Josef Franz. 1980–1985. *Valignano's Mission Principles for Japan*. 2 vols. St. Louis: Institute of Jesuit Sources.

Smith, Jonathan Z. 1998. Religion, Religions, Religious. In *Critical Terms for Religious Studies*. Edited by Mark C. Taylor. Chicago: The University of Chicago Press, pp. 269–85.

Standaert, Nicolas S. J. 1997. New trends in the historiography of Christianity in China. *Catholic Historical Review* 83: 573–613. [CrossRef]

Standaert, Nicolas S. J. 2002. *Methodology in View of Contact between Cultures: The China Case in the 17th Century*. Hong Kong: The Chinese University of Hong Kong.

Standaert, Nicolas S. J. 2008. Jesuits in China. In *The Cambridge Companion to the Jesuits*. Edited by Thomas Worcester. Cambridge: Cambridge University Press, pp. 169–85.

Sun, Anna. 2013. *Confucianism as a World Religion: Contested Histories and Contemporary Realities*. Princeton: Princeton University Press.

Tamburello, Adolfo, M. Antoni J. Ücerler, and Marisa di Russo, eds. 2008. *Alessandro Valignano S.I. Uomo del Rinascimento: Ponte tra Oriente e Occidente*. Rome: IHSI.

Ücerler, Murat Antoni John. 2008. The Jesuit enterprise in sixteenth- and seventeenth-century Japan. In *The Cambridge Companion to the Jesuits*. Edited by Thomas Worcester. Cambridge: Cambridge University Press, pp. 153–68.

Ücerler, Murat Antoni John. 2016. The Jesuits in East Asia in the Early Modern Age: A New 'Aeropagus' and the 'Re-invention' of Christianity. In *Jesuits and Globalization*. Edited by Thomas Banchoff and José Casanova. Washington, DC: Georgetown University Press, pp. 27–48.

Valignano, Alessandro. 1954. *Sumario de las Cosas de Japón (1583)*. Tokyo: Sophia University Press.

Van der Veer, Peter. 2014. *The Modern Spirit of Asia: The Spiritual and the Secular in China and India*. Princeton: Princeton University Press.

Van der Veer, Peter, ed. 2015. *Handbook of Religion and the Asian City: Aspiration and Urbanization in the Twentieth-First Century*. Berkeley: University of California Press.

Zürcher, Erik. 2007. *The Buddhist Conquest of China: The Spread and Adaptation of Buddhism in Early Medieval China*, 3rd ed. Leiden: Brill. First published 1959.

![religions logo] *religions*

MDPI

Article

Religious Belonging in the East Asian Context: An Exploration of Rhizomatic Belonging

Daan F. Oostveen [1,2]

[1] Faculty of Religion and Theology, VU Amsterdam, De Boelelaan 1105, 1081 HV Amsterdam, The Netherlands; dfoostveen@protonmail.com
[2] Faculty of Philosophy, Renmin University, 59 Zhongguangcun Street, Beijing 100872, China

Received: 7 December 2018; Accepted: 7 March 2019; Published: 12 March 2019

Abstract: This article explores the hermeneutical challenges to understand religious belonging and religious identity in the East Asian context. In East Asia, religious identities have not always been as exclusively delineated, as is the case in Western models of religious diversity, for example in the so-called World Religions paradigm. Various theoretical frameworks are discussed in religious studies, sociology and anthropology of religion in China and East Asia, to acquire a better understanding of religious belonging. It is observed that two hermeneutical frameworks are used by scholars to discuss religious diversity: a hermeneutics of multiple religions and a hermeneutics of religiosity. The former analyses "religious belonging" as a "belonging to religious traditions". In the latter, "religious belonging" is understood as transcending particular religious traditions. It is argued that we need to take another look at the philosophical concept of "multiplicity" to understand religious diversity and religious belonging. We can use the Deleuzian concepts of "rhizome" and "assemblage" to describe religious belongings in East Asia specifically and also religion in general. A rhizomatic thinking about religion enables us to reimagine the concept of religious belonging as rhizomatic belonging, and also, as is argued by Haiyan Lee and Mayfair Yang, make it possible to subvert power structures inherent to religion.

Keywords: religiosity; religion; belonging; Daoism; Buddhism; rhizome; hermeneutics

1. Introduction

In East Asia, religious identities have not historically been as clearly demarcated as in cultures which have been dominated by monotheistic religions (Yao and Zhao 2010). Neither Buddhist nor Daoist identities have historically had the same exclusivist connotations as is often the case with people in Christian or Muslim cultures. There appears to be a difference between the laity and religious professionals regarding religious self-identification. Whereas religious professionals in East Asia are usually conscious about religious differences, for the laity the boundaries between religious traditions in East Asia have usually been less clearly demarcated, if not in theory then at least in practice. In his contribution to this special issue, Fenggang Yang explains this as follows: "[. . .] in the Judeo-Christian context, it is assumed that religious identity is exclusive, that every religious person is a member of a local congregation that is part of a denomination or a distinct religion, and that regular activities include weekly attendance at a corporate worship service. However, East Asian religions have distinct characteristics: Religious identity is not necessarily exclusive, religious practice is not based on a weekly rhythm, individual devotion or practice is at least as important as corporate rituals, and the boundaries of religiosity and secularity are ambiguous or blurred" (Yang 2018). In this article I will extend the concept of religious belonging beyond self-identification with religious traditions. I will propose rhizomatic belonging as a form of religious belonging which is suitable for the "hybrid" religious ecology which is characteristic of East Asia. Furthermore, it might be suggested that also in the Western world, religious belonging is increasingly transforming towards this model. I will focus on China as a case study exemplary for East Asia. Though the idea of "religious belonging" does not appear evident in the Chinese setting, I believe it can clarify an important dimension of religion in general.

2. Religious Belonging

What does it mean to have a "religious belonging" in China? What does it mean to be a Daoist? What is a Buddhist identity and is there such thing as a "Buddhist belonging"? Although these questions appear to be straightforward, they open up a whole range of problems. In this article I aim to extend the concept of religious belonging beyond the understanding of this concept as self-identification with a religious tradition. "Belonging" refers to a much deeper amalgam of connections with religious forms then just "identity". Furthermore, it has a strong affective dimension which is often overlooked, and which is not adequately expressed when we understand it only as a concept of classification. If we look into the nature of religion in China and East Asia, we can question whether there exists something we could call a "belonging to Buddhism" or a "belonging to Daoism" in the same way as we immediately understand what a "belonging to Christianity" means. Even if we understand what such a belonging (to Buddhism, or Daoism, or Confucianism) might mean, we could still question what such a belonging would look like. Fenggang Yang states that "[...] there is [...] a cultural tendency of not formally joining any particular religion, which is a consequential 'habit of the heart' formed by centuries of religious repression" (Yang 2016). If we want to understand what religious belonging is, we first have to see what it is not. Therefore, we have to compare various forms of religious belonging in East Asia, such as Buddhist belonging, Daoist belonging, Confucian belonging, Christian belonging, the absence of religious belonging or multiple religious belonging.

In Western theology and religious studies, there has been an increased attention on multiple religious belonging in Western contexts (Schmidt-Leukel and Bernhardt 2008; Cornille 2010; Rajkumar and Dayam 2016; D'Costa and Thompson 2016). So-called "pioneers" are sometimes combining the identities of diverse religions such as Buddhism and Christianity to form a "dual belonging" or a "multiple religious belonging". From this perspective, scholars have sometimes suggested that these Western forms of multiple religious belonging point at an "Easternization" of religious belongings. It is hypothesized that religions in East Asia have not usually been defined by means of exclusive identities with distinct boundaries, as is more common in the Western understanding of religious diversity. Therefore, the assumption goes, individuals can more easily adopt a multiple religious belonging.

These forms of religious belonging, mentioned above, still assume an identification with religious traditions. Next to religious identities and belongings based on self-identification with "religious traditions" we also see phenomena such as popular religiosity, shamanism and hybrid cultural expressions, where the issue of belonging as self-identification is much less clear-cut, if not absent. It seems that "belonging" as a marker of religion can be applied much broader than on self-identification to religious traditions alone. Based on a recent survey on the state of religion in China, it was extrapolated that 215 million Chinese people confessed to believing in the spirits of the ancestors; 362 million Chinese people had participated in divination practices such as face reading and fortune telling in the past year; and a stunning 754 million people practiced ancestor worship (Wenzel-Teuber 2012). There appears to be a stark contrast between practicing "religion", as it is usually understood in Western scholarship, and identifying with (a) religion. Besides an absence of "belonging", even the legitimacy of these practices has also been widely questioned and they have sometimes been labeled as "superstition" or rejected as "magic" (Palmer and Goossaert 2011; Hanegraaff 2016). These numbers are in stark contrast to the official or common understanding of China as a predominantly "atheist" country; they also stand in contrast to the 185 million people who consider themselves as Buddhists (Wenzel-Teuber 2012)—which would be the largest "religion" in China in terms of self-identified adherents.

The situation in the case of Daoism is even more interesting: only 12 million people in the People's Republic of China self-identify as "Daoists", while at the same time 173 million people "had some kind of Daoist practice" (Wenzel-Teuber 2012). Assuming these numbers draw an accurate picture, we could conclude that only approximately 7% of practicing Daoists also self-identity as such.

Palmer and Siegler (2018) notes: "while one can be the disciple of a master or the follower of a specific sect, there has never been a concept of 'membership' in Daoism as a unified 'religion'". As a religious tradition of teachings of self-cultivation and longevity, Daoism appears to eschew the foundational understanding of "religion" as primarily defined by means of exclusive beliefs by "followers" who self-identify with one and only one religion, excluding others. Though we could conclude from this that Daoism is not a "religion" as compared to an ideal type, Daoism might give us the opportunity to even better understand the phenomenon of religion, precisely because it lacks a strong sense of popular self-identification, but instead creates assemblages of ritual and symbols to which many different people can connect.

Historically, religious diversity in China has not been characterized necessarily by competing and exclusive religions with different truth claims, but as complementary, often pragmatically oriented, systems of thought. This is also expressed in the word which was commonly used to refer to Buddhism, Daoism, and Confucianism (or Ruism), namely as jiào教, "teachings". Religious teachings didn't have a similar institutional backing as has been common to the churches in post-reformation Europe. Throughout much of its history, China had a much stronger state bureaucracy than Europe, where church institutions functioned sometimes as de facto states or had a strong influence on politics. Religious traditions in China rarely had this much political clout, were subordinate to strong state structures and therefore their boundaries would often be more porous. The Chinese state and Chinese religions should be seen as inseparable from each other (Lagerwey 2010); emphasis on the "difference" between religions is therefore subordinate to the unity of the Chinese state. In China, "belonging" has not usually been understood as a function of "religions". Instead, "belonging" expresses a relation to the family, to the village, and to the country, to which various ritual obligations are attached.

In the Western world, scholars have witnessed the emergence of hybrid forms of religiosity: individuals who do not identify or belong to one religious tradition but identify with or combine elements from multiple religious traditions. In theology, this phenomenon has been called "multiple religious belonging", with a main focus on dual belongings to Christianity and Buddhism, Judaism and Buddhism or Christianity and Hinduism. Many people, however, appear to combine elements from various religious traditions without feeling a desire to identify or belong to any particular tradition. With this emergence of religious hybridity in the West (Pew Forum on Religion & Public Life 2009; Berghuijs 2017), this understanding of a detachment between "belonging" and "religion" is becoming increasingly relevant in these contexts as well.

In contemporary sociological and anthropological reflections on religious diversity in China, some scholars have emphasized religious practices and the way religion is expressed through various religious modalities (Chau 2011). Chau distinguishes between four such modalities: the discursive or scriptural, the personal-cultivational, the liturgical, the immediate-practical, and the relational. His approach leads the focus away both from the differentiation of "religions" as the primary means of categorization and from an exclusive emphasis on doctrinal content, and instead emphasizes how religion works and what goal it serves. Ordinary Chinese people approach religion often with an aim towards efficacy, and much less towards doctrinal content. Religious teachings are often not entities of which ordinary people are aware, nor something which invokes a feeling of belonging to these teachings and traditions. Only religious elites have a more explicit awareness of distinct religious teachings and traditions, and thus are closer to the notion of "belonging to religions". These elites are specialized in the ritual content of religious traditions. But even for them it is possible to be trained in multiple religious traditions. They would act as either a Buddhist or a Daoist priest for example, depending on the circumstances.

'Religion' as a term is not native to East Asia (Goossaert 2005). Religion has been introduced as a result of Western scholarship and has found application to describe the Three Teachings of China, Daoism, Confucianism and Buddhism, as well as Islam and Christianity. But more contemporary sociological scholarship on religion in China has also applied the term to "popular religion": religious practices which cannot be clearly delineated as part of a single coherent tradition but are diffused practices throughout the country. Also, in the West, "religion" is a contested term (Smith 1998). While in some contexts it refers to "religious traditions", it can also appear in its adjective meaning, namely religion as "the religious" or "religiosity" as a separate domain of human culture, which is commonly contrasted to an oppositional domain of culture, namely "the secular" (Asad [1994] 2009; Yang 2008). Neither of these understandings are native to the historical worldviews of China. As is well known, the term "religion" *zōngjiào*宗教 was only introduced in China in the early 1900s. The development of these understandings of "religion" in modern Western scholarship has had an enormous impact on the self-understanding of cultural diversity in China and East Asia as well. One example is the identification and therefore elevation to the status of World Religion of "Buddhism". Masuzawa (2012) argued that "Buddhism" connected formerly dispersed religious practices throughout Asia and subsumed them under this powerful label (although her analysis has also been disputed by other scholars).

It is important to distinguish between these two meanings of the word "religion" in religious studies—though these two meanings sometimes intersect. The first meaning of "religion" refers to a class concept "religion", with several instantiations, "religions", such as Christianity, Islam, and Buddhism. Within this, what I call, "hermeneutics of multiple religions", individual people belong to one of several "religions" or to none at all. This "hermeneutics of multiple religions" is a generalization of what has been called the "World Religions paradigm" (as it has been proposed by Masuzawa (2012), and in the Chinese context further explained by Hedges (2017)), which is a way of understanding "religions" as exclusive systems of faith, while acknowledging that there are several "options". Hedges (2017) distinguishes three characteristics of the World Religions paradigm. First, the concept of religion in the World Religions paradigm implies bounded territories of belonging. Simply put, one cannot belong to both Christianity and Islam at the same time. Secondly, Hedges argues, belonging to a religion means primarily the belief in a set of principles. Because these principles are perceived to be different in different religions, it follows naturally that an individual cannot belong to more than one religion. Finally, Hedges says, religions are seen as "[their] own internally coherent and regulated entity".

The second meaning of "religion" refers to it as a particular form of human culture: "religious culture". In this meaning, "religion" is more comparable to a concept such as "spirituality"; the class concept of "religion" is rejected. Several social scientists of religion in China, such as Mayfair Yang and Adam Yuet Chau (Chau 2011), have pointed out that the class concept of "religion" does not always make much sense in a non-Western context. Rather, they suggest we should talk about "Chinese religiosities" (Yang 2008). In this "hermeneutics of religiosity", the word "religion" does not refer to "religions" in the meaning of "religious traditions", but rather to an amalgam of different religious life forms.

There has existed a "hermeneutics of multiple religions" throughout the history of China. From the moment Buddhism arrived in China, religious elites have emphasized doctrinal and ritual differentiation as well as legitimation of these differences, although there was an equal amount of borrowing occurring between these traditions. The most important hermeneutical model has been the differentiation and harmonization of the Three Teachings: Confucianism, Buddhism, and Daoism. According to David Palmer, the religious teachings of China have been distinguished in three different ways (Palmer 2013). First, a differentiation between "Inner" and "Outer" teachings. Daoism or Buddhism have often been counted as "Inner", while Confucianism was regarded as an "Outer" teaching. Second there is a differentiation between "Civil" and "Martial" teachings. Civil are the universal teachings, which are applicable to anyone within the Chinese state structure. "Martial" teachings are the locally present religious rituals and deities. The first explanation professes the conviction that the three religious teachings originate from the same source and are thus different expressions of a common religious origin. The second explanation considers the Three Teachings as complementary, but functionally different. Each teaching serves a different goal. Confucianism is then for example a teaching with a mental function, Daoism a teaching with a physical function and Buddhism a teaching with a spiritual function. A third explanation considers different teachings as different methods to reach a common goal. They are distinct roads, which will all lead to the same goal, though some may take longer than others.

3. Reimagining Religious Belonging

I aim at reimagining "belonging" to be applied to religion in East Asia beyond "(self)-identification with religious traditions". The hermeneutics of religiosity and the hermeneutics of multiple religions are two different ways of looking at the same phenomena. The idea of "religious belonging" has been strongly connected to this second framework. But the hermeneutics of religiosity foregrounds the hybrid nature of religious forms, which, we could say, has been more present in East Asia. The context of China teaches us that "belonging" is an idea of connection that generally transcends the mere phenomenology of religious traditions. The feeling of belonging is deeply connected to the religious. Religiosities are constitutive in any person's feeling of belonging. I propose therefore that we reimagine the concept of religious belonging to fit in a hermeneutics of religiosity. Such a belonging can no longer be a function of "religious traditions". However, we should also remain aware not to arrive at a sort of "universal" belonging, which would transcend from all particularity of the context of the individual. Each person finds themselves at a crossroads of cultural forms, and it is out of these interactions that a feeling of belonging arises.

In a hermeneutics of religiosity, "the religious" refers to another form of multiplicity: not the multiplicity of "religious traditions" but, in the words of Hent de Vries, it refers to "words, things, gestures, powers, sounds, silences, smells, sensations, shapes, colors, affects and effects" (De Vries 2008). The French philosopher Gilles Deleuze has developed, together with Félix Guattari, philosophical concepts to deal with such a "multiplicity" (Deleuze and Guattari [1980] 1987). For this work, he is mainly indebted to the philosophical thinking of Henri Bergson. In particular the concepts of the rhizome and assemblage (French: *agencement*) can function to reimagine religious belonging to fit into a hermeneutics of religiosity. The philosophical concept of the rhizome is derived from biology and functions to represent non-hierarchical connections between multiple elements. In biology, the rhizome refers to a subterranean stem of a plant, which sends roots and shoots from its nodes. Deleuze and Guattari use this concept as a metaphor that "'maps' a process of networked, relational and transversal thought, and a way of being without 'tracing' the construction of that map as a fixed entity" (Parr 2010). Furthermore, they see the rhizome as something that "conceives how every thing and every body—all aspects of concrete, abstract and virtual entities and activities—can be seen as multiple in their interrelational movements with other things and bodies" (Parr 2010).

One of the problems of the "arborescent thought" common to a hermeneutics of multiple religions, is that the particulars that are classified under the organizing principle or the taproot have no interaction with each other. In the Deleuze dictionary it is explained that in the arborescent schema "[t]he subordinate elements, once so arranged, are unable to 'move' horizontally in such a way as to establish creative and productive interrelationships with other concepts, particulars or models" (Parr 2010, p. 13). If religious diversity is understood as a diversity of horizontally distinguished religions, as instantiations of an overarching concept "religion", this religious diversity has by definition become solidified and lacks the possibility of "creative and productive interrelationships".

This is opposed by the first two principles of the rhizome according to Deleuze and Guattari [1980] (1987): connection and heterogeneity. They explain the first principle as "any point of a rhizome can be connected to anything other, and must be". A rhizome is characterized by connectivity. To explain heterogeneity, the concept of the assemblage is used to refer to "complex constellations of objects, bodies, expressions, qualities, and territories that come together for varying periods of time to ideally create new ways of functioning" (Parr 2010, p. 18). The connective organization of the rhizome, as opposed to the hierarchic organization of the arborescent schema, enables assemblages to rise from these connections, which are always open to rearrangements.

The third principle of the rhizome is multiplicity. The multiple of the arborescent schema is not considered a real multiplicity, because it is ultimately reduced to the One. Deleuze and Guattari say "it is only when the multiple is effectively treated as a substantive, "multiplicity," that it ceases to have any relation to the One as subject or object, natural or spiritual reality, image and world" (Deleuze and Guattari [1980] 1987, p. 8).

The fourth principle of the rhizome is the principle of asignifying rupture. In the words of Deleuze and Guattari, this principle is directed "against the oversignifying breaks separating structures or cutting across a single structure" (Deleuze and Guattari [1980] 1987, p. 9). Furthermore, the principle describes that a rhizome "may be broken, [. . .] but it will start up again on one of its old lines, or on new lines". This principle of the rhizome accounts for the continuity and discontinuity between religious traditions as structures or assemblages.

Principles five and six of the rhizome are cartography and decalcomania. In the words of Deleuze and Guattari "a rhizome is not amenable to any structural or generative model. It is a stranger to any idea of genetic axis or deep structure" and "the rhizome is altogether different, a map and not a tracing" (Deleuze and Guattari [1980] 1987, p. 12). When applied to religious diversity, these principles teach us that a rhizomatic hermeneutics prompts us not to look for the diachronical origins or the genesis of religion, but to focus on the "map" of religious diversity and the way in which religious phenomena are embedded in their environment.

In this line of thought, Michelle Voss Roberts has argued we should think about religiosity as an "omnicentered model of divine relationality values difference and connection; it helps us imagine persons as nodes in a rhizomatic generation of religious subjects in which no single center definitively determines identity" (Voss Roberts 2010, p. 59). We could say that a "rhizomatic hermeneutics" of religious diversity describes a spatial map of religion in which connections cross transversally. No single religious tradition is traceable back to a first origin. Rather, religiosity originates from many different places at the same time and connects at an immense multiplicity of nodes. What counts is not the unity of the tradition but the diversity of religious elements in the present. "Religions" are assemblages of a variety of heterogeneous religious elements. The concept of assemblage is used to signify social structures from a bottom-up approach. It is used to de-emphasizes fixed religious identities, but instead focuses on the fluidity and exchangeability of religious forms. Individuals connect with different assemblages and with different elements within those assemblages. Instead of a belonging to a fixed identity-structure, individuals should rather be seen as "at home" within fluid and transforming social structures, which emerge from the ground up.

The methodological emphasis on religiosity "as it is lived"—as opposed to an emphasis on theology, doctrine, and religious normativity as expressed by religious elite, was already developed by scholars such as Robert Orsi and David Hall. The framework of "lived religion" does not focus primarily on religious traditions or institutions, but instead on how religious practices are expressed in everyday social contexts. Many anthropologists have noted that the "boundaries" between religious traditions, such as they have been traditionally defined, often do not have much meaning for people in the expression of religiosity in their daily lives. Anthropologist Meredith McGuire writes: "when we focus on religion as lived, we discover that religion—rather than being a single entity—is made up of diverse, complex and ever-changing mixtures of beliefs and practices, as well as relationships, experiences, and commitments" (McGuire 2008). She questions whether boundaries between religious traditions are the best way to describe religious phenomena. She states for example that "[w]e seem to have uncritically accepted definitional boundaries that distinguish religious practices from one religious group from another's, viewing them as mutually exclusive" (McGuire 2008).

4. A Critical Approach to Religion

A rhizomatic hermeneutics, as I coin it, and as has been envisioned by Deleuze and Guattari, aims at destabilizing inherited power structures. Therefore, this conceptual shift has a normative dimension. Power could be regarded as inherent to religion. There exists a complex power dynamic between religious actors, both elites and lay expressions of religion in everyday life, politicians and governments, and religious studies scholars. In order to get a clear image of how religiosity functions in the context of East Asia, we have to consider these power dynamics. According to Mayfair Yang, rhizomatic thinking helps to redress social inequality. The concept of the rhizome takes into account that we can never objectively describe social relationships, especially with respect to religion. The rhizomatic can be understood as a way to subvert vertical structures in societies: structures of hierarchy, structures of transcendence. The Chinese Confucian model often emphasizes these vertical structures. Haiyan Lee talks about a "web of 'rhizomatic' linkages that both support and subvert the vertical, 'arborescent' structures of orthodoxy" (Lee 2010, p. 32). Rhizomatic thinking is therefore particularly important for religion in China. For Lee, there is a strong emancipatory notion associated with the rhizomatic:

> "The rhizomatic realm has little regard for vertical social distinctions such as status, family background, and gender. Although the class hierarchy has always to some extent been mitigated and made porous by the ideal, if not the practice, of meritocracy and men of humble station could always hitch their ambitions of upward mobility to the civil service examinations, women have traditionally had little latitude in circumventing the Confucian gender hierarchy. Besides religious celibacy, entering the rhizomatic realm to become a woman warrior or a courtesan seems to be the only culturally condoned, if not encouraged, avenue of transcending or escaping the Confucian prescriptions of womanhood". (Lee 2010, p. 32)

Mayfair Yang has described how in China, social relationships form the network of society, represented by the concept *guānxi* 关系. From a Confucian point of view, these relations are hierarchical. But if we look closer, you can see how these relationships, constructed on the Confucian model, form large networks of interconnected individuals and communities in which there is no central node: "the 'rhizomatic' (decentered and meandering) growth of practical kinship extends beneath and crisscrosses the centripetal, arborescent structures of the state and is therefore potentially subversive" (Lee's reference to (Yang 1994, pp. 304–11)).

Similar to how C.K. Yang (1961) has shown how "popular religion" functions as the impalpable subcurrent to official religion, Mayfair Yang emphasizes the subversive potential of the rhizomatic structure of Chinese religion and society. Though the official and elite hermeneutics of religious diversity emphasize the tradition of the *jiào* 教, when observing Chinese religion as an anthropologist, a rhizomatic structure emerges, in which religious culture is constituted of a diverse web of practices, beliefs, superstitions, social duties, commitments, and allegiances. This rhizomatic fabric of society enables the possibility to subvert the dominant discourse. In the words of Haiyan Lee:

> "The rhizomatic mode of sentimentality is sustained by a heterogeneity of beliefs, fantasies, and practices that seek to redress the injustices, contradictions, and inadequacies of the dominant social order. Here sentiment is about observing the protocols for dealing with fairies and ghosts or the rules of play between dandies and courtesans in the floating world of sensual pleasures". (Lee 2010)

This analysis of Chinese religion shows us the encounter between a hermeneutics of multiple religions and a hermeneutics of religiosity. The official hermeneutics of the Three Teachings is subverted by the shamanistic and popular practices in the everyday lives of Chinese people. Confucian ethics prescribes loyalty from a son to his father and from a wife to her husband. Lee refers to the Jianhu tales, in which female characters often subvert the common order, in danger of being punished or exorcised by shamans.

> "Martial heroines pride themselves on their valor, martial skills, spirit of righteousness (yiqi), and devotion to sworn brothers and sisters. And yet, like their romantic counterpart, they are also proud of their respect for the moral order and its human embodiments: the emperor and parents. They are often maddening sticklers for decorum, and not a few have become memorable moral paragons in literary and popular histories. It is in this sense that the vertical and horizontal axes of sentimentality are mutually reinforcing. However, with its hidden

transcripts, meandering structures, and fluid identities, the rhizomatic realm is always in excess of orthodoxy and thus a perennial source of anxiety and an intermittent target of appropriation and co-optation". (Lee 2010)

These types of gender-critical approaches to religion, as we see in this citation, show that common understandings of religions and religious orthodoxies often excludes the religious experiences of women. Manuela Kalsky argues that women who experiment with eclectic forms of religiosity should be studied from their own experiences instead of theoretical discourses about faith or religion. She argues: "I would prefer the image of a network of lines. Lines, which are crossing and diverging, and at other moments converging, so that at time boundaries between one and the other are hardly visible". She questions whether "[it is] possible in theology to view religious identity as a part of a transcultural and trans-religious rhizome? Not a root-tree structure, not a solid anchoring in one religion, but a fluid and changeable process of moments of identification" (Kalsky 2017).

Following Mayfair Yang and Haiyan Lee, and also in line with feminist theologians in the West such as Michelle Voss Roberts (2010) and Manuela Kalsky (2017), I think that we should reimagine religious belonging as rhizomatic belonging. The concept "rhizomatic belonging", in my terminology, combines the multiplicity and decentrality of religious forms, with the very unique, personal, and unitary feeling of religious "belonging". Rhizomatic belonging can be applied to both religion in East Asian, and to religion in general. This approach has several advantages. First, I think that the idea of "belonging" in a hermeneutics of multiple religions is too strongly connected to an understanding of belonging as "possessive", as Michelle Voss Roberts (2010) has also argued. The addition of the concept of the "rhizome" liberates the concept of "belonging" from the connotation with possession, as if religions "own" their followers.

Second, the idea of "belonging" in a hermeneutics of multiple religions is not very different from the concept of "identity". Belonging to Christianity means being a Christian. In the sociological understanding of both terms, "belonging" and "identity" are not usually distinguished. There is however, a strong emotional connotation attached to the concept of belonging. The word "belonging" harbors the root of "longing", or desire, and also, belonging is strongly related to a feeling of "being at home" or "being in the right place". It is important to appreciate "belonging" in its semantic dimension of affectivity and interiority. This does not mean that we henceforth all belong to a sort of true principle beyond religious traditions, such as humanity, God, truth or even "the Earth". Although the religious expresses our "ultimate concern" (Tillich [1957] 2009), our feeling of belonging that results from this concern is particular and dynamic.

Therefore, third, the metaphor of the rhizome expresses the dynamic, horizontal, multiple, and interconnected aspects of religious forms and assemblages. The idea of rhizomatic belonging expresses the particular and the interconnected. It does not strongly emphasize religious traditions, without ignoring them altogether. But it also doesn't exchange "religions" for a pluralistic universalism which understands all religions as fundamentally the same. And it is in this sense, I believe, that many people belong religiously. They feel connected to something which transcends them, but this feeling is particular, though not insular. They rhizomatically and transversally encounter movements in religious culture that we, in a hermeneutics of multiple religions, would call traditions, as well as other cultural forms that will inform their religious self-understanding, practices and commitments. Rhizomatic belonging expresses the hybrid nature of the cultural codes that fill individuals lives with meaning.

5. Conclusions

From a rhizomatic perspective, religions are not seen as bounded entities, but rather as networks or assemblages of elements which sometimes group together to form larger networks, sometimes, exclude other structures, but are often connected in many ways to other religious segments of society. What we imagine as "Buddhism" or "Daoism" in a hermeneutics of multiple religions, should better be described as networks of religious "words, things, gestures, powers, sounds, silences, smells, sensations, shapes, colours, affects and effects" (De Vries 2008). My term "rhizomatic belonging" can be used to address religious multiplicities of forms in East Asian religion and religion in general, though it retains the individual sense of unity towards a singular reality. On the one hand these networks have a gravity towards unification and exclusivism, resulting in the "reified imaginative formations" which we call "religions" (Hanegraaff 2016). On the other hand, these networks are fundamentally open, inclusive, connected and transformative. For individuals, it is the challenge to navigate within this religious ecology. What can appear as rhizomatic belonging, as a religious practice observed from an etic perspective, is often much less related to religious identification from an emic perspective (Madsen 2014). We do however also witness the rise of Christian churches and new forms of Buddhism in East Asia, in which religious identity and exclusive belonging in the classical meaning do play a pivotal role (Tang 2013). Religious realities emerge as a result of our theory of religion, and these religious realities in turn inform our theory. Therefore, the relationship between phenomenology of religion and theory of religion can never be completely disentangled. In fact, we have to acknowledge that our conceptualizations of religious diversity are always already influenced by our valuation of those cultural expressions that we have come to call "religious".

Funding: My research on multiple religious belonging was funded by the Netherlands Organisation for Scientific Research (NWO) as part of their research program "Religion in Modern Society" (2013–2018). My PhD Research Fellowship at the Faculty of Philosophy at Renmin University of China in 2018 was funded by the Confucius Institute (Hanban).

Conflicts of Interest: The author declares no conflict of interest. The funders had no role in the design of the study; in the collection, analyses, or interpretation of data; in the writing of the manuscript, or in the decision to publish the results.

References

Asad, Talal. 2009. *Genealogies of Religion: Discipline and Reasons of Power in Christianity and Islam*. Baltimore: Johns Hopkins University Press. First published 1994.

Berghuijs, Joantine. 2017. Multiple Religious Belonging in the Netherlands: An Empirical Approach to Hybrid Religiosity. *Open Theology* 3: 19–37. [CrossRef]

Chau, Adam Yuet. 2011. Modalities of Doing Religion and Ritual Polytropy: Evaluating the Religious Market Model from the Perspective of Chinese Religious History. *Religion* 41: 547–68. [CrossRef]

Cornille, Catherine, ed. 2010. *Many Mansions? Multiple Religious Belonging and Christian Identity*. Eugene: Wipf & Stock Publishers.

D'Costa, Gavin, and Ross Thompson, eds. 2016. *Buddhist-Christian Dual Belonging: Affirmations, Objections, Explorations*. Surrey: Ashgate.

De Vries, Hent. 2008. *Religion: Beyond a Concept*. New York: Fordham University Press.

Deleuze, Gilles, and Félix Guattari. 1987. *A Thousand Plateaus: Capitalism and Schizophrenia*. Minneapolis/London: University of Minnesota Press. First published 1980.

Goossaert, Vincent. 2005. The Concept of Religion in China and the West. *Diogenes* 52: 13–20. [CrossRef]

Hanegraaff, Wouter J. 2016. Reconstructing "Religion" from the Bottom Up. *Numen* 63: 577–606. [CrossRef]

Hedges, Paul. 2017. Multiple Religious Belonging after Religion: Theorising Strategic Religious Participation in a Shared Religious Landscape as a Chinese Model. *Open Theology* 3: 48–72. [CrossRef]

Kalsky, Manuela. 2017. Flexible Believers in the Netherlands: A Paradigm Shift toward Transreligious Multiplicity. *Open Theology* 3: 345–59. [CrossRef]

Lagerwey, John. 2010. *China: A Religious State*. Hong Kong: University of Hong Kong.

Lee, Haiyan. 2010. *Revolution of the Heart: A Genealogy of Love in China, 1900–1950*. Stanford and London: Stanford University Press.

Madsen, Richard. 2014. Secular Belief, Religious Belonging. *Review of Religion and Chinese Society* 1: 13–28. [CrossRef]

Masuzawa, Tomoko. 2012. *The Invention of World Religions: Or, How European Universalism Was Preserved in the Language of Pluralism*. Chicago: University of Chicago Press.

McGuire, Meredith B. 2008. *Lived Religion: Faith and Practice in Everyday Life*. Oxford and New York: Oxford University Press.

Palmer, David. A. 2013. China's Religious Landscape: Models of Religious Pluralism. Paper presented at the Bahá'í Chair for World Peace Fall Lecture, University of Maryland, College Park, MD, USA, November 25.

Palmer, David A., and Vincent Goossaert. 2011. *The Religious Question in Modern China*. Chicago: University of Chicago Press.

Palmer, David A., and Elijah Siegler. 2018. *Dream Trippers: Global Daoism and the Predicament of Modern Spirituality*. Chicago: University of Chicago Press.

Parr, Adrian. 2010. *The Deleuze Dictionary*. Edinburgh: Edinburgh University Press.

Pew Forum on Religion & Public Life. 2009. *Many Americans Mix Multiple Faiths*. Washington: Pew Research Center.

Rajkumar, Peniel Jesudason Rufus, and Joseph Prabhakar Dayam, eds. 2016. *Many yet One?: Multiple Religious Belonging*. Geneva: World Council of Churches Publications.

Schmidt-Leukel, Perry, and Reinhold Bernhardt, eds. 2008. *Multiple Religiöse Identität: Aus Verschiedenen Religiösen Traditionen Schöpfen*. Zürich: Theologischer Verlag.

Smith, Jonathan Z. 1998. Religion, Religions, Religious. In *Critical Terms for Religious Studies*. Edited by Mark C. Taylor. Chicago: University of Chicago Press, pp. 179–96.

Tang, Edmond. 2013. Identity and Marginality—Christianity in East Asia. In *Christianity in Asia*. Edited by Felix Wilfred. Oxford: Oxford University Press, pp. 31–50.

Tillich, Paul. 2009. *Dynamics of Faith*. New York: HarperOne. First published 1957.

Voss Roberts, Michelle. 2010. Religious Belonging and the Multiple. *Journal of Feminist Studies in Religion* 26: 43–62. [CrossRef]

Wenzel-Teuber, Katharina. 2012. People's Republic of China: Religions and Churches Statistical Overview 2011. *Religions & Christianity in Today's China* II: 29–54.

Yang, Ching Kun. 1961. *Religion in Chinese Society: A Study of Contemporary Social Functions of Religion and Some of Their Historical Factors*. Berkeley: University of California Press.

Yang, Mayfair Mei-Hui. 1994. *Gifts, Favors, and Banquets: The Art of Social Relationships in China*. Ithaca: Cornell University Press.

Yang, Mayfair Mei-hui. 2008. *Chinese Religiosities Afflictions of Modernity and State Formation*. Berkeley: University of California Press.

Yang, Fenggang. 2016. Exceptionalism or Chinamerica: Measuring Religious Change in the Globalizing World Today. *Journal for the Scientific Study of Religion* 55: 7–22. [CrossRef]

Yang, Fenggang. 2018. Religion in the Global East: Challenges and Opportunities for the Social Scientific Study of Religion. *Religions* 9: 305. [CrossRef]

Yao, Xinzhong, and Yanxia Zhao. 2010. *Chinese Religion: A Contextual Approach*. London and New York: Continuum.

MDPI

Article

A New Home for New Immigrants? A Case Study of the Role of Soka Gakkai in the Integration of Japanese and Mainland Chinese Immigrants in Hong Kong

Ka Shing Ng

School of Global Humanities and Social Sciences, Nagasaki University, 1-14 Bunkyomachi, Nagasaki, Nagasaki Prefecture 852-8521, Japan; ngkashing@nagasaki-u.ac.jp

Received: 14 September 2018; Accepted: 29 October 2018; Published: 31 October 2018

Abstract: In the discussion of migrant integration into local settings, most scholars agree on the positive linkages between religion and the construction of ethnic identity. However, beyond church and mosque, there appears to be a gap in the research of the roles played by other religions in the process of migrant integration. This paper attempts to fill this gap by studying the role of a new religion, Soka Gakkai (SG), in the integration of Japanese and Mainland Chinese immigrants in Hong Kong. I argue that the social and spiritual support and the ideas of a "big family" and individual empowerment (i.e., empowering oneself to overcome challenges) are important resources for immigrants when starting a new life in Hong Kong. However, the controversial image of SG might also have negative effects on SG members' efforts at integration.

Keywords: Soka Gakkai; Hong Kong; migrant integration

---

1. Introduction

The demographics of Hong Kong are characterized by a huge population of ethnic Chinese and diverse ethnic groups.[1] The continuous movement of people into and out of Hong Kong affects the population dynamics of this small city. The migration patterns and demographics of Hong Kong have attracted a lot of scholarly attention. Many provide excellent analysis of the ties between migration and the issues of identity, integration, and adaptation, but less is discussed from the perspective of religion (e.g., Sussman 2010; Salaff et al. 2010; Shen and Dai 2006). In particular, the possible role of religion in the social integration of migrants into Hong Kong society remains a topic of further exploration. This paper attempts to fill this gap by focusing on the relationships between religion and migration in Hong Kong, using a new religion, Soka Gakkai (SG), as a case study.

Religion and migration has been a topic widely discussed in the United States, the "nation of immigrants", as the interplay between ethnic groups and faith has strong social, economic, and political implications. In *The Churching of America*, for example, Finke and Stark (1992) showed how parishes are dominated by ethnic groups in cities where ethnic neighborhoods are solid, linking the factor of ethnic minorities to the complexity of religious development in the States. From an economic perspective, Iannaccone (1998) reflected on the delicate relationships between religious participation and religious contributions, and sex, age, income, etc. These studies show changing demographics as a result of

---

[1] In 2016, Hong Kong had a total population of 7,336,585, of which 92% were ethnic Chinese and 8.0% ethnic minorities. The latter comprised Filipinos (2.5%), Indonesians (2.1%), White (0.8%), Indians (0.5%), Nepalese (0.3%), Pakistanis (0.2%), Thais (0.1%), Japanese (0.1%), Other Asian (0.3%) and Others (0.9%) (2016 Population By-census, Census and Statistics Department of Hong Kong 2016).

migration will lead to changes in religious behaviors of a particular society and further complicate the dynamics of religious markets.

In the discussion of migrant integration into local settings, it seems that most scholars agree on the positive linkages between religion and the construction of ethnic identity. They contend that religion helps immigrants to establish their identity and community, and settle in the new land. In particular, Wuthnow and Hackett (2003) argued that religion has allowed newcomers to cross social boundaries and forge ties with people, creating linkage, with the host society and a form of identity. Yang's (1999) analysis of Chinese immigrants in America showed how the church has become a place where Chinese can selectively assimilate into American society while simultaneously preserving Chinese values and cultures. Baumann and Salentin (2006) also highlighted the role of religion in the integration process because religion may foster the building of social networks and a sense of community belonging. Even if immigrants are faced with an unfamiliar environment and challenges of settling in an unfamiliar environment, religions in some way "ease the difficulty of adjustment in the host country" (Bonifacio and Angeles 2010, p. 1).

There has been a lack of academic consensus on the definition of integration. Some sociologists (e.g., Gordon 1964) suggest integration as a form of assimilation. Supporters of this idea believe that ethnic groups would become part of the mainstream culture, sharing similar norms and values embraced by the "larger society" over generations. However, assimilation theory tends to focus too much on the homogenization of society and overlook the fact that integration is more than a one-way straight-line progress. Therefore, this paper defines integration as "the process by which individuals become members of society and their multilevel and multiform participation within it" (Anthias et al. 2013, p. 3). Following this line of thought, it could be argued that the success of migrant integration depends on whether migrants receive enough resources, both tangible or intangible, that could facilitate their participation in society in general. Examples of such resources include, information about jobs (for participation in workplace), guidance in legal rights (for participation in civil society), emotional support (for maintaining mental health for social and economic participation), and social relationships (for participation in social activities). In this sense, it is interesting to see whether the resources offered by a religion may be helpful in promoting migrants' participation within a society.

The relationships between religion and migrants in the Hong Kong context have been examined by a few scholars. For example, Cruz (2010) discussed how Christian groups may facilitate the incorporation of Filipina domestic workers (DHs) into Hong Kong society by offering social activities, hotline services, counseling services, legal advice, leadership training, livelihood courses, and shelters for distressed DHs. Constable (2010) also suggested many Hong Kong religious organizations are involved in providing support for migrant workers, and that the church has been playing an important role in the lives of many of Hong Kong's Filipino migrant worker activists. Besides, Knowles and Harper (2009, p. 124) revealed that mosques in Hong Kong supports new Muslim migrants from Pakistan, Bangladesh, India, and, increasingly, from northern Nigeria, Somalia, and other Muslim African countries by providing spiritual support, refreshments, and running supplementary Koran classes, and Arabic classes.

However, beyond the church and mosque, there appears to be a gap in the research of the roles played by other religions in the process of migrant integration. As Bonifacio and Angeles (2010, p. 1) argued, "our understanding of the role of religion and faith-based beliefs in the integration of diverse groups of immigrants [...] seems a bare scratch on the surface of scholarly discourse". In view of this, this paper intends to offer a modest contribution to the study of migrant integration from the perspective of religion using a Japanese new religious movement (NRM), Soka Gakkai, as a case study.[2]

The globalization of SG has drawn a lot of scholarly attention in the US, Brazil, Britain, Italy, and Southeast Asia (e.g., Metraux 1988, 1994, 1996, 1997, 2000, 2001, 2010; Wilson and Dobbelaere 1994; Dobbelaere 2001; Machacek and Wilson 2000; Hammond and Machacek 1999). These studies focus on the development of SG in different regions and argue how SG has applied the Buddhist concept of *zuiho-bini* (spread of Buddhism according to local cultures) in the localization process. In the USA, for example, SG meetings are held on Sunday to suit the church-going habits of westerners, whereas meetings are usually scheduled on weekdays in Japan. In this way, Hammond and Machacek (1999, p. 282) argue that SG's "tranquil experience in the USA lies in SGI USA's compliance with American social institutions and a history of reforms designed to make this Japanese religion look as American as possible". Hammond and Machacek also touched upon the issue of migrants in their study. They found that, in the early development of SGI-USA, it mainly targeted Japanese immigrants and SG acted as a community to connect Japanese immigrants together. Meetings were held in traditional ways in which "participants spoke Japanese, removed their shoes at the door, and knelt on the floor to chant" and sat "in sex segregated groups" (Hammond and Machacek 1999, pp. 25, 98). Their study hints that SGI-USA has a role in helping Japanese migrants maintain their Japanese traditions and religious identity in a society where Christian cultures are prevalent.

In his case study of SGI-Canada, Metraux also held a similar argument. He wrote "the sizeable growth of immigrants have left any Canadians with an uncomfortable feeling that they are without firm roots and a group to belong to" (Metraux 1996, p. 81). Especially, Canada is a major educational center which attracts many overseas students, who usually come to Canada on their own and are living separately from their families and friends. Some see SGI-Canada as a "home" for them to make friends, where they can find a sense of home and community. In addition, SGI-Canada has tried to portray itself as a migrant-welcoming organization by emphasizing its multi-ethnic memberships with people of different origins and colors. This strategy seems to be rather effective as seen from the large number of foreign immigrants in SGI-Canada (45% white, 24% Asian and 19% black people) (Metraux 1996, p. 82).

The case of Singapore Soka Gakkai (SSA) is also worth discussing. One of the characteristics of SSA, as pointed out by Metraux (2001, p. 47), is a strong sense of national pride in Singapore. Singapore is a young nation that gained its independence in 1965. The Singaporean government therefore puts a lot of effort into building a national identity. Numerous ceremonies and festivals are organized by the government to develop a sense of patriotism among its young citizens. To echo with the national policy, SSA portrays itself as an organization which promotes patriotic values. Its members have been active in The National Day Parade and Singapore Youth Festival. Singaporean members, especially the young ones, believe that they are working for the better future of society. In fact, Singapore has attracted many new migrants working in the financial sector as it has established itself as an international financial center. SSA may appeal to these new migrants who agree with the "Singaporean identity", which emphasizes excellence and hard-work.

From the above case studies, we can see SG is related to migrant integration in different ways. It may serve as an ethnic community preserving the traditions and a sense of identity of migrants (Japanese migrants in early SGI-USA), as a multi-ethnic community where migrants of different origins feel free to get together (SGI-Canada), or as a facilitator to help migrants identify themselves with the values and identities in that country (SSA). These studies suggest that SGI branches show different

---

[2] According to Helen Hardacre, "new religions" (shinko shukyo) appeared around 1800 in Japan. They have a great variety of doctrines, but "share a unity of aspiration and worldview significantly different from those of secular society and from the so-called established religions". They emphasize "this-worldly-benefits" by improving spiritual health, family relationships, and material prosperity. The founders of these religions are always charismatic individuals who attract followers through faith healing (see Hardacre (1986), pp. 3–5).

strategies in migrant integration as these regions possess different social, cultural, and demographic features. The reason for choosing HKSGI in this study is therefore to fill the gap in the studies of SGI and migrant integration, where the number of Japanese migrants and Mainland Chinese migrants is increasing due to rapid cross-broader economic activities and migrations.

In addition to the above reason, the amounts of research on SG in the Chinese contexts in general remains inadequate. Through the case study of HKSGI, we may understand the internationalization strategies of SG in the Chinese settings.

This paper starts with an introduction of the immigration patterns in Hong Kong, which is followed by an overview of SG development in Japan and Hong Kong. Then, it discusses how the resources provided by HKSGI may facilitate the integration of Japanese and Mainland Chinese immigrants. In particular, this paper argues that the informational, social, and spiritual support provided by HKSGI, particularly the ideas of a "big family" and individual empowerment, are important resources for immigrants when starting a new life in Hong Kong.

2. Immigration Patterns in Hong Kong

Many migration theories hold that work opportunities and higher wages are two of the main incentives for migrant workers to travel to a new environment (e.g., Ravenstein 1885; Sjaastad 1962; Todaro 1969; Piore 1979; Sassen 1988).[3] Hong Kong has been one of the popular destinations for a large amount of workers from the Philippines, Thailand, Nepal, Indonesia, and other less developed regions to seek jobs. For instance, at the end of 2017, there were 369,651 domestic helpers working in Hong Kong, of whom about 43.2% were from Indonesia and 54.4% from the Philippines (Hong Kong Government 2017, p. 117). According to the Asian Development Bank (Asian Development Bank), the largest migrant-sending country to Hong Kong is the Philippines (142,000), followed by Indonesia (108,000), the United States (not available), Thailand (30,000), and other Asian countries such as India, Japan, and Nepal (Asian Development Bank 2006, p. 4). The remittances they send to their homelands not only can improve their families' living standards, but also provide the labor exporting country with steady inflows of external income.[4] After working in Hong Kong for an average of five (Indonesia) to eight (the Philippines) years, most of these temporary workers return to their homeland after fulfilling their role of *dekasegi* (working away from home) (Asian Development Bank 2006, p. 56). Some may wish to reside permanently in Hong Kong after seven years of stay.[5]

Another type of migrant workers are self-motivated individuals and expatriate workers sent by their host companies to stay in Hong Kong on a temporary or semi-permanent basis. In fact, many Japanese migrants in Hong Kong fall into this category. For instance, the number of Japanese nationals who work or live in Hong Kong in 2017 amount to 25,527, of whome 17,834 work in the business sector, 49 in media, 1256 are self-employed, and 691 are students, researchers, or teachers (Ministry of Foreign Affairs Japan 2018). These Japanese workers may return to their home country after a short period of stay, or eventually settle permanently in Hong Kong. Two well-established Japanese communities can be found in Whampoa Po and Taikoo Shing where Japanese restaurants and shops run by ethnic Japanese can be easily seen. The Hong Kong Japanese Club, and the Japan Society of Hong Kong are organizations that aim to promote cultural exchanges between Hong Kong and Japanese people, but less is concerned about the social and religious well-being of Japanese migrants.

Migration in Hong Kong is also characterized by the emerging population inflow of Chinese from the Mainland in recent decades. As of 2017, there were 47,000 Mainland Chinese who moved to

---

3 Ravenstein's (1885) laws of migration (economic opportunity), Sjaastad (1962) and Todaro's (1969) neoclassical economic theories (global supply and demand of labor), Piore's (1979) segmented labor-market theory (immigrants to fill secondary market), and Sassen's (1988) world-systems theory (migration as a by-product of capitalism) offer some explanations to the large amount of foreign workers in Hong Kong.

4 According to the Asian Development Bank (2006), Filipino and Indonesian migrants living and working in Hong Kong transact an average of US$300 each time with an annual average number of transactions of 11 and 15, respectively.

5 The original Japanese word *dekasegi* (出稼ぎ) means "working away from home".

Hong Kong with the one-way permit (Hong Kong Government 2017, p. 286).[6] These new immigrants mainly come for work, education, and family reunion, but they also constitute a major proportion of Hong Kong's impoverished underclass (Law and Lee 2006). Governmental surveys reveal that many of them still receive little education and engage in low-wage jobs. According to a report released by the Research Office of the Legislative Council Secretariat (2018), the median monthly family income of new-arrival households is HK$ 17,500 in 2016, while that of all households is HK$ 25,000. The same report also suggests the poverty rate of new-arrival households is 30.1%, compared to 14.7% for all households.[7] In addition, the public impression on Mainland Chinese immigrants varies among Hong Kong people. Some criticized them as unproductive and dependent on social welfare and public assistance, and even label them as "locusts" (which travel great distances, rapidly stripping fields and greatly damaging crops), whereas some employers recognized them as hardworking and trustworthy.[8]

Regardless of the forms of migration, new immigrants may have to face new challenges in the unfamiliar environments. Separated from their homelands and detached from the original social networks and cultural settings, they lose the attachment they once enjoyed and may feel lonely, lost, and long for various forms of support. Before examining how SG may function as a source of social and spiritual support to new immigrants, the following offers an overview of the history and teachings of SG and the methodologies adopted in this study.

3. Overview of SG

The steady and non-threatening patterns of migration, institutions of religious diversity, and various social structures and organizations have promoted religious harmony in Hong Kong (Bouma and Singleton 2004). Religious pluralism not only gives rise to the flourishing of indigenous religions but also the steady development of new religious movements (NRMs). SG is one of the latter, and its growth in Hong Kong is partly attributed to the open religious market and a high degree of religious freedom enjoyed by Hong Kong residents and religious producers.

Tracing back to the Kamakura period of Japan, a series of disasters (domestic strife, natural disasters, and Mongolian invasion) that hit the island country made Nichiren (1222–1282), the founder of Nichiren Buddhism, subscribe to the belief that Japanese people were living in the age of *mappo* 末法 (the age of degeneration of the Dharma) when people turned away from the saving truths of Buddhist scripture and turned to evil and violence (Kirimura 1980, p. xxiii). He prescribed a simple mantra, *nam-myoho-renge-kyo* 南無妙法蓮華経 (literally meaning "devotion to the mystic law of the *Lotus Sutra*", also known as *daimoku* 題目) and a mandala, *Gohonzon* 御本尊. Based on his teachings, all individuals may attain perfect enlightenment through chanting *daimoku* (Kirimura 1980).

In 1928, the Japanese educator Makiguchi Tsunesaburō became a true believer of Nichiren Buddhism. Two years later, he founded the education reformist group Soka Kyōiku Gakkai (SKG, literally "Value-Creation Education Society") to promote the reformation of the educational system in Japan. The group criticized the educational system at that time for being centered too much on obedience and rote memorization and promoted critical thinking as a key to achieve personal goals and interests. He thought that students should also be taught to pursue values and make positive contributions to society (Nishihara 2008, p. 54).

After World War Two, Toda Josei reorganized SKG by dropping the word *kyoiku* (education) from the name and formed SG. An organization originally with an emphasis on educational reform became

---

6   "One way-Permit" is a document issued by the People's Republic of China allowing residents of mainland China to leave the mainland for permanent residence in Hong Kong. Before 1995, 75 permits were issued on a daily basis. The number has since increased to 150.

7   New Chinese migrants had often been associated with the image of being poor and uneducated. In recent years, however, the number of Chinese migrants who belong to the well-off class is increasing. Some of them make investments in real estate and start businesses in Hong Kong.

8   While the term has been widely used in anti-Chinese movements in Hong Kong, many criticized it for being discriminative and fueling hatred and intolerance.

a religion following the teaching of the *Lotus Sutra* and Nichiren Buddhism. Under the leadership of Toda, the organization successfully recruited over one million households in the postwar era through vigorous recruitment strategies known as *shakubuku* (approaching strangers in public places and coaxing them to visit SG meetings), and massive rallies, and parades (Yano and Shimada 2010, p. 81). In the 1960s, Toda's successor Ikeda Daisaku successfully developed this Japanese religion into a world religion by establishing Soka Gakkai International (SGI) with its headquarters located in Shinjuku, Japan, to coordinate overseas branches in North and South America, Europe, and Asia.

Starting with only 15 members in 1961, the membership of Hong Kong Soka Gakkai International (HKSGI) has now reached 50,000 (HKSGI 2011). The steady growth in membership may be attributed to its localization policies and recruitment strategies (Ng 2012), as well as the socio-political and religious background of Hong Kong. The organization has also built a very strong grass-roots network by organizing different cultural and social activities. Recently, the organization has successfully recruited more social elites, such as businessmen, lawyers, professors, and doctors; their participation further legitimizes SG development in Hong Kong.

Nowadays, HKSGI has eleven community headquarters all over Hong Kong Island, Kowloon, and the New Territories. Nine headquarters serve the ethnic Chinese, one serves non-Chinese English speakers including Filipinos, Indians, Americans and British, and the remaining one serves Japanese speakers. HKSGI runs four cultural centers in Kowloon Tong, Causeway Bay and Tuen Mun, and Sai Wan Ho; one kindergarten in Kowloon Tong; and a recreational center in Tai Po.

4. Research Methods

HKSGI shows a diverse ethnic make-up in its membership. From the latest figures, there are around 400 Japanese and 400 English-speaking foreigners among the 50,000 members (HKSGI 2011). The number of members migrating from Mainland China, however, is not available. The 400 Japanese members in the 11th headquarters can roughly be classified into three categories: (1) first generation that joined SG in Japan and settled in Hong Kong; (2) second and third generation who were born in Hong Kong, mostly from SG family; and (3) few Japanese exchange students and temporary workers who only stay in Hong Kong for a short period of time. Due to the high proportion of ethnic Japanese registered to the 11th headquarters, it is one of the main focuses of my study. However, the facts that Mainland Chinese immigrants are assigned to the first to ninth headquarters based on their place of residence in Hong Kong, and that the organization does not record whether members came from the Mainland, pose difficulties in locating this group of people. Therefore, my study focuses on the Tuen Mun Cultural Center, which mainly serves members living in Tin Shui Wai and Tuen Mun, where the number of Mainland Chinese immigrants are said to be high.

The methodology adopted in this paper includes participant observations in SG activities, semi-structured interviews of SG members and staff conducted from 2009 to 2011, additional follow-up interviews from 2011 to 2015, and analysis of official publications of SG. In this paper, pseudonyms are used for all informants.

5. HKSGI: A Home for New Immigrants?

SG views migration as one of the many common social phenomena nowadays which volume, scale, and speed are further catalyzed by modernization and globalization. To Ikeda, however, migration may also be harmful to human civilizations. He is concerned about the "intolerance based on ethnic or national differences, often aggravated by international movements of population" which "has been the cause of conflict and criminal violence, and many societies are experiencing severe divisions" (Ikeda 2006, p. 1). On this account, Ikeda envisions a sense of global citizenship that promotes an interconnecting humanity bonded by Buddhist teachings. He believes that "the only way to create global unity is to build a world civilization linking together all humanity [sic] which, while preserving and making positive use of local traditions, at the same time, is a truly international culture"

(Ikeda 1981–1987, pp. 32–33). To him, Buddhist ideas are the important antidote to the problems associated with migration.

At the organizational level, however, HKSGI does not have a specific supporting system or recruitment strategy targeting new immigrants. This point is clearly and repeatedly mentioned by both SG staffs and members.

> HKSGI does not have special preferences in recruiting or supporting new immigrants. Our organization sees every human being equally. And our members are encouraged to promote SG teachings to all people regardless of their ethnicity and social status. (Interview with Miss K, SG staff)

> HKSGI is not providing support to migrants at all because it is a matter related to the laws and administration of a nation. And we, SG members do not specifically target new immigrants. (Interview with Mr. I, SG member)

> We do not offer material or financial support to them [new immigrants]. We help them through religious means, such as chanting *daimoku* and sharing Buddhist teachings. Encouraging them to apply the teachings of SG to their life is the fundamental way to achieve real happiness instead of offering temporary monetary or material assistance. (Interview with Miss Y, SG staff)

In addition, SG applies what Dawson (1998, p. 68) called the "friends recruit friends, family members each other, and neighbors recruit neighbors" strategy. Only for the very close people and at the very appropriate timing (when they are stressed out or suffering illness), members will try to introduce SG to them.

The official stance and recruitment policy stated above tend to suggest one thing: SG plays a passive role in the integration of new immigrants. In this paper, I try to offer some arguments supporting the opposite. I want to discuss three *resources* provided by HKSGI that Japanese and Mainland Chinese new immigrants consider useful in promoting their participation and integration in Hong Kong society: (1) promoting a strong network between local and overseas SG branches and members; (2) providing religious support; and (3) upholding the ideas of a "big family", human dignity, and human revolution.

5.1. A Strong Network among SG Branches and Members

The efficiency of migrant integration into a new environment depends strongly on whether supporting agents and social networks are available when one arrives in the host country. In the case of SGI, communication networks among SG branches in Japan and overseas are very well-established, which ensures that the movements of members are informed to the new branches in advance so that the concerned members will be taken good care of in the new place. In this way, whenever there is a foreign member going to Hong Kong, the headquarters in Hong Kong will get informed and members can get prepared to offer support to the new-coming members from the very first day of their arrival. The following interviews with Mr. I and Miss T show how such a strong network among SG branches and assistance from local members were helpful during their stay in Hong Kong.

Mr. I is an ethnic Japanese who was born in a SG family in Japan. His parents registered him as a SG member when he was only a child. In his younger days, although he actively participated in SG meetings and cultural activities, he was not a devoted believer of SG and sometimes even doubted whether chanting could really achieve personal goals. At the age of eighteen, he failed his university entrance examination. Since then, he chanted more frequently and studied hard in the hope of entering a good university. A year later, he successfully passed the entrance examination of Soka University, a university affiliated with SG. Believing it was the reward of his intense chanting, he became more devoted to SG teachings and activities.

In 2002, Mr. I came to Hong Kong and started teaching Japanese language in a few local universities and several Japanese language schools. Prior to his departure from Japan, he consulted some senior members and SG staff and was given a reference letter that proved his SG membership. The staff also gave him the contacts of HKSGI, therefore he was able to inform the Hong Kong staff of the date and details of his arrival, and exchange some personal information for future contacts. Once Mr. I arrived in Hong Kong, he was able to resume his religious practice and make new friends within the new organization quickly thanks to the smooth transition of his membership.

Moreover, Japanese members in the 11th headquarters have formed a strong network and community for promoting mutual support, such as sharing jobs and housing information, which Gordon (2009, p. 259) also found in SG Japan. From this network Mr. I received information about housing and could eventually share an apartment with another Japanese SG member (coincidently, he was also a Japanese language teacher) with a lower rent, where they lived for almost a year.

The 11th headquarters is also a place where he could communicate effectively with other Japanese members in his mother tongue, and exchange important news and useful information about living in Hong Kong, easing most of the inconvenience he encountered. The SG community as a source of information is especially important for Japanese members like Mr. I who have not yet mastered the Cantonese and English languages. Similarly, when Mr. I went to the U.S. to further his studies in 2008, he received support from the American members, which was made possible because of the strong network among SG branches and members.[9]

Miss T, who is also ethnic Japanese, shared a similar experience with Mr. I. When she was an undergraduate student at Soka University, she went on a one-year exchange a local university in Hong Kong in 2010. She received a reference letter from the SG branch office in Japan to which she had belonged and contacted the Hong Kong branch office before she set off. When she arrived in Hong Kong, members of the HKSGI Student Division, which includes many college students, were helpful in providing her with various kinds of assistance, such as taking her to different spots and teaching her about Hong Kong cultures, and a little bit of Cantonese language skills. According to another SG staff that I interviewed, there is also a "supporter system" for newcomers. Supporters are local Hong Kong SG members recruited from the organization who usually live in the same district as the newcomers. They are responsible for informing and reminding the newcomers of the meeting time and places and providing spiritual support by sharing Buddhist teachings. Eventually, some supporters and newcomers develop a close friendship, going out together very often for social activities (e.g., refreshments, dining out, and going to the movies) and giving a helping hand to each other when necessary (e.g., going to a clinic together).

The majority of members in the 11th headquarters of HKSGI are ethnic Japanese.[10] Having gone through similar adaptation process, these *senpais* (seniors) can often give useful advice to their new-coming *kouhais* (juniors). For instance, Mr. O, a senior Japanese member working in the SG Translation Department, and Publication Bureau of HKSGI noted:

> In our gathering, members share their worries with others. These worries can sometimes be spiritual and sometimes practical, for example, being unemployed. After listening to their worries, we will offer our own opinions. Depending on the situations, some members may ask the person 'what kind of job can you do?' and even introduce a job to him. (Interview with Mr. O, SG staff)

---

[9] According to another Japanese informant, there are actually many ways to transfer membership from one branch to another, depending on different regions and circumstances. In his case, he had to return his SG membership card to the current branch, which was then sent to the new branch on behalf of him. Regardless of the methods, the important idea behind this is that new members would be able to resume their religious and social life in a new place as soon as possible.

[10] There are also a few ethnic Chinese who are the spouses of Japanese members in the 11th headquarters.

He also added that some Japanese members complained to him over "everyday life" issues in Hong Kong. For instance, a member asked Mr. O "Cantonese food is too spicy and oily. What can I do?" He told the member that "no specific Buddhist teaching can help you solve this problem". He then asked the member to "try his best to adapt to local cultures" and suggested that he "go and eat Japanese food" because there are plenty Japanese restaurants available in Hong Kong. Their conversation then moved naturally to the discussion of where they could find the best Japanese cuisines such as *ramen* and *sushi* or nice *izakaya* (Japanese pub) in Hong Kong. They also talked about the culture shock they encountered and what it meant to live in Hong Kong as Japanese people. These conversations did not necessarily have any conclusion, but most members, especially newcomers, looked relieved after attending these sharing sessions.

From this example, we can see the difficulties experienced by members range from the most basic needs, such as housing and job, to something more casual, like appetite. The practical advice from these *senpais* are helpful for these newcomers to solve daily problems. What is more important is probably the presence of those who are experienced and could understand the difficulties facing the newcomers because they all shared life journeys, cultural identities, and religious backgrounds. In this sense, the Japanese community in HKSGI also serves as a source of reaffirmation of identity for Japanese members whose cultural identity might have been challenged in their everyday life in Hong Kong.

Although Japanese SG members in HKSGI may often rely on their Japanese counterparts and *senpais* for guidance, it is unlikely the 11th headquarters will become an ethnic enclave that hinders their interactions with Hong Kong people and the wider society. This is because HKSGI is an organization that actively promotes social engagement and cultural exchanges. For instance, Ikeda, the Honorary President of SGI, strongly believes in the power of dialogue in enhancing mutual understanding and solving conflicts among different civilizations. In *Embracing the Future*, he wrote "the distances between people need not act as barriers that wound and harm. Rather, these very differences among cultures and civilizations should be recognized and appreciated as creating richer value for all" (Ikeda 2009, p. 160). Practicing what he believes, Ikeda has been traveling to different places to conduct peace dialogues with various renowned political (e.g., Zhou Enlai), cultural (e.g., Jin Yong), and academic figures (e.g., Bryan Wilson) (Bauhinia Magazine 2007).

Following Ikeda's lead, HKSGI highly encourages its fellow members to link up with and spread the teachings of SG to local people through dialogue. Japanese members in Hong Kong are also mobilized to participate in many public activities, such as exhibitions and cultural festivals, in which they have many opportunities to cooperate and work with local Hong Kong people and other foreign members.

The following is an interview with Miss M, an ethnic Japanese who has lived in Hong Kong for almost 20 years. Miss M was assigned to lead the 1600 person choir in the Cultural Festival 2011. Since the choir is composed of various sub-groups containing members from Hong Kong, Taiwan, Malaysia, Singapore, the Philippines, Japan, and South Korea, she was worried that the huge size of the choir would make it difficult to coordinate, and that language barriers would cause misunderstandings among members. To take on this challenge, Miss M and the choir members formed the "confidence-filling station", a temporary group for members to get to know each other, chant, and share ideas, to unite members of different ethnicities and burst their confidence to work for the best outcome.

During the preparation, Miss M travelled to different headquarters regularly to meet with various sub-groups of the choir. She wanted to make sure that performers from different districts, divisions, or groups were delivered the correct instructions, thereby minimizing any mistake or confusion that might arise due to misunderstanding and miscommunication. Eventually, the large and multi-national choir was able to "turn the poison into medicine" (convert risks into opportunities) and accomplished this difficult task.

From the perspective of SG, the success of the choir in the cultural festival may as well be attributed to the power of dialogue, which brought culturally diverse members together to strive for the same goal. Believing in the power of dialogue as a key to peace and harmony may also be one of the reasons why many Japanese members are more than willing to interact with the local communities through education (e.g., teaching Japanese language), business (e.g., opening Japanese restaurants), and participating in voluntary activities (e.g., Japanese festivals). Isolating themselves by forming an ethnic enclave is not the case among Japanese members in HKSGI, although it may be true for some other ethnic-religious groups.

It is also worth noting that HKSGI organizes peace exhibitions and cultural seminars at local universities on a regular basis. SG members visit various universities and share with local students and teachers about the importance of peace. While no direct evidence is available at this time, this kind of outreach activities might have the potential to serve as a bridge between members and the larger Hong Kong society as members may build new social networks beyond the SG circle. The effects of participating in outreach activities on the social inclusion of Japanese members in Hong Kong society is another topic that needs to be explored in the future.

In short, the support Japanese members gain in the 11th headquarters is mostly emotional and religious, and in the form of experiences and information (e.g., housing and job). Senior members can help frustrated members through giving guidance and sharing. The organization also encourages Japanese members to bring their skills into full play by mobilizing them to participate in various SG activities. Through working and having dialogues with Hong Kong members, they understand better the local cultures and expand their social networks beyond the Japanese community. Although HKSGI enjoys high autonomy in terms of administration, management, recruitment, and finance, it still maintains a close relationship with the Japanese headquarters that allows rapid information exchanges. This communication mechanism, together with the supporter-system, ensures members who travel overseas are taken good care of by the local SG branches.

5.2. Religious Supports

Immigration can be considered as a "theologizing experience" since immigrants often make sense of the alienation that is inherent in migration in religious terms (Smith 1978). Casanova also argued, "The uprootedness which accompanied emigration meant that 'faith' could no longer be taken for granted. It had to be actively and voluntarily 'kept' or 'revived'" (Casanova 1980, p. 177), and that "the uprootedness it entails from traditional ways, the uncertainty of the journey and the anomic experience of being strangers in a new land calls forth a religious response" (Casanova 2007, p. 66). Similarly, SG members seek explanations for their new adventures and definitions of identities in the new place from the teachings of Nichiren and Ikeda, which eventually leads to the enhancement of faith towards SG. The following presents some examples of how SG teachings might serve as important resources for members to facilitate their new journeys in Hong Kong.

Lee Kon Sau, an ethnic Japanese whose original name was Kajiura Hisashi, was the president of HKSGI from 1966 to 2009. Lee first came to Hong Kong as a university exchange student at New Asia College, Chinese University of Hong Kong (CUHK) in 1964. The two-year university life in Hong Kong enabled Lee to acquire knowledge of Hong Kong culture and Cantonese language. This experience also laid a good groundwork for the next mission appointed to Lee in 1966: to lead SG development in Hong Kong. Motivated by Ikeda in 1974, he changed his name to Lee Kon Sau, which means "just became 35 years old" in Chinese (Lee 2009, p. 185). His familiarity with and respect for Cantonese dialects and cultures, as well as the social networks established with the locals, has facilitated his leadership in Hong Kong.

Nevertheless, promoting a new religious organization in a foreign environment is more challenging than just being an exchange student. When he recalls his life journey in Hong Kong (Lee 2009, p. 192), Lee quotes the words of Nichiren in *Risshōankokuron* (Treatise on securing the peace of the land through the establishment of the correct, 1260): "A blue fly, if it clings to the tail of a thoroughbred horse, can travel ten thousand miles, and the green ivy that twines around the tall pine can grow to a thousand feet" (Nichiren 2003, p. 17). It seems that the vitality of the blue fly and green ivy that allows them to travel a long distance and develop to the fullest, which also symbolizes the unbounded potential and power of life, has been one of the many of Nichiren's words that maintained his faith throughout his 45-year mission of *kosen-rufu* (promotion of Buddhism). Lee's life journey in Hong Kong also resembles Nichiren's vivid analogy of the blue fly and green ivy, as he carried the seed of Nichiren Buddhism from Japan and cultivated it in new soils.

Mr. I, a SG member mentioned above, regarded Nichiren's teachings in *Gosho* (the individual and collected writings of Nichiren) as important resources for him to "define" himself when he was lost and regain confidence in the time of difficulties. "Whenever I have doubts in my life, especially when I just arrived in Hong Kong and everything was unfamiliar to me, chanting and reading Nichiren's teachings helped me a lot" said Mr. I. His favorite chapter is "On Rebuking Slander of the Law and Eradicating Sins":

> I am praying that, no matter how troubled the times may become, the *Lotus Sutra* and the ten demon daughters will protect all of you, praying as earnestly as though to produce fire from damp wood, or to obtain water from parched ground. (Nichiren 2003, p. 444)

Neither producing fire from damp wood nor obtaining water from parched ground is an easy task in reality, but Mr. I believes that through chanting *daimoku* with a strong determination to convert the impossible into possible, he could overcome challenges in his life and stand up from where he falls. At the time of the interview, he was also planning to have three children after getting married to his Hong Kong girlfriend in the near future. In the midst of uncertainty and countless challenges, Mr. I referred to the teachings of Ikeda and Nichiren for a source of power to stay optimistic about his future.

SG teachings are also important guidance for Japanese people who are starting businesses in Hong Kong. The experience of Mr. H provides us an illustration in this regard (Lung 2011, pp. 22–23). Mr. H was ethnic Japanese who joined SG in Japan when he was two years old. In 1989, he traveled to Hong Kong with his wife and started working in a sushi restaurant. After a long period of planning and intensive chanting, he successfully opened his own sushi restaurant in 2002. He also attributed his recovery from heart disease to chanting *daimoku* and encouragement from other SG members. After the Great East Japan Earthquake in 2011, however, Mr. H's sushi restaurant was badly affected because the public feared that food imported from Japan might be contaminated by radiation. Facing this unheralded business crisis, he resorted to chanting *daimoku* and the teachings of Nichiren and Ikeda. For example:

> Employ the strategy of the *Lotus Sutra* before any other. (Nichiren 2003, p. 1001)

> [The *Lotus Sutra* is] like a great physician who can change poison to medicine. (Nichiren 2003, p. 146)

The following two incidents made him believed that his intense chanting moved the *shoten-zenshin* 諸天善神 (gods in heaven): on 21 May, the Prime Minister of the People's Republic of China, Wen Jiaobao, visited Fukushima and ate the local agricultural products; on 23 May, Chief Executive of Hong Kong at that time, Donald Tsang, attended a banquet which promoted Japanese food safety. In the banquet, Tsang, who was not a fan of sushi, went to the sushi counter and ate one made by Mr. H. These events helped relieve some public fear of Japanese food products in Hong Kong and restored people's confidence in dining in Japanese restaurants. He concluded by quoting Ikeda's words: "the greater challenges and difficulties we face, the greater opportunity we have to grow." The teachings of SG and Ikeda have been, and will still be, the "medicine" for Mr. H whenever he faces difficulties in the future. From these examples, SG may serve as "confluences of organic-cultural flows that intensify joy and comfort suffering by drawing on human and suprahuman forces to make homes and cross boundaries"[11] (Tweed 2006, p. 54).

In the 1990s, when Hong Kong was about to be handed over from Britain to China, many Hong Kong people worried that the transition would bring about drastic changes to their lifestyles and living standards. There was even a mass migration to Canada, Australia, and the US because of the fears of the Communist takeover. Seeing the social unrest in Hong Kong, Ikeda encouraged members to be more optimistic, as he strongly believed that Hong Kong would have a better future after the transition of sovereignty because of this city's energy and vitality (Jin and Ikeda 1998, pp. 46–47). Ikeda's positive attitude toward Hong Kong's future eased the anxiety of many, including the Japanese members, who decided to stay in Hong Kong because they realized this small city has already become not only their new homes, but also an important window to further promote SG to the world.

5.3. Ideology of Itaidōshin, Dai-Ga-Ting, and Ningenkakumei

SG emphasizes a sense of family and that members are spiritually linked together based on the idea of *itai-dōshin* 異体同心 and *dai-ga-ting* 大家庭. *Itai-dōshin*, literally meaning "different bodies, same soul", emphasizes the idea that different individuals could work together and create the desired outcome. This expression is constantly used by members and leaders in both private conversation and public speech.

Dai-ga-ting, or the big family analogy, which also symbolizes a sense of collectiveness and solidarity, is also frequently used by members to describe their organization as family-like. For example, "my life has improved a lot after joining the SG big family" or "I feel very warm in this big family,". While Confucianism has been heavily shaken in the encounter with the modern age (Chan and Lee 1995) and the idea of a big family is losing some of its importance, SG fosters the community bonding and strengthens social cohesion by linking members under a family ideology. As Metraux (2000, p. 425) put it, "SG has succeeded in Asia also because it provides members with a new extended family".

It also seems that the ideology of family and a sense of collectiveness are especially attractive to those new immigrants who are suddenly detached from their previous social networks. Many foreign members found it more enjoyable and comfortable to spend time in the HKSGI big family since members share the same beliefs and can mutually support each other through the discussion of Buddhist teachings. They also felt that the positive and warm atmosphere cultivated in SG contrasts with the competitive and individualistic environment found in their workplaces.

While SG does not particularly intend to convert new immigrants, it always encourages members to promote Buddhist teachings to their acquaintances such as neighbors, colleagues, classmates and relatives. Derived from Mahayana Buddhism and embracing the teachings of *Lotus Sutra*, SG has the grand objective of improving the well-being of all people and enlightening all mankind, based on the idea of equity and that everyone bears the seed to enlightenment. When asked about their recruitment strategies, a SG staff noted:

We do not force our members to promote SG, like forcing them to convert ten people a day. No. We never do this. Instead, we hope our members will take the initiative to promote

---

[11] In the end of the American occupation of Japan in the 1950s, some American soldiers returned to the US with their Japanese wives. Some of these wives were SG believers and thus they brought their religion to the US. However, these Japanese wives were struggling in the new host country due to language barriers and culture shock. On 5 October 1960, Ikeda visited North America and encouraged these frustrated SG members to respond to the challenges positively by doing three specific things: to get a green card, to learn how to drive, and to learn English well. He believed that only by achieving these could they settle well in America. In this case, Ikeda's advice was practical and strategically targeted the difficulties facing the Japanese migrants. What is more important is also the symbolic meaning of Ikeda's visit. Another story happened in France in which a Japanese member was frustrated because he could not afford to buy his own house. Ikeda asked him to reflect on his intention of buying a house: whether it is just for his own happiness or for the spread of Buddhist teachings (as a meeting place for members). Significantly inspirited by Ikeda's words, the member recognized that his goal of buying a house was for the latter purpose and he worked harder and finally realized this ultimate objective.

Buddhist teaching to people around them [. . .] because one can only gain real happiness by experiencing the power of Buddhist teachings. And we are happy to let more people experience this mighty power. (Interview with Miss K, SG staff)

The aspiration of saving oneself and others has become a strong motivation for individual members to preach SG within their social networks. For instance, some Hong Kong members, especial women, promote SG teachings to new immigrants regardless of their ethnicity or social status, including those migrants from Mainland China. Many SG members approach these new immigrants kindly, showing their care and concern through home visits, gatherings (dining and chatting), and telephone calls. They then invite these potential converts to SG *zadankai* (sit-and-talk meeting) and "seminars of Buddhist teachings for new friends" if they show interests in the religion. Although no official record has been made available, the presence of Mainland Chinese immigrants in HKSGI, who include university students, businessmen, and housewives, is growing gradually.

In response to the increasing number of Mainland Chinese immigrants and the growing anti-Chinese sentiment in Hong Kong, a SG staff that I interviewed replied in a positive way:

We treasure the dignity of all human lives. We do not see Mainlanders as trouble-makers. Actually, people of other origins are causing some kinds of social problems in Hong Kong. We do not have a bias towards Mainlanders. Everyone bears the seed to enlightenment according to the *Lotus Sutra*. (Interview with Miss K, SG staff)

The ideas of anti-discrimination and respect for human dignity found in the *Lotus Sutra* are also emphasized in Toda's essay *Ningen-kakumei* (Human Revolution) and Ikeda's book series *Shin-ningen-kakumei* (New Human Revolution) (Ikeda 1995–2018). The concept *ningen-kakumei*, or human revolution, refers to the process of inner transformation from a self-concerned and egoistic "lesser self" toward an altruistic "greater self" capable of caring for all humanity. Following this idea, the human revolution of all individuals will lead to the revolution of the whole society, and the world will become the paradise depicted in Buddhist teachings.[12] Most importantly, according to SG teachings, the path to human revolution is indiscriminate because everyone bears the seed to enlightenment.

Human revolution also bears a strong this-worldly orientation that promotes positive thinking and actions to improve one's current conditions (Ikeda 1995–2018). According to SG teachings, any physical benefits brought by chanting are regarded as proof of the ongoing process of human revolution in one's life and society. Therefore, chanting and working hard for this-worldly benefits such as wealth, health, and love is not only acceptable but also preferable as receiving benefits implies one's human revolution is in progress.

Throughout my study, I found that the idea of individual empowerment has played an important role in the life of some Mainland Chinese immigrants. Especially, the financially less-privileged tend to find the idea of human revolution especially charming, as they want to seek a religious explanation and solution to their current financial difficulties. They want to believe that the challenges facing them are just temporary and changeable, and that they have the potential to achieve a better life through hardwork and chanting.

Mrs. L, an ethnic Chinese who migrated from the Mainland to Hong Kong in 2001 for family union, was deeply attracted by SG teachings, especially the notion of individual empowerment. Living with her husband in Tin Shui Wai,[13] one could hardly see any sorrows from her face, even though

---

[12] "We can change our own lives and the world for the better. While the role of institutions or governments is important, change that starts with each person's life is seen as the surest way to tackle the problems facing the world in the 21st century. Many people feel hopeless about these issues, but SGI stresses that people have the power to change their circumstances, and its public education and outreach projects aim to inspire people and equip them with information that they can use to make a difference in their communities" (see Soka Gakkai International 2018).

[13] From 2000 to 2007, about twenty people died in six suicides in this city. For instance, in April 2004, a man attempted suicide after killing his wife, a Mainland Chinese migrant, and two children in a quarrel. In November 2007, a mother,

the district is also known as the "city of sadness" for its high rate of unemployment, suicides, and spousal and child abuse. Mrs. L was satisfied with her family and social life, and she described her encounter with SG as miraculous. Her life did not seem to be smooth in the early 2000s. Similar to many less well-off families, both she and her husband (a local Hong Kong person) had to work in order to support the family. She recalled how the life of her family has changed after joining SG:

> One day I was really stressed out because of money. Then one of my colleagues, who I didn't know she was a SG member before, came to comfort me and asked me to try chanting at home. Coincidently, I received a small rise in salary after I chanted and the financial problem was somehow solved. Although it might seem mysterious to some people, I regard it as a miracle. After a few months of chanting and learning from my SG colleague, I found this religion can give me power and confidence, and I eventually became a member in 2003. My husband also tried chanting, after seeing the positive changes in my life. The bad-tempered man is gradually becoming gentler. Our family is also filled with more "positive power". I understand that everything we have faced in the past, are facing now, or will face in the future, including happiness, sadness, difficulties, or success, is related to our *shukumei* (past fates). It is only through chanting, our fates can be transformed and life improved. (Interview with Mrs. L, SG member)

SG also teaches its members to stay confident, optimistic, and positive toward life when facing challenges. A SG staff said:

> If they [new immigrants] face difficulties in a new environment, it doesn't mean that the problems will disappear when they return to their own countries; other problems may arise instead. It is only through practicing Buddhist teachings, one can transform their past fate and live a happy life. (Interview with Miss K, SG staff)

Convinced of the power of chanting *daimoku* in bringing about *shukumei-tenkan* 宿命転換 (transformation of one's fate), not few Mainland Chinese immigrants that I encountered in HKSGI believe they could achieve both spiritual and material happiness in this life. In the sharing session, they gratefully gave testimonies of how practicing SG teachings enabled them to overcome illnesses, get rid of frustration, improve family relationships, get better jobs, enter universities, etc. Although the benefits reported by members varied according to age, sex, occupations and some other attributes, these testimonies all pointed to and reinforced the very core belief of SG: all kinds of rewards are revelations and consequences of the transformation of past fates and the ongoing process of human revolution, as a result of chanting. In this way, SG provides a way for individuals to experience a sense of empowerment in their lives throughout the continuous process of chanting *daimoku*, transforming one's *shukumei*, and undergoing *ningen-kakumei*.

To take the discussion further, the participation of Mainland Chinese immigrants in HKSGI may be related to a "hunger for religion" among Mainland Chinese people. In his study on the religious market in China, Yang (2005, p. 432) argued that many Chinese people, who are struggling in "the wild market with existential anxieties", begin to seek "peace, security, and meaning in religion". However, religion remains a very controversial and sensitive issue in China and its religious market is still highly regulated. Although basic religious freedom is guaranteed according to the Constitution, religious seekers in China can only participate in the five approved religions (Christianity, Protestantism, Buddhism, Daoism, and Islam) under the umbrella of "patriotic associations". However, since these religions have strong communist color, and their operation and beliefs are subject to government regulation and censorship, some Chinese have lost their interest in these "compromised" patriotic

---

also a Mainland Chinese migrant, tied her nine-year-old son and eleven-year-old daughter up and dropped them from the twenty-fourth floor. The mother, who committed suicide afterward, and the two children were found dead.

religions and take the high risk to join illegal underground religious groups. Contrary to China, in a free market such as Hong Kong, citizens are free to practice any form of religions and are not exposed to any fear or risk of government suppression. Living in a vibrant marketplace of religions founded on cultural pluralism and a high degree of religious freedom, these "spiritually starving" Mainland Chinese immigrants in Hong Kong are happy to shop in the religious market and try various religious goods and services in a censorship-free and fear-free environment.

Mrs. C, who migrated from the Mainland to Hong Kong in 1998, was uncomfortable with the busy city life and a sudden detachment from her original social networks. Born in the 1970s in China, she also experienced the breakdown of social norms and moral values as a result of rapid modernization. To compensate for her spiritual lost, she started to explore the religious market.

> I did have some interest in traditional Buddhism and Taoism, but they are quite detached from the society and social life. It is not so good for a new-migrant like me to further isolate myself from the society ... Some of my housewives friends took me to a local Church. The people there were very nice and I could make friends inside the organization ... I admit that Christianity is a good religion but I am not convinced by the idea that human beings can only achieve salvation in the afterlife ... One day, I was invited by a friend to a Buddhist seminar organized by SG. I wasn't very interested at first and wanted to reject her. But my friend said "this seminar welcomes non-believers, and this religion is quite different from traditional Buddhism. So please come with me and try to experience something different". In fact, the meeting was not very different from the Christian fellowship; people talked about how their lives are improved by chanting and so on. But what caught my attention was the confidence and happy faces shown by the members. When I knew that people could indeed achieve enlightenment in this life through human revolution, I realized that this religion may be the religion that I have been seeking. (Interview with Mrs. C, SG member)

A religion which is not yet approved to operate in China succeeded in attracting Mainland Chinese religious seekers in Hong Kong, whose religious demands had long been suppressed by the strict religious policies imposed by the Chinese government.[14]

In short, the idea of a big family, the emphasis on human dignity and respect for all mankind, and the idea of individual empowerment are three important backbones in SG teachings that make SG "approachable" and "attractive" to Mainland Chinese immigrants. SG teachings are world-affirming and suggest the possibility of changing one's misfortune, which is the source of faith and courage to live a better life in Hong Kong for many newcomers who tend to be less well-off. In this sense, the deprivation theory may also explain the conversion of some new immigrants to SG because of their marginalized social status. The stories of Mrs. L and Mrs. C further show that the idea of human revolution is particular charming as it provides a religious worldview to explain the causes of their misfortunes (i.e., bad karma) and offers them possible solutions to fulfill their potential and achieve happiness (transformation of bad karma into good through chanting).

6. Problems Facing SG Members

One of the challenges faced by SG members in their integration in Hong Kong society is the negative images associated with the organization. SG is often criticized for its relationship with the political party *Komeito* (Clean Government Party). In Japan, SG was involved in the controversial "freedom of the press incident" in which Komeito tried to obstruct Professor Fujiwara Hirotatsu (Meiji University) from publishing a book called *Soka Gakkai wo Kiru* (Critic of Soka Gakkai).

---

14 In addition, HKSGI refrains from proselytizing Mainland Chinese people who do not have a Hong Kong Identification Card (HKID), since it violates the verbal agreement Ikeda made with Zhou Enlai that SG would enter China only if it is permitted by the government and the people of China "welcome" them.

The political participation of SG in politics is also criticized for violating the idea of separation of religion from politics stated in Article 20 of the Constitution of Japan. Apart from the connections between SG and politics in Japan, Ikeda Daisaku, the President of SGI, is criticized as a "fame and power seeker" for he has received honorary doctorate degrees from more than 380 universities.

People in Hong Kong who are aware of the news of SG have a negative perception of HKSGI as well as its members. For instance, SG's donation to a local university stirred up serious debate in 2009. Two donors wanted to donate 10 million Hong Kong dollars to a local university in Hong Kong. However, they also demanded the university to rename one of its student hostels to "Ikeda Daisaku Hostel". When this plan was announced, students, teachers, and alumni of that university expressed their concerns about the incentives of the donors and fear of political interventions from SG. At the end, the two donors and the university agreed to receive the donation but instead rename the hostel to "Sun Yat-sen Hall" in anticipation of the 100th anniversary of the Xinhai Revolution. Similarly, SG's donation to another local university in Hong Kong also drew opposition from their students and teachers because they feared SG was a "cult".

The negative perceptions of SG held by some people in Hong Kong might become an obstacles in migrant integration. For instance, at least two migrants told me they have experienced being treated unfairly in the workplace when their colleagues knew of their SG identity. Mr. I, for example, was mocked by his colleague because of his beliefs, and was asked why he chose to join a "strange" organization when there are so many other options such as Christianity. While many migrants I encountered in my study agreed that the various kinds of support from HKSGI can promote their participation in society, their SG identity, if exposed, may cause them unnecessary pressure in the workplace.

7. Conclusions

Existing SG literature on migrant integration has centered on the role of SGI in countries with high ethnic and cultural diversities. These studies hint that SGI branches in different demographic and cultural settings may adopt different strategies to respond to the needs of migrants. For instance, SGI may promote migrant integration by serving as: (1) an ethnic community to preserve migrants' traditional cultures (Japanese migrants in early SGI-USA); (2) a welcoming multi-ethnic community (SGI-Canada); or (3) a community fostering migrants' identification with the host society (SSA). However, the role of SGI on migrant integration in societies dominated by a single ethnic group is yet to be examined. Hong Kong, where the majority of the population is ethnic Chinese and is witnessing an increase in the number of Japanese migrants and Mainland Chinese migrants due to rapid cross-broader economic activities and migrations, serves as an important case study to fill the gap in the current SG literatures.

Besides, existing studies on migrant integration in Hong Kong have primarily focused on the various kinds of support offered by churches and mosques. The role of other religions in the process remains unclear. This paper contributes to the studies of migration and integration by evaluating how non-Christian and non-Muslim groups in Hong Kong, such as SG, have played a part in the lives of new migrants.

This paper shows Japanese and Mainland Chinese migrants found the informational, social, and religious resources offered by HKSGI helpful in starting their new life in Hong Kong. The integration of Japanese members is largely facilitated by the Japanese-speaking community in the 11th headquarters of HKSGI. Japanese newcomers receive such information as housing, job, and food from their Japanese counterparts, which is useful for them to start a new life in Hong Kong. Emotional support from senior members is also important when they experience culture shock and seek reaffirmation of a Japanese identity. For Chinese newcomers who are frustrated about their current financial conditions, SG teachings, especially the idea of human revolution, which serves as a source of energy to improve their lives, are considered appealing and helpful. The idea of SG as a "big family" is also appealing to some newcomers who have become detached from their original social networks.

In terms of religious beliefs, both Chinese and Japanese members believe that the challenges they encounter in Hong Kong are the consequences of their past fate, which can be transformed by chanting *daimoku*. The idea that one is able to convert bad karma into good is appealing to those who wish to unleash the burden of the past and starting a new life in Hong Kong. Moreover, SG teachings suggest that the path to human revolution is open for all, something all mankind can achieve through chanting and hardwork regardless of ethnicities and origins. In this sense, openness of theology and simplicity of practice make SG look more approachable to religious seekers. On many occasions, the words of Nichiren and Ikeda are perceived by the migrants as sources of power to help them stay positive and confident when facing ups and downs in life.

Two important remarks can be made based on the above findings. First, instead of being a welcoming multi-ethnic community or fostering a new identity among migrants as in the case of the North America and Singapore, HKSGI's strategies on migrant integration are inclined to the provision of informational, social, and religious resources. In particular, the ideas of "a big SG family" and "human revolution" are constantly emphasized. In brief, as Japanese migrants in Hong Kong are usually dispatched workers or exchange students who stay in Hong Kong alone on a short-term basis, many see HKSGI as a "temporary" family for them where they can seek information, guidance, and emotional support. In this sense, HKSGI may play a similar role to SGI-USA in the social integration of Japanese migrants in the US. In addition, some Japanese migrants who encounter difficulties in their business or workplace, and Chinese migrants who are financially challenged, often find the idea of "human revolution" as a source of confidence for them to overcome these challenges.

Second, this case study also suggests HKSGI has applied different strategies in migrant integration compared to churches and mosques in Hong Kong. Christian and Islamic groups have organized specific programs targeting migrants in Hong Kong, such as counselling services, legal advice, leadership training, and language classes. On the other hand, HKSGI has not been engaged in these kinds of programs. One of the possible explanations is that the notion of "equity" in SG teachings may have hindered the organization from targeting a specific group of members in society. If everyone is equal and can achieve a better future through their own efforts, they may see no reason to purposely "single out" a group.

This study suggests the positive influences of HKSGI on migrant integrations. However, the image of SG may affect how SG members are received in Hong Kong. How HKSGI should improve its public image in Hong Kong remains an important topic for the organization.

Funding: This research received no external funding.

Acknowledgments: The author gratefully thanks the editors and anonymous referees for their constructive comments and recommendations.

Conflicts of Interest: The author declares no conflicts of interest.

References

Anthias, Floya, Maria Kontos, and Mirjana Morokvasić, eds. 2013. *Paradoxes of Integration: Female Migrants in Europe*. Dordrecht: Springer.

Asian Development Bank. 2006. *Workers' Remittance Flow in Southeast Asia*. Manila: Asian Development Bank.

Bauhinia Magazine. 2007. Special edition vol. 2. Hong Kong: Thousand Wisdom Ltd.

Baumann, Martin, and Kurt Salentin. 2006. Migrant Religiousness and Social Incorporation: Tamil Hindus from Sri Lanka in Germany. *Journal of Contemporary Religion* 21: 297–323. [CrossRef]

Bonifacio, Glenda Tibe, and Vivienne S. M. Angeles, eds. 2010. *Gender, Religion, and Migration: Pathways of Integration*. Lanham: Lexington Books.

Bouma, Gary, and Andrew Singleton. 2004. A Comparative Study of the Successful Management of Religious Diversity: Melbourne and Hong Kong. *International Sociology* 19: 5–24. [CrossRef]

Casanova, José. 1980. *Public Religions in the Modern World*. Chicago and London: The University of Chicago Press.

Casanova, José. 2007. Immigration and the New Religious Pluralism: A European Union/United States Comparison. In *Democracy and the New Religious Pluralism*. Edited by Thomas Banchoff. New York: Oxford University Press, pp. 59–84.

Census and Statistics Department of Hong Kong. 2016. 2016 Population By-census. Available online: https://www.bycensus2016.gov.hk/en/ (accessed on 11 September 2018).

Chan, Hoiman, and Rance Pui Leung Lee. 1995. Hong Kong Families: At the Crossroads of Modernism and Traditionalism. *Journal of Comparative Family Studies* 26: 83–99.

Constable, Nicole. 2010. Telling Tales of Migrant Workers in Hong Kong: Transformations of Faith, Life Scripts, and Activism. *Asia Pacific Journal of Anthropology* 11: 311–29. [CrossRef]

Cruz, Gemma Tulud. 2010. It Cuts Both Ways: Religion and Filipina Domestic Workers in Hong Kong. In *Gender, Religion, and Migration: Pathways of Integration*. Edited by Glenda Tibe Bonifacio and Vivienne S. M. Angeles. Lanham: Lexington Books, pp. 17–36.

Dawson, Lorne. 1998. *Cults in Context: Readings in the Study of New Religious Movements*. Toronto: Canadian Scholars' Press.

Dobbelaere, Karel. 2001. *Soka Gakkai: From Lay Movement to Religion*. Salt Lake City: Signature Books.

Finke, Roger, and Rodney Stark. 1992. *The Churching of America, 1776–1990: Winners and Losers in Our Religious Economy*. New Brunswick: Rutgers University Press.

Gordon, Milton Myron. 1964. *Assimilation in American Life: The Role of Race, Religion, and National Origins*. New York: Oxford University Press.

Gordon, Andrew. 2009. *A Modern History of Japan: From Tokugawa Times to the Present*. New York: Oxford University Press.

Hammond, Phillip, and David Machacek. 1999. *Soka Gakkai in America: Accommodation and Conversion*. New York: Oxford University Press.

Hardacre, Helen. 1986. *Kurozumikyo and the New Religions of Japan*. Princeton: Princeton University Press.

Hong Kong Soka Gakkai International (HKSGI). 2011. *Brochure of HKSGI Cultural Festival 2011*. Hong Kong: HKSGI.

Hong Kong Government. 2017. Hong Kong Year Book 2017. Available online: https://www.yearbook.gov.hk/2017/en/ (accessed on 11 September 2018).

Iannaccone, Laurence Robert. 1998. Introduction to the Economics of Religion. *Journal of Economic Literature* XXXVI: 1465–96.

Ikeda, Daisaku. 1981–1987. *A Lasting Peace: Collected Addresses of Daisaku Ikeda*. New York: Weatherhill.

Ikeda, Daisaku. 1995–2018. *The New Human Revolution*. Santa Monica: World Tribune Press, vol. 1–30.

Ikeda, Daisaku. 2006. 2006: Peace Proposal. A New Era of the People: Forging a Global Network of Robust Individuals. Available online: http://www.daisakuikeda.org/assets/files/pp2006.pdf (accessed on 11 September 2018).

Ikeda, Daisaku. 2009. *Embracing the Future*. Hong Kong: Bauhinia Publication.

Jin, Yong, and Daisaku Ikeda. 1998. *Looking for a Bright Century*. Hong Kong: Ming Ho Publications Corporation Limited. (In Chinese)

Kirimura, Yasuji. 1980. *The Life of Nichiren Daishonin*. Tokyo: Nichiren Shoshu International Center.

Knowles, Caroline, and Douglas Harper. 2009. *Hong Kong: Migrant Lives, Landscapes, and Journeys*. Chicago: University of Chicago Press.

Law, Kam-Yee, and Kim-Ming Lee. 2006. Citizenship, Economy and Social Exclusion of Mainland Chinese Immigrants in Hong Kong. *Journal of Contemporary Asia* 36: 217–42. [CrossRef]

Lee, Kon Sau. 2009. A Blue Fly, If It Clings to the Tail of a Thoroughbred Horse, Can Travel Ten Thousand Miles. In *Cherry Blossom Memories: CUHK Alumni in Japan*. Edited by CUHK Alumni Association in Japan. Hong Kong: Comos Books, pp. 182–92.

Lung, W. Y. 2011. Defeat the 311 Disaster with the Strategy of the *Lotus Sutra*. *New Century Monthly* 215: 22–23.

Machacek, David, and Bryan Wilson. 2000. *Global Citizens: the Soka Gakkai Buddhist Movement in the World*. New York: Oxford University Press.

Metraux, Daniel Alfred. 1988. *The History and Theology of Soka Gakkai: A Japanese New Religion*. Lewiston: Edwin Mellen Press.

Metraux, Daniel Alfred. 1994. *The Soka Gakkai Revolution*. Lanham: University Press of America.

Metraux, Daniel Alfred. 1996. *The Lotus and the Maple Leaf: The Soka Gakkai Buddhist Movement in Canada*. New York: University Press of America.

Metraux, Daniel Alfred. 1997. *The Soka Gakkai Buddhist Movement in Quebec: The Lotus and the Fleur De Lys (Canadian Studies)*. Lewiston: Edwin Mellen Press.

Metraux, Daniel Alfred. 2000. The Expansion of Soka Gakkai into Southeast Asia. In *Global Citizens: The Soka Gakkai Buddhist Movement in the World*. Edited by David W. Machacek and Bryan R. Wilson. New York: Oxford University Press, pp. 402–29.

Metraux, Daniel Alfred. 2001. *The International Expansion of a Modern Buddhist Movement: The Soka Gakkai in Southeast Asia and Australia*. Lanham: University Press of America.

Metraux, Daniel Alfred. 2010. *How Soka Gakkai Became a Global Buddhist Movement: The Internationalization of a Japanese Religion*. Lewiston: Edwin Mellen Press.

Ministry of Foreign Affairs Japan. 2018. Annual Report of Statistics on Japanese Nationals Overseas 2017. Available online: https://www.mofa.go.jp/mofaj/files/000368754.pdf (accessed on 11 September 2018).

Ng, Ka Shing. 2012. The Development of Soka Gakkai in Hong Kong. *Journal of the Graduate School of Letters* 7: 77–85.

Nichiren. 2003. *The Writings of Nichiren Daishonin*. Edited and translated by The Gosho Translation Committee. Tokyo: Soka Gakkai.

Nishihara, Kentaro. 2008. *Soka kyoiku no genryu: makiguchi tsunesaburo* (The Origin of Soka Education: Makiguchi Tsunesaburo). Tokyo: Ushio Suppansha.

Piore, Michael. 1979. *Birds of Passage: Migrant Labor in Industrial Societies*. Cambridge: Cambridge University Press.

Ravenstein, Ernst Georg. 1885. The Laws of Migration. *Journal of the Statistical Society of London* 48: 167–235. [CrossRef]

Research Office of the Legislative Council Secretariat. 2018. Livelihood of New Arrivals from the Mainland. Available online: https://www.legco.gov.hk/research-publications/english/1718issh18-livelihood-of-new-arrivals-from-the-mainland-20180323-e.pdf (accessed on 11 September 2018).

Salaff, Janet, Siu-Lun Wong, and Arent Greve. 2010. *Hong Kong Movers and Stayers: Narratives of Family Migration*. Urbana: University of Illinois Press.

Sassen, Saskia. 1988. *The Mobility of Labor and Capital: A Study in International Investment and Labor Flow*. Cambridge: Cambridge University Press.

Shen, Jianfa, and Erbiao Dai. 2006. *Population Growth, Fertility Decline, and Ageing in Hong Kong: The Perceived and Real Demographic Effects of Migration*. Hong Kong: Hong Kong Institute of Asia-Pacific Studies.

Sjaastad, Larry. 1962. The Costs and Returns of Human Migration. *Journal of Political Economy* 70: 80–93. [CrossRef]

Smith, Timothy. 1978. Religion and Ethnicity in America. *American Historical Review* 83: 1155–85. [CrossRef]

Soka Gakkai International. 2018. Human Revolution. Official Homepage. Available online: https://www.sgi.org/about-us/buddhist-concepts/human-revolution.html (accessed on 12 September 2018).

Sussman, Nan. 2010. *Return Migration and Identity: A Global Phenomenon, A Hong Kong Case*. Hong Kong: Hong Kong University Press.

Todaro, Michael. 1969. A Model of Labor Migration and Urban Unemployment in Less Developing Countries. *American Economic Review* 59: 138–48.

Tweed, Thomas. 2006. *Crossing and Dwelling: A Theory of Religion*. Cambridge and London: Harvard University Press.

Wilson, Bryan, and Karel Dobbelaere. 1994. *A Time to Chant: The Soka Gakkai. Buddhists in Britain*. Oxford: Clarendon Press.

Wuthnow, Robert, and Conrad Hackett. 2003. The Social Integration of Practitioners of Non-Western Religions in the United States. *Journal for the Scientific Study of Religion* 42: 651–67. [CrossRef]

Yang, Fenggang. 1999. *Chinese Christians in America: Conversion, Assimilation, and Adhesive Identities*. University Park: Pennsylvania State University Press.

Yang, Fenggang. 2005. Lost in the Market, Saved at McDonald's: Conversion to Christianity in Urban China. *Journal for the Scientific Study of Religion* 44: 423–41. [CrossRef]

Yano, Jyunya, and Hitomi Shimada. 2010. *Soka Gakkai: mou hitotsu no nihon* (Soka Gakkai: One More Japan). Tokyo: Koudansha. (In Japanese)

religions

Article

Expansion of Religious Pluralism in Korean Civil Society: A Case Study of Conscientious Objection in South Korea

Kwang Suk Yoo

Sociology, Kyung Hee University, Seoul 02447, Korea; ksyooii@khu.ac.kr

Received: 15 September 2018; Accepted: 22 October 2018; Published: 24 October 2018

Abstract: This paper analyzes a socio-cultural adaptation of the concept of religious pluralism, focusing on the matter of conscientious objection in Korean pluralistic situation. The issue of conscientious objection in Korea has extended from a religious and philosophical field to a political, diplomatic, and international problem, being influenced heavily by IRFR and UNHRC. Regardless of their numerical marginality, its social implication is revealed more clearly in recent decisions of local or higher courts and triggers another significant public discourse on how Korean civil society should expand a concept of pluralism to integrate them. The paper concludes that the concept of pluralism advances into an operational principle to prop up the civil society of Korea beyond the narrow concept of religious pluralism.

Keywords: Korean conscientious objection; pluralism in Korea; Korean religious market; sectarian pacifism; Korean civil society

1. Introduction

Conscientious objection based on religious belief makes the most significant discourse of how religious pluralism has been evolved in Korean public sphere. Especially the International Religious Freedom Reports (IRFR) issued by the U.S. government since 1999 has touched the imprisonment of conscientious objectors in Korea (IRFR 1998–2017), which caused both religious majority and minority to be engaged in the public discourse. The U.N. Human Rights Commission (UNHRC) has recommended the Korean government introduce an alternative service for conscientious objectors many times since 1984. Although the IRFR and U.N. recommendations have no legal binding in Korea, their impact on Korea is never slight, socially and politically, because the Korean government greatly depends on moral as well as political or diplomatic support of the U.S. and U.N. in a global society. In this context, Korean society is now under pressure to find a new way of relieving about 600 conscientious objectors who are imprisoned every year.

This paper analyzes a socio-cultural adaptation of the concept of religious pluralism, focusing on the matter of conscientious objection in Korea's pluralistic situation, even if it is a universal principle of law binding global as well as Korean society. While such international norms as U.N. recommendations and the IRFR invokes religious freedom as a necessary condition of religious pluralism in a Christian or American way (Smith 2001, p. 153), both religious freedom and pluralism are new concepts that could not be made in Korean culture before the era of colonialism and modernization. From the first Korean constitution of 1948 on, the Korean legal system has obviously codified the separation of state and religion and guaranteed religious freedom as one of the basic human rights, but those fundamental principles have not strictly been kept in real religious market. Similar to the monopolistic Confucianism of the *Chosun* dynasty, which served as a political ideology to justify an absolute authority of the King, religious majorities such as Korean Protestantism and Buddhism have made a strong alliance with an absolute sovereign of national state during the period of modernization.

This unequal structure of the Korean religious market controlled by the existing religious and state powers in Korea encouraged the issue of conscientious objection, mostly Jehovah's Witnesses, to be closed within the conceptual framework of religious pluralism. In fact, Korean religious majorities focused mainly on attacking conscientious objectors' morality in the field of public discourse, not on the concept of conscientious objection itself, criticizing them for conspiring to avoid a compulsory military service in Korea. The national demographic census of Statistics Korea shows clearly that religious minorities occupy no more than 5% of the whole Korean population (K. Yoo 2015). An extreme imbalance of religious majority and minority has remained rarely unchanged since 1985 when religious affiliation was initially asked (Statistics Korea 2017).

Under this socio-religious structure, it is reported that 92.5% of conscientious objectors worldwide are South Korean nationals (IRFR 1998–2017)[1] and that 17,000 Jehovah's Witnesses have been imprisoned due to conscientious objection since 1950 in Korea (WOL 1930–2018)[2]. American Jehovah's Witnesses press the U.S. government to intervene in the issue of Korean conscientious objectors in terms of universal human rights. As a result, the issue of conscientious objection in Korea has extended from a religious and philosophical field to a political, diplomatic, and international problem, being influenced heavily by IRFR and UNHRC. Now the issue of conscientious objectors, regardless of their numerical marginality, triggers another significant public discourse on how Korean civil society should expand the concept of pluralism to integrate them.

In short, this paper focuses on a semantic expansion of pluralism from religious to secular fields through tracking down the following questions: how religious majorities have comprehended religious minorities with conscientious objectors; how the latter have adapted to the established order supporting religious majorities; and how pluralism has changed into a functional principle inherent in Korean civil society. For a theoretical analysis, this article compares Jehovah's Witnesses with Seventh-Day Adventists in terms of religious market strategy in Korea, because the two minority groups have in common a tradition of conscientious objection based on Christian pacifism.

2. Previous Studies

A substantial amount of literature and empirical research exists on the issue of conscientious objection in Europe and America. Among them, the legal approach to religious minorities has become a dominant research trend, enough to overwhelm all other studies on historical, sociological, psychological, political, and economic relationship (Kaplan 1989; Richardson 1995; Peters 2000; Richardson and Introvigne 2001). Analysis and interpretation of changing court judgments, laws, acts, and constitutions are very useful for understanding various legal aspects concerning conscientious objection based on religious belief (Todd 1969; Barker 1982; Flowers 2002; Wah 2002; Richardson 2006). Another research paradigm of conscientious objection comes from a socio-historical approach in that religious pacifism is a historically important tradition to understand its various successors in Catholicism and Protestantism (Stevenson 1934; Sibley 1943; Brock 1968; Walters 1973; Moskos and Chambers 1993). These historical studies greatly contribute to a better understanding of conscientious objection based on religious belief. Robert C. Stevenson's article, "The Evolution of Pacifism," explains very well how Western society evolved from individualistic pacifism to collective or social pacifism in Christian tradition, ranging from early Christians such as Augustine or Ambrose to the present Quakers known as unique pacifists (Stevenson 1934, pp. 439–40). Likewise, Korean research on conscientious objection is mostly biased on the aspects of religious freedom, human rights, sociological theory of law, comparative study of law, and social ethics (S. Kim 2002; S.-S. Kang 2005; K.-D. Yoo 2005; Chin 2006), and there are only a few studies of Jehovah's Witnesses dealing limitedly with the issue

---

[1] See 2013.
[2] See yb14, p. 40.

of conscientious objection (D. Kang 2006; Yoon 2007) unless many Christian theological articles are considered (D. Kim 2002; Shin 2004; K.-D. Yoo 2005).

This article pays more attention to a socio-cultural aspect of pluralistic religious market which has rarely been handled by previous studies. As Korean conscientious objectors belong to Jehovah's Witnesses without great exception, a multi-dimensional approach on them is necessarily required for a better understanding of their behavior as a religious minority. The unique pacifism of Jehovah's Witnesses cannot be understood without considering a historical, social, and cultural expansion of Christian pacifism. For example, while conscientious objectors belonging to Jehovah's Witnesses can be considered as a relatively radical wing of the American Christian tradition, they are apt to be regarded simply as a deviant cult which deny both legal justification of social order and historical tradition in Korean culture. While they can be good citizens that the legal system of society should protect in American civil society, in Korea they have been only criminals who cannot be tolerated socially, culturally, and legally. This multi-dimensional difference is not only a matter of the legal system, but also a matter of socio-cultural tradition to justify such a legal system. In short, a new religiosity adhering to conscientious objection makes both religious and secular citizens internalize a pluralistic nature of civil society in a different way that imported religions such as Buddhism, Confucianism and Christianity grew into a religiously monopolistic majority throughout all Korean history. Given that there are no sociological studies on the social impact of Korean conscientious objectors (I. Kang 2003, 2005), it is meaningful to analyze drastic changes of recent judicial judgments surrounding conscientious objection in Korea rather than an unchanging principle of law or human rights. After all, the paper examines not only the actual impact on Korean religious policy and pluralistic features of the Korean religious market, but also how such international norms as the International Covenant on Civil and Political Rights (ICCPR) and international recommendations issued by IRFR and U.N. Human Rights Commission (UNHRC) has influenced the qualitative progress of Korean civil society.

3. A Historical Review of Korean Religious Regulation

Korea has a long history of religious regulation since the era of the *Chosŏn* Dynasty in the 14th century. From its beginning, the Dynasty officially announced and enforced its policy to promote Confucianism and oppress Buddhism, because it had been founded on the Confucian political philosophy and bureaucratic system. In addition to Buddhism, it expelled almost all traditional religions out of the capital of Seoul and prohibited Buddhists and shamans from entering the capital of the Dynasty. Historically, this represented the start of religious regulations based on the national legal system in Korea, although it was only partially valid and very limited in the scope and extent of its regulations. As soon as the Japanese colonialists occupied Korea in 1910, religious regulation became more systematic and oppressive to make Korean religious organizations accommodating to Japanese colonialism. Various religious restrictions during the period of Japanese rule mainly focused on institutional religions that had organizational networks across the country. From the start of Japanese rule, Korean Buddhism and Catholicism were cooperative with the colonialist government, while Korean Protestantism and nationalistic new religious movements protested against it. Non-institutional and non-organizational religions such as shamanism or folk religions were regarded as superstition or pseudo-religion, and frequently punished as frauds. When shamans wanted to perform rituals, called *kut*, they had to show a registration card issued by the Japanese government (Cho 1988, p. 324). Despite this Japanese restriction, fortune-telling practices were generally found across the nation. Murayama's 1933 survey sponsored by the *Chosŏn* Governor-General of Japan shows the widespread popularity of fortune-telling at that time (Murayama [1993] 2005). However, things changed after the 1945 Liberation. The legal structure of the religious market turned out to be even more favorable for major official religions such as Buddhism, Catholicism, and Protestantism. In 1948, the first constitution of the Republic of Korea announced in *Article 12: (1) All people have the freedom of faith and conscience. (2) An establishment of religion is denied, and religion is separate from state.*

Article 12 remains even through the ninth amendment since 1948 without any serious revisions, but the idea of equality between religions is controlled by a legal system of hierarchy that consists of the constitution, laws, regulations, judicial decisions, customs, and so on. As the Korean government had the independent right to enact laws and regulations under the centralized presidential system, it was and is still the most influential actor of religious enactments except for the National Assembly in Korea. With regard to religious policy, it is noteworthy to recognize two Korean Presidents who had a remarkable impacts on both the pattern of religious enactment and eventually the structure of the Korean religious market. *Syng-man Rhee*, who took power from 1948 to 1961, established very clearly a religious policy based on Christian political ideals. He, as an elder of a Korean Protestant church, pursued a relationship between religion and state to serve his Christian ideals. After the Korean War, his regime was heavily dependent on Protestantism because many American assistance groups such as Team Mission, World Vision, and Compassion International, actively engaged in various activities for reconstructing post-war Korean society, as well as supporting Korean Protestant churches (I. Kim 2003, p. 338). In 1952, President *Rhee* allowed Protestant chaplains to be assigned to all military bases, which was stipulated in 1961. This contributed to the basis of an evangelical movement to convert all military men into Protestants in the 1970s (I. Kim 2003, p. 379). Given that all male citizens have an obligatory military duty in Korea, such stipulations on the level of law or regulations caused to empty the ideal of religious freedom on the level of the constitution.

Chung-hee Park, who ruled from 1962 to 1979, was known to be a Buddhist, but he separated his religious conviction from the political reality because he especially considered major institutional religions as political resources. Similar to *Rhee*'s administration, *Park* still pushed an evolutionary concept of religion under which world religions such as Buddhism and Christianity would be "developed religions," while Confucianism and folk religions were remains of pre-modern and anachronistic traditions. Religion had to become a cultural resource of economic development to be modernized as soon as possible. In this point of view, the state intervened actively in the religious as well as economic market. *The Law of Hyangkyo* (Confucian shrine) *Properties* and *the Law of Management of Buddhist Properties* in 1962 legalized the direct control of Confucian and Buddhist properties by the military regime (K. Yoo 2012, p. 73; Kamibeppu 2011, pp. 325–39). *Hyangkyos* and Buddhist temples were restricted severely in terms of the management and possession of their properties because the laws imposed complex administrative procedures and requirements on their economic activities. Protestantism and Catholicism faced no limitations in terms of taking advantage of their own economic resources, whereas the special laws seriously limited Buddhism and Confucianism in accessing various economic resources. The special laws remain even today.

4. Conscientious Objectors in the Korea Religious Market

This brief review of the historical changes in the religious regulations of Korea suggests that the Korean religious market remains structurally unequal, depending on the religious preferences of political regimes. However, as the imprisonment of conscientious objectors belonging to Jehovah's Witnesses in Korea was declared by UHHRC in 1987 in violation of Article 18 of ICCPR, the Korean religious market began to be under serious pressure from various international norms and organizations, including the U.N. Human Rights Council, U.N. Human Rights Commission, European Court of Human Rights, IRFR of U.S., and so on. Given that the ruling institutions of administration, National Assembly, and judicial courts regarded conscientious objection as a purely domestic issue, they could not recognize a pluralistic nature of the Korean religious market concerned with the issue of conscientious objection. Historically, both the rapid growth of Christianity and the decline of Confucianism in modern Korea resulted in a socio-cultural internalization of the Christian dualistic worldview: the only god vs. idolatry, religion vs. superstition, good vs. evil, rationality vs. irrationality, modernity vs. feudality, etc. In this context, the governmental attitude toward conscientious objectors was compatible with the oligopolistic structure of the Korean religious market controlled explicitly by Christianity and implicitly by Buddhism. The extreme pacifism as a religious doctrine, especially for Korean regimes and religious majorities, was stigmatized simply as a reflection of "irrational and fanatic" religiosity that could never be matched up with the post-war Korean political situation. In fact, the Ministry of Defense of Korea claimed continuously that conscientious objection eventually denies a nation-state ideology in which national security comes prior to religious faith. As the police physically oppressed shamanistic rituals (G. Kim 2007, p. 289), the ruling system of administration, National Assembly, and judicial courts did not hesitate to put conscientious objectors in jail because it could not integrate such practices into the ready-made category of "religion." They were even treated as "para-religions" or "pseudo-religions" in actual execution of religious laws, even though it is never possible to find a definition of religion in any Korean laws.

R.R. Holister and W.J. Holister brought some literature of Jehovah's Witnesses to Korea from Japan and also got the first Korean convert in 1914 (WOL 1930–2018).[3] During the period of the Japanese imperialist wars in the 1930s in East Asia, similar to Jehovah's Witnesses in Japan and Taiwan, 38 conscientious objectors in Korea were first imprisoned as traitors in 1939 because they refused to take up arms for Japanese imperialist wars. Ironically, some documents issued by Korean government describe the *deungdaesa* (燈臺社) incident as part of Independence movement (Han 2004). After the Liberation from the Japanese in 1945, 12 believers composed the first Korean congregation of Jehovah's Witnesses in 1949 and became organizationally independent of their Japanese center. Don and Earlene Steele sent by the IBSA (International Bible Students Association) had 417 publishers in seven congregations in 1953 (WOL 1930–2018)[4]. As fundamentalist Protestants come to occupy a religious hegemony in Korea since the Liberation, the legal, social and political persecution of conscientious objectors has strengthened to justify morally the anti-communist ideology of military regimes and dictatorship. Since the Korean War, the Witnesses' uncompromising pacifism, refusal of blood transfusion, and door-to-door visits made them more isolated and sectarian from the established order of the post-war society. Both religious majorities and social elites did not hesitate to regard them as a dangerous and anti-social fanatic community. It seems that this social circumstance had a negative influence on the increase of their religious membership, even though they have about 99,000 members and 1300 congregations in 2011 (MCST 2011, p. 43). It was until the 1990s that international political organizations such as the UN recognized Korean conscientious objectors' reality because both North and South Korea were allowed to join the UN in 1991. Since then, the Korean government had to report its situation of human rights regularly and simultaneously many international norms such as ICCPR came into effect equal to domestic laws. Based on the reports of the Korean government, UNHRC continue to recommend to make conscientious objectors free and enact an alternative service for them in 1987, 1989, 1993, 1995, 1998 and 2004.

Meanwhile, the IRFR first included a brief description of conscientious objection in its 2004 issue. This impact of IRFR was very different from that of UNHRC recommendations because any decisions of the U.S. government based on the IRFR could determine the political, economic, and socio-cultural future of Korea, and in reality the U.S. embassy's deputy chief of mission discussed the problem of conscientious objectors with representatives of Jehovah's Witnesses and then asked Korean government to introduce an alternative service as soon as possible (IRFR 1998–2017).[5] In response to this international pressure, the Ministry of National Defense of Korea "established a seventeen-member committee, made up of scholars, lawyers, journalists, religious leaders, civic activists, and military officials, to study ways to introduce and to establish the standards for such alternative service" (IRFR 1998–2017).[6] Despite a negative conclusion of the committee against the introduction of alternative service, the administration announced the introduction of an alternative service for conscientious

---

3 https://wol.jw.org/en/wol/d/r1/lp-e/301988011?q=Hollister&p=par (accessed on 20 October 2018). See yb88, p. 155.
4 See yb88, p. 187.
5 See 2007.
6 See 2007.

objectors on 18 September 2007, but cancelled its plan on 24 December 2008 after the launch of *Myung Bak Lee's* conservative regime.

About 1000 conscientious objectors, as Figure 1 shows, have been put in jail or on judicial trial every year for the last ten years. It is reported that 20,000 young people were imprisoned due to conscientious objection so far, even if there is no official statistics issued by the government.

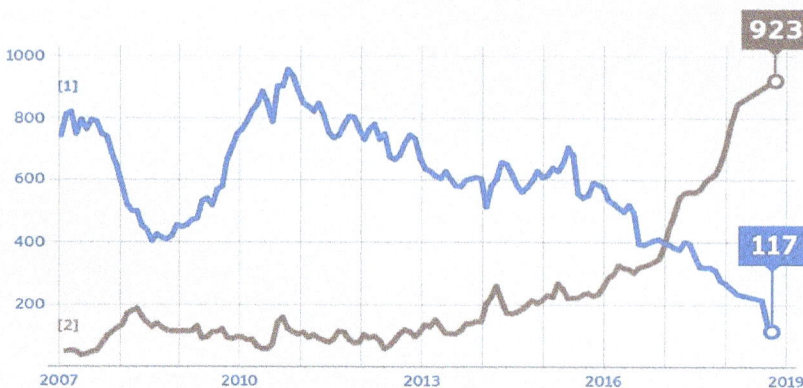

Figure 1. (1) Conscientious objectors imprisoned; and (2) pending cases of conscientious objectors.[7]

A groundbreaking change was made in 2004 by a local court of Seoul district (2002kodan3941), which declared conscientious objectors from Jehovah's Witnesses not guilty of violating military law. For the first time, the local court as a government institution regarded conscientious objection as a just reason to avoid the compulsory conscription. Since then, many local or high courts found religious conscientious objectors innocent of violating military law in totally 104 cases (Hankyoreh 23 August 2018).[8] Nonetheless, both the Supreme Court and the Constitutional Court would not change their previous decisions and judgments which conscientious objectors are still violating the current positive law of Korea, while asking the National Assembly to revise the military law for introducing an alternative service (2004do2965; 2007do7941; 2002hunga1; 2008hunga22). Finally, the Constitutional Court of Korea declared on 28 June 2018 that the current military law should be revised to introduce an alternative service by 31 December 2019 because it excessively violates conscientious objectors' human rights (2011hunba379).

5. From Sectarian Pacifism to Democratic Pluralism

Although 92.5% of conscientious objectors worldwide are imprisoned in Korea (IRFR 1998–2017),[9] almost all of them stick to a unique pacifism of Jehovah's Witnesses (JW) which can be interpreted as a sectarian choice made in a competitive religious market. From its beginning, Jehovah's Witnesses shared common roots with Seventh-Day Adventists (SDA) who believed in imminent eschatology derived from the Millerite movement in the 1840s. The two groups were not only initially very similar, but on other measures, such as international spread, growth rates, and total membership, have also remained remarkably alike (Lawson 1995, p. 353). Especially during World Wars I and II, sectarian conscientious objectors became well known for their rigid attitude toward conscription and military

---

[7] https://www.jw.org/en/news/legal/by-region/south-korea/jehovahs-witnesses-in-prison (accessed on 10 September 2018).
[8] http://www.hani.co.kr/arti/society/society_general/858916.html (accessed on 12 September 2018).
[9] See 2013.

service, which caused a very serious persecution of them across the world (Penton 1985; Wah 2002; Brock 2004; Stoltzfus 2013).

JW and SDA started to dispatch their missionaries into Korea in 1914 and 1904, respectively, and, during the period of Japanese rule, they were seriously persecuted by the Japanese colonialist government. It was not until the end of the Korean War that Jehovah's Witnesses and Seventh-Day Adventists did their missionary work intensively in Korea. In the 1960s, however, the Seven-Day Adventists allowed their members to decide freely on the issue of completing Korean military service in various ways, whereas Jehovah's Witnesses adhered to their unique pacifism and hence refused to compromise with secular authorities. Following the sectarian pacifism of the Mennonites, Brethren, and Quakers, who do not adopt the theory of just war as a traditional doctrine of Christianity, JW never gave up their resistance against the Korean conscription system, leading to about 20,000 conscientious objectors being put in jail thus far. The first federal conscription law of America allowed draft substitution upon payment of $300 as early as 1863 and further Congress enacted the Selective Service Act in 1940 (Todd 1969, p. 1734), whereas Korean politicians and bureaucrats have been unwilling to introduce an alternative service.

Especially there is no cultural tradition of such sectarian pacifism in Korean history, even if a historical origin of conscientious objection can be traced back to Chinese Taoism, Buddhism, and Christian Reformation groups such as the Waldensians and Anabaptists (Kauffman 1989, p. 368). Rather, Korean Buddhism is well known for "*Hokuk Bulkyo* (Patriotic Buddhism)" because Korean Buddhists have never hesitated to participate in various wars and power struggles throughout all Korean history. Korean Protestantism has also played an important role in supporting or justifying Korean political regimes since its introduction in the 19th century. Korean people have never had a cultural experience to imagine the unique pacifism which transcends both national interest and security. After all, conscientious objectors of JW have failed to draw any political or emotional support even from mainstream Protestants as well as other religious majorities, because they would not consider any cultural adaptation or compromise in contrast with the flexible strategy of SDA.

Obviously, conscientious objection is only one sectarian market strategy in terms of religious market theory (K. Yoo 2014, pp. 114–32). Especially, religious market theorists such as Rodney Stark, Roger Finke, and L. R. Iannaccone regard it as a rational strategy to exclude free riders out the sectarian organization (Iannaccone 1992; Stark and Iannaccone 1997; Stark and Finke 2002, p. 149). This strategy proved very effective for the growth of religious membership in the American cultural context, whether belonging to sectarian or church-like organizations (Finke and Iannaccone 1993; Iannaccone 1994; Finke 1997). According to Grim and Finke's research to verify the pluralism thesis of religious market theory, the increase of religious freedom tends to promote social peace, while the price of religious freedom being denied is social conflict (Grim and Finke 2011). In short, to legally protect a free and fair competition system between religious majorities and minorities now becomes one of the most important duties of democratic civil society in realizing religious freedom as human rights. Nonetheless, as the concept of conscientious objection based on a sectarian pacifism itself is still very foreign in the Korean civil society, the Supreme Court of Korea (SCK) has consistently confirmed the legitimacy of the current military service law which punishes conscientious objectors based on the sectarian pacifism of JW. A public poll conducted by the government in 2008 also showed that 68.1% of respondents objected to the introduction of an alternative service (*Hankyoreh 21*, 29 December 2008).[10]

It was the local courts across the country that began to protect the sectarian pacifism under the principle of pluralism, interpreting it as a basic operational rule of every democratic civil society. Since the 2004 decision of "not guilty", many local courts followed the judgment of acquittal, criticizing both legal interpretations and logical impropriety inherent in the previous SCK judgments. A local court in

---

[10] http://h21.hani.co.kr/arti/COLUMN/32/24057.html (accessed on 11 September 2018).

the city of Gwangju justified its decision of "not guilty", citing a judgment of the European Court of Human Right (Bayatyan vs. Armenia):

> As democracy should guarantee a fair and reasonable treatment to the minorities instead of the abuse of the ruling power by the majorities, giving religious minorities the chance to serve the entire society implies not that it, as the government claims, causes an inequality and a unfair discrimination, but that it promotes the tolerance and harmony among religions and brings a stable pluralism. The European Court of Human Rights explained the features of democracy as pluralism, tolerance, and broadmindedness.... The democratic majorities of a society should be responsible for realizing such democracy and social integration through protecting human rights of the minorities and making the protection of the socially weak institutionalized. If there are the majorities who neglect this duty in a society, the political system run by them is nothing but a nominal democracy because they are just the oppressive and numerical majorities. (2015no1181)

Given that mainstream Korean Protestants have shown a strong hatred against the word "pluralism" itself and both Korean politicians and scholars of religion have been unwilling to use it in a field of public discourse, this judicial interpretation of pluralism by the local courts was a significant and historical turning point on which one should acknowledge that pluralism is bound to function as an essential principle of the Korean civil society. Besides, a few social polls in 2016 showed an important change in the necessity of introducing an alternative service as soon as possible. A relative majority of respondents examined by Amnesty International and by the Bar Association in Seoul began to support the introduction of an alternative service by 70% and by 80.5%, respectively, even if most of them answered that they cannot entirely accept a logical ground of conscientious objection. Thanks to these changes in public polls and many challenging decisions of local courts, the Constitutional Court of Korea (CCK) finally ordered on 28 June 2018 that the government and National Assembly introduce an alternative service in accordance with the higher idea of the Korean Constitution to protect conscientious freedom (2011hunba379).

The issue of conscientious objection in recent Korea concerns not only the socio-religious dimension, but also the construction of collective identity of a nation state (Pace 2011, p. 445). That makes Korean civil society rethink what pluralism is and how it works in the Korean context. The drastic decision of CCK is not a final solution, but only a new starting point for answering the self-reflective questions of Korean civil society. The integration of sectarian pacifism into a macro-level principle of pluralism was never touched in the 2018 CCK decision in contrast with many decisions of the local courts concerned with conscientious objectors. In addition to domestic conditions, the above-mentioned international factors such as IRFR and UNHRC make it much more complicated to understand the meaning of pluralism in a process of globalization, because it is invoked in different ways such as a political ideology, a religious creed, and a basic principle of society, as the issue of conscientious objection in Korea shows clearly.

6. Conclusions

This paper focuses on the case of conscientious objection in the Korean socio-cultural context, which cannot be entirely comprehended by a religious concept of pluralism, particularly explaining how the concept of pluralism could be expanded through integrating a sectarian pacifism of JW into the entire civil society of Korea. Since Korea joined the U.N. in 1991, the criminal punishment and imprisonment of conscientious objectors in Korea has become a more complicated international issue because both the U.S. and U.N. have intervened in this issue in the diplomatic, legal, or moral dimension. Although there was no sectarian and unique pacifism in the Korean cultural tradition, international powers forced Korean society to comprehend the non-Korean worldview in the name of human rights and pluralism.

Except for conscientious objectors, Jehovah's Witnesses in Korea have enjoyed a high level of religious freedom for their missionary activities, including door-to-door visits, whereas their colleagues in European countries are in trouble legally or socially (Stark and Finke 2002, pp. 233–35; Richardson and Introvigne 2001). Unlike SDA, it is noteworthy that they chose conscientious objection as a market strategy in the Korean religious market. Indeed, religious market theorists tend to attribute their growth in American membership to this kind of religious strictness and conservativeness. However, they remain a sectarian minority isolated from the Korean civil society. The absolute majority of Korean people, including politicians and bureaucrats, do not agree with conscientious objectors in a moral, religious, or logical dimension.

The first judgment of acquittal by a local court in Seoul in 2004 has been followed by many decisions of the local or higher courts across the country. In parallel with the increasing religious diversity in contemporary Korea, the local courts tried to interpret the concept of pluralism in a much broader context of meaning than dealing with the matter of conscientious objection as a by-product of sectarian pacifism. That changed the matter of how Korean civil society should protect pluralism as a necessary element of democracy, and hence how pluralism in the Korean context can work in harmony with a global expansion of pluralism motivated by international powers.

Funding: This research was funded by the National Research Foundation of Korea funded by the Ministry of Education of the Republic of Korea (NRF-2016S1A2A2915833).

Conflicts of Interest: The author declares no conflict of interest.

References

Barker, Rachel. 1982. *Conscientious, Government and War: Conscientious Objection in Great Britain 1939–1945*. London and Boston: Routledge & Kegan Paul.

Brock, Peter. 1968. *Radical Pacifists in Antebellum America*. Princeton: Princeton University Press.

Brock, Peter. 2004. *These Strange Criminals: An Anthology of Prison Memoirs by Conscientious Objectors from the Great War to the Cold War*. Toronto: University of Toronto Press.

Chin, Sang-Beom. 2006. Hankuksahoi Yangshimjuk Byungyeok Kuboo ei daehan Kukga wa Jongkyo ui Daeung (Confrontation of State and Religions against Conscientious Objectors in Contemporary Korean Society). *Religion and Culture Studies* 8: 191–217.

Cho, Hung-youn. 1988. Mukyo Sasangsa (History of Korean Shamanism). In *Hankuk Jongkyo Sasangsa IV*. Seoul: Yonsei University Press, pp. 221–333.

Finke, Roger. 1997. The Illusion of Shifting Demand: Supply-Side Interpretations of American Religious History. In *Retelling U.S. Religious History*. Edited by Thomas Tweed. Berkeley and London: University of California Press, pp. 108–24.

Finke, Roger, and Laurence R. Iannaccone. 1993. Supply-Side Explanation for Religious Change in America. *The Annals* 527: 27–39.

Flowers, Ronald B. 2002. *To Defend the Constitution: Religion, Conscientious Objection, Naturalization, and the Supreme Court*. Lanham: Scarecrow Press.

Grim, Brian J., and Roger Finke. 2011. *The Price of Freedom Denied: Religious Persecution and Conflict in the Twentieth Century*. New York: Cambridge University Press.

Han, Hong-Gu. 2004. 'yeohowa ui jeungin' apeseo pookeulupda (Shameful in Front of Jehovah's Witnesses). *Hankyoreh 21*, May 27. Available online: http://legacy.h21.hani.co.kr/section-021075000/2004/05/021075000200405270511062.html (accessed on 31 August 2018).

Iannaccone, Laurence R. 1992. Sacrifice and Stigma: Reducing Free-Riding in Cults, Communes, and Other Collectives. *Journal of Political Economy* 100: 271–92. [CrossRef]

Iannaccone, Laurence R. 1994. Why Strict Churches Are Strong. *American Journal of Sociology* 99: 1180–211. [CrossRef]

International Religious Freedom Report (IRFR). 1998–2017. Issued by U.S. Department of State. Available online: http://www.state.gov/j/drl/irf/rpt/index.htm (accessed on 10 September 2018).

Kamibeppu, Masanobu. 2011. *Keunhyundai Hanil Jongkyojungchaek Bikyoyeonku (A Comparative Study of Korean and Japanese Religious Policy in Pre-Modern and Modern Ear)*. Seoul: Jishik kwa Kyoyang.

Kang, Incheol. 2003. *Cheonjaing kwa Jongkyo (War and Religion)*. Osan: Hanshin University Press.

Kang, Incheol. 2005. Hankuksahoi wa Yangshimjuk Byungyeok Kuboo: Yeoksa wa TeuksungHistory (Korean Society and Conscientious Objection: History and Features). *Religious and Cultural Studies* 7: 103–41.

Kang, Seung-Sik. 2005. Mikuk Hunbupsang Jongkyo ui Jayoo (Freedom of Religion in the United States Constitution). *The Korean Journal of American History* 22: 223–57.

Kang, Dongu. 2006. Yeohowa ui Joungin ui Teukjing kwa Jeongae (The Characteristics and Development of 'Jehovah's Witness'). *Korean Journal of Religious Studies* 43: 45–69.

Kaplan, William. 1989. *State and Salvation: The Jehovah's Witnesses and Their Fight for Civil Rights*. Toronto: University of Toronto Press.

Kauffman, J. Howard. 1989. Dilemmas of Christian Pacifism within a Historic Peace Church. *Sociological Analysis* 49: 368–85. [CrossRef]

Kim, Dushik. 2002. Yangshimjuk Byungyeok Kubooj wa Kidokkyo (Conscientious Objection and Christianity). *Human Rights and Justice* 309: 140–53.

Kim, Suntaek. 2002. *Hankunae Yangshimjuk Byungyeok Kubooja ei daehan Daechebokmoo Injungyeoboo ei kwanhan Ironjuk Shiljoungjuk Yeonku (A Theoretical and Empirical Research on Alternative Service of Conscientious Objector in Korea)*. Seoul: National Human Rights Commission of Korea.

Kim, Insoo. 2003. *Hankukkidokyo Kyohoisa (History of Korean Christianity)*. Seoul: Korean Presbyterian Publishing Company.

Kim, Geumhwa. 2007. *Bidankot Neomsae (Silk Flower called as Neomsae)*. Seoul: Sangkak ui Namu.

Lawson, Ronald. 1995. Sect-State Relations: Accounting for the Differing Trajectories of Seventh-Day Adventists and Jehovah's Witnesses. *Sociology of Religion* 56: 351–77. [CrossRef]

Ministry of Culture, Sports and Tourism of Korea (MCST). 2011. *Hankukui Jongkyohyunwhang (The Index of Korean Reliigons)*; Seoul: Religious Affairs Office.

Moskos, Charles C., and John Whiteclay Chambers, II, eds. 1993. *The New Conscientious Objection: From Sacred to Secular Resistance*. New York: Oxford University Press.

Murayama, Jijun. 2005. *Chosun ui Jeombok kua Yeiun (Divination and Prophecy in Chosun)*. Translated by Heekyung Kim. Seoul: Dongmunsun. First published 1993.

Pace, Enzo. 2011. The Socio-Cultural and Socio-Religious Origins of Human Rights. In *The Oxford Handbook of the Sociology of Religion*. Edited by Peter Clarke. New York: Oxford University Press, pp. 432–48.

Penton, M. James. 1985. *Apocalypse Delayed: The Story of Jehovah's Witnesses*. Toronto, Buffalo and London: University of Toronto Press.

Peters, Shawn F. 2000. *Judging Jehovah's Witnesses—Religious Persecution and the Dawn of the Rights Revolution*. Lawrence: University Press of Kansas.

Richardson, James. T. 1995. Legal Status of Minority Religions in the United States. *Social Compass* 42: 249–64. [CrossRef]

Richardson, James. T. 2006. The Sociology of Religious Freedom: A Structural and Socio-Legal Analysis. *Sociology of Religion* 67: 271–94. [CrossRef]

Richardson, James T., and Massimo Introvigne. 2001. Brainwashing Theories in European Parliamentary and Administrative Reports on Cults and Sects. *Journal for the Scientific Study of Religion* 40: 143–68. [CrossRef]

Shin, Wonha. 2004. Yangshimjuk JipchongKuboo Uthukkae Boaya hana? (How Should We See Conscientious Objection?). *Ministry and Theology* January: 241–45.

Sibley, Mulford Q. 1943. The Political Theories of Modern Religious Pacifism. *The American Political Science Review* 37: 439–54. [CrossRef]

Smith, Thomas W. 2001. Review: Religious Freedom as Foreign Policy Priority. *International Studies Review* 3: 152–56.

Stark, Rodney, and Roger Finke. 2002. *Acts of Faith: Explaining the Human Side of Religion*. Berkeley and London: University of California Press.

Stark, Rodney, and Laurence R. Iannaccone. 1997. Why the Jehovah's Witnesses Grow So Rapidly: A Theoretical Application. *Journal of Contemporary Religion* 12: 133–57. [CrossRef]

Statistics Korea. 2017. Population Census 2015. Available online: http://kosis.kr/eng/statisticsList/statisticsList_01List.jsp?vwcd=MT_ETITLE&parentId=A (accessed on 2 September 2018).

Stevenson, Robert C. 1934. The Evolution of Pacifism. *International Journal of Ethics* 44: 437–51. [CrossRef]

Stoltzfus, Duane C. S. 2013. *Pacifists in Chains: The Persecution of Hutterites during the Great War*. Baltimore: Johns Hopkins University Press.

Todd, Timothy G. 1969. Religious and Conscientious Objection. *Stanford Law Review* 21: 1734–49. [CrossRef]

Wah, Carolyn R. 2002. Jehovah's Witnesses and the Empire of the Sun: A Clash of Faith and Religion during World War II. *Journal of Church and State* 44: 45–72. [CrossRef]

Walters, LeRoy. 1973. A Historical Perspective on Selective Conscientious Objection. *Journal of the American Academy of Religion* 41: 201–11. [CrossRef]

Watchtower Online Library (WOL). 1930–2018. *Yearbook of Jehovah's Witnesses*. New York: Watch Tower Bible and Track Society. Available online: https://wol.jw.org/en/wol/h/r1/lp-e (accessed on 20 October 2018).

Yoo, Kyung-Dong. 2005. Yangshimjuk Byungyeok Juboo wa Kidokkyo Sahoiyoonli (Conscientious Objection and Christian Social Ethics). *Theology and World* 52: 192–220.

Yoo, Kwangsuk. 2012. Applicability of Religious Economy Model (REM) to the Growth of Fortune-telling in Contemporary Korea. Ph.D. dissertation, The University of Ottawa, Ottawa, ON, Canada.

Yoo, Kwangsuk. 2014. *Jongkyo Shichang ui Lihai (Understanding of Religious Market)*. Seoul: Dasan Publication.

Yoo, Kwangsuk. 2015. Numbers and Categorization of Korean Religious Minorities: A Comparison of Demographic Census and International Religious Databases. *Discourse* 201: 43–63.

Yoon, Yong-Bok. 2007. Yeohowa ui Joungin ui Yeoksa wa Teuksung (The History and Characteristic of 'Jehovah's Witnesses'). *Korean Journal of Religious Studies* 47: 289–313.

![religions logo] *religions*

MDPI

Article

Exegetical Resistance: The Bible and Protestant Critical Insiders in South Korea

Seung Min Hong

Independent Scholar, Kwang Ju, Kyong Gi, Korea; seung.min.hong2018@gmail.com

Received: 13 September 2018; Accepted: 3 October 2018; Published: 7 October 2018

Abstract: South Korean Protestantism has attracted scholars for a number of reasons including its almost unrivaled numeric growth and vibrancy in East Asia. Recent observations, however, have also noticed its negative perceptions among the general public in Korea, including those who profess to be Protestants. This study focuses on movements by Protestant "critical insiders," namely, those who are committed to their Protestant faiths yet are highly critical of the ways in which the Protestant religion is taught, believed, and practiced in South Korea. Such emphasis on resistance fits well the scholarly agenda of cultural studies. The subjects of observation in this study, however, can take the cultural studies orthodoxy and flip it on its head. In cultural studies, it has been asserted that unintended-creative readings of cultural—and religious—texts on the part of the readers indicate their resistive agency rather than subjugation. Korean Protestant critical insiders' various activities pertaining to the Bible, however, entail reversing such observations about interpreting cultural texts and empowerment. Instead of turning the signs upside down, as typically celebrated in cultural studies, what they aspire to do is follow more radically the intended meanings/readings of the text. Rescuing the text, so to speak, is paramount for religiously loyal resistance.

Keywords: Korea; Protestantism; cultural studies

1. The Topic: Religious Critical Insiders—A South Korean Protestant Case

Among scholars of religion, Protestant Christianity in South Korea has been a notable case for various reasons, including (a) its rapid and massive growth that is unparalleled compared to most other parts of Asia, (b) its churches, some of which are the world's largest Protestant churches—both in terms of building size and number of congregation—and (c) the fact that South Korea is now the second largest overseas missionary sending country in the world. Such facts have all encouraged scholars of religion to look more deeply into Protestantism in South Korea to gain insight into how major religious traditions travel around the world and interact with various social and cultural settings. Nowadays, scholarly literature on South Korean Protestantism abounds in various disciplines.[1]

Despite its highly visible growth in the numeric sense, or perhaps partly because of it, various statistics show that Protestantism, for many years now, has been rated by the general public as the most despised religious tradition believed and practiced in South Korea.[2] The hostility is specifically toward Protestant Christianity, as opposed to Roman Catholicism,[3] but the object of animosity is not further divided into specific denominations (e.g., Presbyterians, Baptists, Methodists, Anglicans,

---

[1] For a most up-to-date English monograph on Korean Protestantism, see Timothy Lee's *Born Again: Evangelicalism in Korea* (Lee 2010). Also helpful, though less recent, are the various essays found in the edited volume *Christianity in Korea* (Buswell and Lee 2006). There are also other works that focus more on specific issues: for example, Korean Protestant Christianity and gender (Kim 2016; Choi 2009) or North Korean migrants (Jung 2015).

[2] See the various survey results, for example, in Chong 2012; Lee 2010.

[3] The presence of Eastern Orthodoxy and other branches of Christianity is minimal in Korea.

etc.). In other words, when it comes to the general public's negative views against Christianity, they do make the distinction between Protestantism and Catholicism, but generally not between various Protestant groups.[4] Reasons for such negative perceptions are manifold and complicated as is the case with any religion that is the object of animosity and dispute. Some of the major reasons, however, include (a) extreme collusion with the political right (Kim 2016), (b) hostility toward other religions and self-righteous demarcation of the self, which is returned in response from the public by also demarcating Protestant Christianity from all other religions (Park 2005), (c) perceived moral corruption of Protestants, often represented by their religious authorities (Lee 2010, pp. 139–51), and (d) pro-Western attitude of Korean Protestantism often at the risk of alienating Korean traditional customs and culture (Hong 2016b).

While it is in general the non-Protestant population that expresses contempt toward Korean Protestantism most vociferously, there are also those who remain deeply committed to their Protestant faiths yet are highly critical of, and distance themselves from, the dominant and popular ways in which it is institutionalized and followed. I refer to such social actors—who are critical of a particular religion from that very religion's perspective—as religious "critical insiders." This paper's topic of research is critical insiders of Protestant Christianity in South Korea.

To these critical insiders, the fact that Protestant Christianity is so strongly present and supported by so many believers in Korea and yet so highly despised arouses serious questions about how the Protestant tradition is actually being taught and lived out in the Korean society. In addition to the negative perceptions of Protestant Christianity among the general public in Korea, statistics also show that a small yet noticeably growing number of Protestants are leaving the institutionalized church, not because of their loss of faith but because of the inconsistency they perceive between the way Protestant Christianity ought to be taught, believed, and practiced and the ways in which it is actually embodied in Korea (Chong 2015). Such perceived discrepancies between "true Protestant Christianity" and Korean Protestantism include not only moral aspects—such as financial, political, sexual, and other abuses by pastors—but also doctrinal/theological aspects as can be seen in critical insiders' critiques of popular teachings concerning mandatory tithing or the divinely sanctioned authority of the pastorate. These two aspects can also overlap as is often the case (e.g., the correlation of compulsory tithing to pastors' financial abuses).

In such a context, Protestant critical insiders in South Korea can be further defined as those who (a) identify themselves as Protestant Christians and hold accordingly to fundamental Protestant beliefs—such as the tenets of the Trinity, the life, death, and resurrection of Jesus as a historical figure, and the (Protestant) Bible as the divinely inspired word of God—as well as the resulting actions/practices of such beliefs, (b) yet are critical of the actual teachings and beliefs held by, as well as behaviors practiced by, the majority of Protestant institutions (mostly churches) and their adherents in South Korea.

In this paper, I capture a particular aspect of Korean Protestant critical insider resistance to dominant Protestantism in South Korea. The study of resistance in the realm of culture—which certainly includes religion—is most pertinent to the field of cultural studies. Critical insider "resistance," however, is not anti-religious but religiously loyal. They protest the dominant institutions and offer alternative visions not by negating Protestant beliefs but by relying more radically on them. An important ramification of such religiously loyal resistance, the key argument of this paper, is stated below in Section 3. Before that, however, a brief note on the objects of analysis is in order.

2. Objects of Analysis

Some critical insiders of Korean Protestantism go public, and their movements are the bulk of what I analyze in this paper. They include both individual actors as well as organized movements that

---

[4]   In South Korea, the number of Protestant denominations are in hundreds.

publically deliver critiques and alternative views. They are the leading individuals and organizations that are more fully and formally committed to the task of challenging the dominant voices. In addition to facilitating gatherings and activities that require physical presence, many of them have been highly reliant upon new media by creating web/mobile content while not completely ignoring traditional "old media" such as broadcast TV, radio, or print magazines and newspapers. Major examples of such Protestant critical insider institutes in South Korea include educational ones such as Nehemiah Institute for Christian Studies, Holywave Academy, and Chungeoram ARMC, as well as journalistic ones represented by NewsNJoy.

More recently, there were two TV talk shows that were broadcast through CBS (Christian Broadcasting System), a major Protestant TV network, and tried to bring together these critical insiders and collectively disseminate their voices to a wider circle. These two shows are *CBS Christian Now* and *Nancy Lang's Theology Punch*.[5] In addition to analyzing all of these media texts available on the Internet, I also incorporate into my analysis the interviews I conducted with fourteen individuals who are involved in the production of the two TV shows, most of whom are also involved in other critical insider movements. All of the interviews were carried out during the summer of 2015.

3. The Argument: Religion, Cultural Studies, and Exegetical Resistance

As briefly mentioned earlier, critical insider movements in South Korea is a suitable topic for cultural studies—a field that specializes in capturing the struggle between domination and resistance in the realm of culture, which includes religion. Such resistance does not refer to physical violence against the oppressors but mainly revolves around recognizing hegemonic processes in social and cultural discourses and challenging dominant ideologies with alternative voices. Among other contributions, cultural studies has offered an observation that has become an orthodoxy: that unintended-creative readings of cultural texts on the part of the recipients indicate their active agency for resistance. Likewise, the pleasures and practical benefits people get from such readings have also been taken as indications of empowerment rather than subjugation.

As cultural resistors who protest dominant religious institutions and disseminate alternative voices, Protestant critical insiders also have imperatives regarding reading and interpreting a particular cultural text, the central religious text of Protestantism, the Bible. Their view of textual interpretation and resistance, however, flips this cultural studies orthodoxy on its head; resistance to authority here comes not from reading against the grain but from using intended meanings of the text against its abusers. Exegesis, discovering authorial and intended meanings, is not taken as a practice that perpetuates Western Christian imperialism. Instead, it serves as the very foundation for religiously motivated resistance.

4. Literature Review: Reading of Cultural Texts and Resistance in Cultural Studies

Concerning the relationship between resistance and cultural texts, including religious texts, the cultural studies tradition has given us the long cherished observation of how such texts can be read in resistive ways. While a number of founders of cultural studies have provided the theoretical groundwork for such an observation, the foundational articulation of resistive reading on the part of the audience/reader is still that of Hall (1980). As a key figure in cultural studies, Hall showed how cultural texts, delivered through mass media, can be read by the recipients in ways not intended by the producers. Even when the intended purposes of popular cultural texts are to inform and shape the audience in ways that perpetuate dominant power structures, Hall argued that such cultural texts are not always interpreted according to authorial intentions. Instead, the readers bring into the process of decoding their own experiences, background, and insight that can modify, twist, or outrightly

---

5 See Hong 2016a for an in-depth exploration of this particular TV show.

challenge intended readings.[6] One of Hall's real examples of such resistive interpretation in relation to religion was Rastafarianism, a Jamaican religious movement that re-read Western Christianity, the religion of the dominant Europeans, and reshaped it in ways that advocate for the colonized and the oppressed (Chen 1996, pp. 492–93). Hall's idea of encoding/decoding has since become a prominent theoretical framework and served as a common reference point to debunk what has been caricatured—and exaggerated—as "the hypodermic needle model," the idea that people in general are passive dupes who just get injected with ideologies by whatever cultural texts that are given to them.

While the idea of audiences as more than passive consumers is celebrated as a major contribution of cultural studies, it actually has an older lineage. As a pioneer of what is called "uses and gratification theory," Herzog (1941) emphasized the audiences' (listeners of radio broadcast programs in her case) active role in choosing to consume—or not consume—particular texts as well as what they do with them. For Herzog, the fact that audiences discern and use the emotional satisfaction as well as practical help from popular cultural texts to their own benefit points to their active involvement in the process of mass communication. Unlike Hall's and cultural studies' approach, Herzog's perspective on how cultural texts are actually consumed shows that one need not necessarily recognize ideological struggles when looking for the audiences' agency. From a uses-and-gratifications perspective, one does not need to have sophisticated interpretive strategies and discern ideological aspects in popular culture in order to avoid being passive consumers. Instead, even the very pleasure of enjoying cultural products can indicate people's agency.[7] Theories put forth by pioneering scholars such as Hall and Herzog have developed over the years, and it has now become a major trend in cultural studies to emphasize what the audiences can do with given cultural texts as indications of their agency (Fiske 1987; Jenkins 1992).

Religion being an integral part of culture, people's arbitrary interpretation and/or creative appropriation of religious texts can also be seen from these cultural studies perspectives as indications of empowerment. I explore what Protestant critical insider movements in South Korea can bring to the discussion. What might these particular social actors have to say about cultural resistance and textual reading? More specifically, the (Protestant) Bible being the central source for religious thought and practice of both the critical insiders and the dominant Korean Protestant institutions, how do these loyal religious protesters relate reading and interpreting the Christian scripture to resistance?

In what follows, I engage these questions by exploring Korean Protestant critical insiders' view of reading the Bible and religiously loyal resistance. Essentially, what I argue is that, in the particular context of Korean Protestantism, their view of religious resistance and textual reading brings a corrective to the views of unintended reading and uses-and-gratification/pleasure as agency. Quite to the contrary, it is the dominant institutions keeping the laity from discovering "intended" meanings of the Protestant canon and even encouraging Bible-reading for reader-gratification that sap the knowledge and insight crucial for resistance from a genuinely Protestant worldview. And, in light of all this, the critical insider movements' attempts to equip the laity with interpretive capabilities also become a form of resistance: what I call *exegetical* resistance.

5. Clarification of Concepts: Exegesis vs. Eisegesis

In biblical studies, the term reserved for the act of discovering biblical authors' communicative intent is *exegesis* (Snodgrass 2005, p. 203), the opposite of which—importing meaning unrelated to the text—is *eisegesis* (p. 203). It is also to be noted that eisegesis is generally a derogatory term in the theological community (Grenz et al. 1999, p. 49). What is important to recognize, then, is that even though actual conclusions of proper exegesis regarding specific biblical passages have always

---

[6] Hall categorizes different levels of resistive reading into dominant-hegemonic, negotiated, and oppositional codes of reading (Hall 1980).
[7] It must be noted, however, that Herzog herself was often highly cynical about the audiences she studied. For more information on later scholars who took the more celebratory approach to uses-and-gratification theory, especially in the global media context, see Mirrlees 2013, p. 230.

been debated, the method of exegesis has still been the norm while eisegesis has been taken as a fallacy. In other words, what the biblical authors' intended meanings were have been the points of debate, not whether the endeavor of discovering such intended meanings is the legitimate method in biblical studies.

Notably, the terms exegesis and eisegesis have been borrowed in media/cultural studies. In the context of discussing how Hollywood films enable global audiences to go beyond intended readings and inject their own meanings to the text. Olson (2004) specifically employs the terms and flips them around to argue the positive role of eisegesis (pp. 122–23). Olson's attempt at switching the status of exegesis and eisegesis is in line with cultural studies' celebration of reading cultural texts against the grain as audience agency. Indeed, in Hall (1980), "dominant" reading, which is equivalent to intended reading, is the opposite of "oppositional" reading.

John Storey, however, raises an astute question in relation to the general trend in cultural studies regarding reading cultural texts and resistance: "what happens to the model when the encoded message is 'radical' or 'progressive'?" (Storey 2010, p. 41). Indeed, I argue that, at least from the South Korean Protestant critical insiders' perspective, what Hall and others might call "dominant" reading is precisely the interpretive imperative for resistance when it comes to reading their sacred text.

6. Evidence of the Argument: Examples of Rescuing the Text as Critical Insiders' Resistance

Upon looking into the materials listed in the Objects of Analysis section above, it becomes clear that one of the core tasks of critical insider activities in Korea is critically examining popular ways in which the biblical text is interpreted and preached. This often takes the form of exploring certain biblical passages with the agenda of critiquing/debunking what is commonly taught out of those passages in Korean churches. This is especially true of educational organizations such as Holy Wave Academy or Chungeoram ARMC that offer courses on proper interpretations of various books in the Bible. In the case of Nehemiah Institute for Christian Studies, another educational organization, it can be said that one of the core purposes of the institute's alternative seminary courses for the laity is providing skills for proper exegesis. The TV show *CBS Christian Now* was where these and other movements were introduced to a wider viewership via broadcast television. In addition to content provided through such organized movements, some critical insiders also publish individual works, such as Hyung Kook Kim's *Kyohoe anŭi kŏchitmal (Lies in the Church)* (Kim 2013), which focuses on debunking commonly misunderstood/misinterpreted and abused biblical teachings. Another TV show by CBS, *Nancy Lang's Theology Punch*, was aimed at inviting theologians to discuss and debate about a variety of teachings in the church that can be misunderstood, misleading, one-sided, or outright manipulative.

Critical insider resistance via recovering intended meanings of the Bible—what I call "rescuing the text"—can be roughly divided into two categories, both of which revolve around the idea of not reading into the text—eisegesis—but recovering authorial intentions—exegesis. The first is more pertinent to bringing to light the textual abuses of dominant Protestant institutions and authorities, while the second is a response to popular ways in which the Protestant canon is used or appropriated by the laity for their gratification. There are, indeed, overlaps between the two as they are often correlated (e.g., where do popular readings come from? How are dominant teachings perpetuated? etc.). Nevertheless, the two categories are helpful in highlighting different aspects of rescuing the biblical text and promoting proper exegesis.

The examples below represent these aspects of critical insider movements. While there can be many more examples, excluded here are mostly forms of either delivering similar messages via different venues (e.g., appearing both on a TV show and writing an article on a website) or using similar venues with different contents (e.g., a critical insider theologian writing several books to debunk inappropriate interpretations of several biblical passages respectively).

6.1. Rescuing the Text from the Authorities

A major approach that critical insiders take with the biblical text is unmistakably debunking unwarranted ways of how dominant Protestant institutions use biblical passages to justify and perpetuate their power at the expense of proper exegesis. One of the best sample passages is Romans 13:1,[8] which is the verse that is used regularly as a proof text for justifying conservative Protestant institutions supporting certain political authorities or parties. NewsNJoy, the most representative critical insider online newspaper, has devoted several articles for critiquing how Protestant churches in Korea use the verse to preach that believers ought not to protest the governmental authorities but obey them as appointed rulers of God. Organizations like Holy Wave Academy held a lecture on the history of the verse's use. *CBS Christian Now*, a TV talk show devoted to the cause of critical insider movements, also had several episodes in which the panels argued about problematic usages of the passage in the context of discussing Korean Protestant church's popular sermons of obedience to the government at the expense of social justice. Likewise, *Nancy Lang's Theology Punch* had an episode that deconstructed the notion of "authorities granted by God" in which Romans 13:1 was also discussed. Yeon Kyung Kwon, a theologian who teaches at Nehemiah Institute for Christian Studies and also appeared in *Theology Punch* regularly, recently published a book that focuses on properly explicating Romans 13 (Kwon 2017).

Common counter arguments in all of these efforts against Korean Protestant churches' use of the passage are actually very simple and are what anyone who reads the biblical text holistically in context can discover. For example, even a cursory reading of the entire chapter of Romans 13 reveals that (a) the author (Paul) is talking about governmental systems that reward good and punish evil, and that (b) his main point in context is that Christians ought to pay tax just like everyone else. The fact that there are so many other passages in the Bible—especially the prophetic writings—that strongly condemn and protest against authoritative institutions, political and/or religious, that ignore justice and side with the rich and the powerful is also noted. Why are those passages against corrupt political powers not evoked even nearly as often as Romans 13:1—interpreted out of context—when the church talks about faith and politics? From the critical insiders' perspective, the fundamental problem of dominant Protestant institutions and their adherents in Korea is *not* that they lack the creativity to use the text in unintended ways. Quite to the contrary, it is failing to grasp the intended meanings, the authorial intentions of the religious text that is called the Bible.[9]

There are a number of similar examples, such as (mis)interpreting passages on gender roles, theodicy, or the antichrist, all of which have been dealt with by many of the critical insider movements. When I conducted interviews during the summer of 2015 with some of the leading figures of these movements, most of the informants—especially the theologians—highlighted such interpretive issues. Instead of elaborating upon problematic readings of specific texts as they did in the TV shows or other mediated venues, they stated more about the problematic modes of reading the Bible during the interviews.

> "Protestant Christianity is all about (properly interpreting) scripture, but they (Korean Protestant churches) are not really interested in it. Rather, they only want to use it to their advantage." (Interviewed on 27 July 2015)

> "They seem to think that they already have all the answers, and that all they need to do is finding proof texts." (Interviewed on 16 July 2015)

---

[8] "Everyone must submit himself to the governing authorities, for there is no authority except that which God has established. The authorities that exist have been established by God" (NIV).

[9] Another problem that they point out is the inconsistency of the Protestant institutions appealing to the verse only when the conservative party is ruling; when it is a liberal party, the churches contradict what they preach by "protesting" the government. Since an important part of Romans 13 is the argument that Christians are not exempt from the duty to pay tax as citizens, critical insiders also ask why affluent pastors—mostly in megachurches—refuse to pay tax.

The second informant was arguing that, instead of discovering the intended meanings of the biblical text, church authorities already have what they want to say and that what they desire to do with the Bible is simply finding passages that look most suitable for their pre-determined arguments. The first comment above, on the other hand, is a most telling example of critiquing the uses-and-gratification approach to the Bible on the part of the readers. It also points out that the dominant Protestant institutions are the ones doing "textual poaching," to borrow Jenkins' term (Jenkins 1992), to perpetuate institutional status. In his influential book *Textual Poachers* (Jenkins 1992), Jenkins saw popular culture fans' various creative uses of film and television texts in ways that are out of contexts of the movies and the TV shows as indications of their active and resistive agency. According to the critical insiders of South Korean Protestantism, however, things are the opposite in their context. Instead of turning the signs upside down, recognizing and challenging the deviations from authorial intentions of the biblical text is the way forward for their religiously motivated resistance.

6.2. Rescuing the Text from the Popular

Let the readers be reminded that textual manipulations at the institutional and the popular level are not mutually exclusive. Far from arguing that they are, what I show in this section is how critical insiders' perspectives on the Bible and popular Protestant beliefs in Korea can inform, and challenge, the idea of seeing a cultural text's readers' uses-and-gratification and pleasure as audience agency. The section above was more about how the institutional authorities appropriate the biblical text, from critical insiders' perspectives, to perpetuate their authorities. This section is more about how "popular" readings of the Bible among the laity may not be indications of resistance but rather co-optation.

While there is much critical insider content on the topic of popular readings of the Bible, one episode of *Nancy Lang's Theology Punch* really spells out what they have to say about textual reading and interpretation at the popular level. The title of this particular episode is "What is wrong with reading the Bible for QT?" QT is an acronym for Quiet Time and is a widely used term in Korea that basically means devotional reading of the Bible. The Protestant ideal of every single believer having the right—and responsibility—to read and interpret scripture is not what is challenged by the critical insider theologians in this episode. What that Protestant ideal does *not* entail for the theologians in this episode, however, is that any—creative or otherwise—reading goes as long as the reader feels empowered. Quite to the contrary, the critique is that arbitrary interpretations give the illusion of empowerment, while the technical act of exegesis—exploring the biblical authors' intended meanings—is delegated to the authorities who do not actually perform appropriate exegesis but instead take advantage of the perception that serious biblical exegesis is their privilege. As a response, this episode of *Theology Punch* along with other critical insider programs try to equip the laity by providing them with commonsensical skills for adequately grasping authorial intentions of the biblical books without overly relying on the pastoral authorities. Various sample passages are discussed in the episode to give examples of arbitrary and appropriate biblical interpretation.

This aspect of critical insiders' view on the relation between textual reading of the Bible and resistance can conflict with how some media/cultural studies scholars might see the same phenomenon with a more positive perspective (i.e., as something that indicates the readers' agency) in light of the uses-and-gratification approach, or some variations of it. It should be remembered that, for critical insiders of Protestantism, their kind of resistance is not against the Protestant religion altogether. It is not anti-Protestantism that they pursue; it is rather Protestant Christianity that is authentic/real/appropriate (one can come up with numerous terms here) that they are after. From such a religiously loyal perspective, reading into the text (eisegesis) that satisfies the reader is not an act of empowering the reader of the Bible. A popular phrase in Korean churches that the QT episode of *Theology Punch* challenged was "see what the word of God is saying *to you*." What the theologians in this episode and other similar critical insider programs are saying is "first and foremost, it is

NOT about you."[10] Popular readings of the Bible often encourage the readers—and thus bring emotional gratification—in ways not intended by the biblical authors, and that often inevitably involves false hopes and promises. In that sense, far from empowering the readers, it might be perceivable that it can actually become something like an opiate of the people.

Some of the episodes of *CBS Christian Now* and *Nancy Lang's Theology Punch*, as well as content provided by critical insider websites and lecture events, also pinpoint specific beliefs resulting from popular readings. Such readings, they argue, bring gratification to many Protestants in Korea, and deconstructing their hopes deriving from such popular readings can be quite unpleasant to those who think they have benefited from such readings. One example is the belief in there being a "soul mate" for every single believer who did not receive from God "the gift of celibacy" (1 Corinthians 7). Based upon several passages in the Christian Bible that depict male characters meeting female partners (e.g., Genesis 2:20–25, Genesis 24, or the book of Ruth), this popular belief suggests that, except for those whom God destined to live—and gave the ability to cope with—a celibate life, God has already prepared a soul mate to all sincere Christians. Marriage is guaranteed for every single desiring believer. This belief is quite pertinent to contemporary South Korean Protestant churches in which females significantly outnumber males, yet it is taught that Protestants should marry fellow Protestants. *Theology Punch* actually had a separate episode to address this belief. The episode's title was "did God prepare a soul mate for me?" to which the theologians basically answered "we cannot know that, and that is not what those passages are there for." They also elaborated upon how such popular beliefs can be taken advantage of by the church in dangerous ways: for example, demanding that believers should not seek "worldly" means, such as blind dates, but spend their time at church so that they can see how God brings their soul mates to them.

Critical insider content also addresses many other issues on popular readings of the biblical text. A common thread in those various critiques, however, as can be found in the one on soul mates, is that the problematic readings are unwarranted interpretations from an exegetical (as opposed to eisegetical) standpoint, yet they bring immediate gratification to the readers. Several articles in NewsNJoy as well as two episodes of *Christian Now* specifically targeted popular books sold in millions at Christian bookstores, ones that encourage readers to read meanings into the biblical texts to find promises desired by themselves. Numerous books on "answered prayers" with such a popular approach encourage the readers to also seek what the authors of those books have experienced. According to critical insiders' assessment, one of the major problems with such books, supported by popular readings of the Christian Bible, is that their promises—disguised as biblical teachings but theologically unfounded—will prove to be wrong/inapplicable/unrealized sooner or later to many of the readers. To speak in religious terms, being confident about what God does not even promise, by means of reading into God's word, speaks nothing positively about the laity's agency. Instead, the concern is that such popularized unintended readings of the Bible, which can bring emotional satisfaction to the audience, will actually be detrimental to the agency of lay Protestants who have the right and responsibility to read and interpret authorial intentions/intended meanings of the biblical text made available to them. Critical insiders' concern is that, when such desired readings are welcome, encouraged, and facilitated by the dominant institutions, what may appear to be empowerment will actually become subservience.

Speaking of critical insiders' resistance against (propagation and encouragement of) unintended readings of the biblical text and unwarranted promises that bring gratification to the audience, a mention must be made on a too well-known topic in contemporary Protestant Christianity that is all-inclusive of the two categories discussed so far.

---

[10]   Keun Ju Kim, a full-time Old Testament faculty member at Nehemiah Institute for Christian Studies, recently published a book on this topic (Kim 2017), the title of which can be translated as "Bible Reading that Looks Beyond One's Self."

6.3. Prosperity Gospel: The Default Mode of Reading into the Text

During my interviews, it was almost always presupposed—given as a fact that is too obvious—in the conversations that Korean Protestantism pretty much equates to what is known as "prosperity gospel."

> "What we hear from the pulpit is, by default, prosperity gospel." (Interviewed on 20 July 2015)

> "It's prosperity theology, which, after all, has a lot to do with the influence of Yoido.[11]" (Interviewed on 9 July 2015)

For those who are familiar with criticism of Korean Protestantism, the critique of how prosperity gospel can be detrimental to the laity is perhaps all too common.[12] The prosperity gospel here simply refers to the common understanding of the term as the belief in the positive correlation between one's financial/social success and God's blessing/approval.[13] It is hard to trace its singular origin in Korea; as mentioned by the second interviewee cited above, it is seen, on the one hand, as something that was brought from America by a popular charismatic preacher and intensified in the Korean soil; on the other hand, other scholars also find its origin in the syncretization of Christianity and popular folk beliefs in Korea (e.g., Chang 2007). Regardless of its origin, prosperity gospel is, as a theologian stated in an interview (Interviewed on 27 July 2015), what satisfies both the institutions' desire for their adherents' loyalty and the laity's pleasure of hearing what they desire.

What makes the critique of prosperity gospel important for this essay is its relevance to the problem of biblical exegesis and agency from Protestant critical insiders' perspectives. So many lectures, episodes, and other content provided by them address it as central to problematic Korean Protestant beliefs. Prosperity gospel is seen as the epitome of both how the institutions secure the congregations' loyalty and how the laity finds their desired gratification by an unwarranted reading of, or reading into, the biblical text.

From a non-religious outsider perspective, perhaps a theological critique of prosperity gospel is problematic. After all, what is wrong with people finding gratification and expectation for material success and well being? Should they rather be always depressed by the harsh realities? Even when they do not receive what they believe to be promised, would not the message of divinely sanctioned financial success in the future continue to give them hope and a sense of empowerment? Is it not better than the "other-worldly" Christian religion, the one Marx so harshly criticized, that discouraged its believers from engaging with this world and encouraged them to keep their eyes only on heaven? Perhaps so, at least at the individual level, from an outsider perspective. From the (critical) insider view, however, such a gratifying interpretation of the religious text, one that is not in accordance with the authorial intentions, is actually what saps the agency of the laity and secures their institutional loyalty instead. Quite to the contrary of what Marx worried about, it is prosperity gospel's focus on "worldly" matters—albeit in a different sense—that distracts the laity as potential social agents from appropriate religious knowledge and values that ought to be concerned with social justice and critical examination of unchecked religious authority and institutional domination. It is not my purpose here to weigh on the possible outsider-insider debate. Rather, my purpose has been to show that the critical "insider" perspective on religion, resistance, and textual interpretation can be quite different from conventional views in cultural studies.

---

[11] This is a reference to the charismatic Yoido Full Gospel Church, which has been known as the world's largest Protestant church and also seen by many critics as the key propagator of prosperity gospel in Korea.

[12] See, for instance, Kim 2011, pp. 126–30, p. 171 or Kim 2012, pp. 61–106.

[13] For a succinct history and development of prosperity gospel/theology, see Prothero 2007, p. 183.

7. A Caveat: Rescuing the Text without Guarantees

One more subject must be addressed for the discussion of intended readings of the Bible as resistance. My argument in this paper has been that, in the particular context of critical insiders in South Korean Protestantism, it is not unintended interpretation/appropriation of the religious text—the Christian Bible—that counts as what cultural studies advocates like to see: resistance and agency. Instead, to them, it is proper exegesis, discovering authorial intentions and intended meanings of the sacred text that enables religious resistance. But one might be troubled at this point. If discovering intended meanings is the key here, that entails that not all interpretations are equally legitimate. How can one (or who can) decide which interpretation is right and which is wrong? Is, for instance, Stuart Hall's example of Rastafarianism a faithful reading, or is it closer to what critical insiders are critiquing?

Three responses can be given to this legitimate and important question. First, this paper is not about advocating particular schools of theological interpretation over others. Indeed, theological literature abounds in the disciplines' methodologies as well as the topic of bibliology, not to mention different schools of interpretation critiquing each other. Instead, this paper's aim is more modest in that it simply shows how the act of exegesis—contrary to a key theoretical view in cultural studies—can be seen as cultural resistance. The complication brought by the resultant multiplicity of exegetical conclusions in Protestantism is another matter, which has been dealt with by theologians from various perspectives (e.g., Vanhoozer 2016).

Second, the fact that there is a multiplicity of *competing* exegeses shows that such multiplicity is not an endorsement of relativism but rather an indication of Protestant theological communities' efforts for appropriate interpretations while at the same time betraying its difficulties. On the flipside, it is also a refutation of the notion that there are always obvious meanings that can be easily discovered as long as the readers' religious commitments are secured. Far from insisting upon simple literal interpretations of the Christian canon all the time, what the interpretive imperative that critical insiders' resistance entails is *literary* readings,[14] which includes the process of judging whether certain statements are meant to be taken literally or not. It is rather the suppression of literary interpretation that my informants challenged. There are meanings to be discovered, yet the discovery is not guaranteed. That is why it is dangerous for interpretation to be dictated by church authorities. To put a check on such interpretive dictatorship, Protestants are to examine and take part in the uneasy process of literary engagement. Protestantism's interpretive imperative on its sacred text just might be the most demanding enjoinment for its lay followers!

Third, and in a similar vein, one must not confuse the idea of *contextualization* with the notion of any-reading-goes. Many non-Western theologies that are resistive to Western colonialism are *not* attempts at ascribing unintended meanings into the text. Rather, they aspire to ask legitimate questions of the text, questions that the oppressors/rulers do not wish to address, and discover (divinely) intended answers to those questions.[15] For instance, they may ask "what did biblical authors intend to say about oppressive economic structures such as ones we see in capitalism?" or "what does the Bible say about ancestors?"[16] Far from reading into the text with wishful thinking, such contextualized theologies are more akin to the critical insider movements in South Korea in that they seek to resist with religious aspirations coupled with uninhibited exegesis.

8. Conclusions

> "It seems like they (Korean Protestants) lost their ability to simply read the bible as a written document." (Interviewed on 29 July 2015)

---

14 For an argument for literary, as opposed to literal, reading, see Vanhoozer 2013.
15 For more insight on non-Western theologies, see Tennent 2007.
16 For an example of a non-Western theological engagement with this question, see Hong 2017.

In this paper, I argued that cultural studies' traditional approach of seeing unintended and creative readings of cultural texts as resistance and agency may need reconsideration in certain religious contexts. Unlike circumstances in which the oppressed protests against the dominant's religious tradition, Protestants protesting against dominant and popular institutionalized Protestantism renders a situation in which manipulative/creative/unintended readings of the Christian Bible becomes the very means through which the dominant actually perpetuate their status. In such contexts, it is the act of rescuing the text—endeavoring to discover authorial intentions—and asking "is there a meaning in this text" (Vanhoozer 1998) that opens the door for agency and becomes the mode of resistance.

Conflicts of Interest: The author declares no conflicts of interest.

References

Buswell, Robert E., and Timothy S. Lee, eds. 2006. *Christianity in Korea*. Honolulu: University of Hawaii Press. ISBN-13: 978-0-8248-2912-4.

Chang, Nam Hyuk. 2007. *Kyohoesokŭi Shamanism (Shamanism in the Church)*. Paju: Chipmundang. ISBN 89-303-0942-9.

Chen, Kuan Hsing. 1996. The formation of a diasporic intellectual: An interview with Stuart Hall by Kuan-Hsing Chen. In *Stuart Hall: Critical Dialogues in Cultural Studies*. Edited by David Morley and Kuan Hsing Chen. New York: Routledge, pp. 486–505. ISBN 0-415-08804-6.

Choi, Hyaeweol. 2009. *Gender and Mission Encounters in Korea: New Women, Old Ways*. Berkeley and Los Angeles: University of California Press. ISBN 978-0-520-09869-5.

Chong, Chae Yong. 2012. *Han'guk kyohoe ŭi chongkyo sahoehakchŏk ihae (Understanding the Korean Church through the Sociology of Religion)*. Seoul: Yŏllin ch'ulp'ansa. ISBN 978-89-87548-98-2.

Chong, Chae Yong. 2015. *Kyohoe annakanŭn kŭrisŭtoin: Kanaan sŏngtorŭl ŏttŏke* ihaehal kŏtinka (Churchless Christians: How to Understand Canaanite Believers). Seoul: InterVarsity Press. ISBN 978-89-328-1422-3.

Fiske, John. 1987. *Television Culture*. New York: Routledge. ISBN 0-415-03934-7.

Grenz, Stanley J., David Guretzki, and Cherith Fee Nordling. 1999. *Pocket DictionaHallry of Theological Terms*. Downers Grove: InterVarsity Press. ISBN 0-8308-1448-3.

Hall, Stuart. 1980. Encoding/decoding. In *Culture, Media, Language*. Edited by Stuart Hall, Dorothy Hobson, Andrew Lowe and Paul Willis. London: Hutchinson, pp. 128–38. ISBN 0-415-07906-3.

Herzog, Herta. 1941. On borrowed experience: An analysis of listening to daytime sketches. *Studies in Philosophy and Social Science* 11: 65–95. [CrossRef]

Hong, Seung Min. 2016a. Punching Korean Protestantism: Challenging from within through a televised theological roundtable. *Journal of Korean Religions* 7: 99–121. [CrossRef]

Hong, Seung Min. 2016b. Uncomfortable proximity: Perception of Christianity as a cultural villain in South Korea. *International Journal of Communication* 10: 4532–4549.

Hong, Seung Min. 2017. Toward Korean Contextualization: An Evangelical Perspective. *International Bulleting of Mission Research* 41: 18–28. [CrossRef]

Jenkins, Henry. 1992. *Textual Poachers: Television Fans and Participatory Culture*. New York: Routledge. ISBN 0-415-90571-0.

Jung, Jin Heon. 2015. *Migration and Religion in East Asia: North Korean Migrants' Evangelical Encounters*. New York: Palgrave Macmillan. ISBN 978-1-349-56673-0.

Kim, Sung Gun. 2011. *Han'guk kyohoe ŭi hyŏnsil kwa chaengjŏm (Realities and Issues of the Korean Protestant Church)*. Yongin: Preaching Academy. ISBN 978-89-6640-000-3.

Kim, Jin Ho. 2012. *Simin K kyohoerŭl nakata (Citizen K Goes to—Or leaves—Church)*. Seoul: Hyŏnamsa. ISBN 978-89-323-1617-8.

Kim, Hyung Kook. 2013. *Kyohoe anŭi kŏchitmal (Lies in the Church)*. Seoul: Poiema. ISBN 978-89-977-6041-1.

Kim, Nami. 2016. *The Gendered Politics of the Korean Protestant Right: Hegemonic Masculinity*. Cham: Springer. ISBN 978-3-319-39977-5.

Kim, Keun Ju. 2017. *Narŭl nŏmŏsŏnŭn sŏngkyŏng ilki (Bible Reading That Looks beyond One's Self)*. Seoul: Scripture Union Korea. ISBN 978-89-325-2122-0.

Kwon, Yeon Kyung. 2017. *Romasŏ sipsamchang tasi ilki (Understanding Romans 13)*. Seoul: NewsNJoy. ISBN 978-89-909-2839-9.

Lee, Timothy. 2010. *Born Again: Evangelicalism in Korea*. Honolulu: University of Hawaii Press. ISBN 978-0-8248-3375-6.

Lee, Won Kyu. 2010. *Chongkyosahoehakchŏk kwanchŏmesŏ pon hankukkyohoeŭi wikiwa hŭimang (Crisis and Hope of the Korean Church: From the Perspective of Sociology of Religion)*. Seoul: The KMC Press. ISBN 978-89-8430-454-3.

Mirrlees, Tanner. 2013. *Global Entertainment Media: Between Cultural Imperialism and Cultural Globalization*. New York: Routledge. ISBN 978-0-415-51982-3.

Olson, Scott Robert. 2004. Hollywood planet: Global media and the competitive advantage of narrative transparency. In *The Television Studies Reader*. Edited by Robert Clyde Allen and Annette Hill. New York: Routledge, pp. 111–29. ISBN 0-415-28324-8.

Park, Jin Kyu. 2005. "Are you Christian? I'm the other": The demarcation of Christianity and the other in popular Korean television. *Studies in World Christianity* 11: 106–24. [CrossRef]

Prothero, Stephen. 2007. *Religious Literacy: What Every American Needs to Know and Doesn't*. New York: HarperCollins. ISBN 978-0-06-085952-7.

Snodgrass, Klyne. 2005. Exegesis. In *Dictionary for Theological Interpretation of the Bible*. Edited by Kevin J. Vanhoozer. Grand Rapids: Baker Academic, pp. 203–6. ISBN 978-0-8010-2694-2.

Storey, John. 2010. *Cultural Studies and the Study of Popular Culture*, 3rd ed. Edinburgh: Edinburgh University Press. ISBN 978-0-7486-4038-6.

Tennent, Timothy C. 2007. *Theology in the Context of World Christianity: How the Global Church Is Influencing the Way We Think about and Discuss Theology*. Grand Rapids: Zondervan. ISBN 13:978-0-310-27511-4.

Vanhoozer, Kevin J. 1998. *Is There a Meaning in This Text?* Grand Rapids: Zondervan. ISBN 0-310-21156-5.

Vanhoozer, Kevin J. 2013. Augustinian inerrancy: Literary meaning, literal truth, and literate interpretation in the economy of biblical discourse. In *Five Views on Biblical Inerrancy*. Edited by James Merrick and Stephen M. Garrett. Grand Rapids: Zondervan, pp. 199–235. ISBN 978-0-310-33136-0.

Vanhoozer, Kevin J. 2016. *Biblical Authority after Babel: Retrieving the Solas in the Spirit of Mere Protestant Christianity*. Grand Rapids: Brazos Press. ISBN 978-1-5874-3393-1.

religions

MDPI

Article

Shaping the Religiosity of Chinese University Students: Science Education and Political Indoctrination

Miao Li [1], Yun Lu [2,*] and Fenggang Yang [3]

1   Department of Sociology, Notre Dame University, Notre Dame, IN 46556, USA; mli13@nd.edu
2   Department of Sociology and Social Work, Sun Yat-sen University, Guangzhou 510275, China
3   Department of Sociology, Purdue University, West Lafayette, IN 47907, USA; fyang@purdue.edu
*   Correspondence: luyun7@mail.sysu.edu.cn

Received: 10 September 2018; Accepted: 4 October 2018; Published: 11 October 2018

Abstract: Our study examined the respective relationships between two components of higher education in mainland China—science education and political indoctrination—and the religiosity of university students. Using a cross-sectional, representative sample of about 1700 college students in Beijing, we found first that students studying natural/applied sciences were less likely to perceive Protestantism, Catholicism, and Islam as plausible and less likely to have supernatural belief, relative to students in humanities/social sciences. In addition, the more students positively evaluated the political education courses—which indicates students' acceptance of political indoctrination—the less likely they reported Protestantism and Catholicism as being plausible. Nevertheless, neither science education nor political indoctrination was associated with the perceived plausibility of Buddhism and Daoism or the worshipping behavior of students. We discuss the implications of these findings in light of the secularization debate and the research on education, religion, and state atheism.

Keywords: higher education; religiosity; science education; political indoctrination; atheism

1. Introduction

Influences of higher education on religiosity have attracted much scholarly attention. While many studies have portrayed universities as unfriendly places for religion (e.g., Caplovitz 1977; Hunter 1983), others have documented stable rates of religious commitment of college students (e.g., Hill 2009, 2011; Mayrl and Uecker 2011; McFarland et al. 2011; Reimer 2010). Most studies on the topic have been done in the United States, where religious freedom is protected. Nevertheless, it is unclear how higher education influences students' religiosity in places where religious freedom is restricted and where the state-enforced secularization curriculum tries to systematically undermine the plausibility of religion.

Governments in many countries have practiced or are practicing state atheism, a secularization movement with a goal of eradicating religion. These governments often take a series of radical measures to secularize higher education, such as forbidding religious preaching on campus and enforcing anti-religious curricula. So far, only a few studies have examined the relationship between higher education and religion in these antireligious settings, and the findings have been mixed (Sacerdote and Glaeser 2001; Schwadel 2015; Wang and Uecker 2017; Xie et al. 2017). These mixed findings may be due to the fact that the studies generally compared religiosity between populations of different education levels, an approach that fails to untangle the various components of higher education and so does not shed much light on the mechanisms through which higher education shapes students' religiosity. Scholars have identified multiple components of modern higher education that may undermine students' religiosity, with natural science education often invoked as the most prominent one (Halman and Draulans 2006; Johnson 1997; Schwadel 2011). In countries with state-enforced secularization, however, there are additional components to be considered, most notably the mandatory political indoctrination of students with atheism and nationalism.

The purpose of the present study is to examine the extent to which two important components of higher education in China—science education and political indoctrination—influence students' religiosity. Through focusing on the religiosity of college students, this study helps shed light on the influences of higher education on the overall religious landscape. In China, there exists a religion–science–conflict discourse in which religions have been labelled with superstition and backwardness, while science has been labelled with modernity and progressiveness and has been embedded in science education. In addition, the Communist Party of China (CPC, hereafter) is indoctrinating university students with an atheist ideology through political education programs. Therefore, we hypothesized that science education and political indoctrination would impair religiosity among Chinese college students. We also argue that the negative influences of this political indoctrination on religiosity may be particularly pronounced for Christianity, a religion that has been historically linked with Western colonialism and has a strong mobilization capacity. The current study is based on a representative sample of university students in Beijing, the capital city of China, which has the highest concentration of higher education institutions in the country. Findings from this study will advance our understanding of the relationship between higher education and religion in countries with state-enforced secularization by unpacking the "black box" of the mechanisms via which higher education influences religiosity in an antireligious setting.

2. Science Education and Religiosity

A popular narrative in social sciences predicts that exposure to science and its epistemological approach to knowledge will undermine religion (e.g., Comte 2015; Ruiter and van Tubergen 2009; Weber 1993). Scholars following this education-religion-conflict narrative argue that science and religion use different methods for making truth claims about the natural world. Embracing the epistemological view of natural and applied sciences therefore is believed to impair the religious faith and activity of students (Evans and Evans 2008). One approach that past works in the U.S. have taken to examine this science-religion-conflict argument is to compare the religiosity between scholars and college students from different academic backgrounds. However, the evidence in this approach is mixed. For example, one study found that students in natural science/engineering tended to favor science over religion compared to those in social sciences/humanities (Scheitle 2011). In contrast, other studies contended that scholars in social sciences/humanities were not less religious than natural scientists (Gross and Simmons 2009; Stark and Finke 2000), or they found that there were no significant differences in the view of the religion–science relationship between the two groups of scholars (Ecklund and Park 2009). There are some potential explanations for why science education may not weaken religiosity among students. First, people may perceive science and religion as being separate instead of as being alternatives. It may be that the subject matter and methods of natural science do not directly examine religion itself and also that many individuals still understand their daily life through a religious lens (Lehman and Shriver 1968; O'Brien and Noy 2015). Second, vibrant ministry work on campuses provides opportunities for students to engage in various forms of religious worship, which may offset the effect of natural science education (Cherry et al. 2001; Uecker et al. 2007).

Although the findings on the science education-religion link are mixed in the U.S., we expected an undermining effect of science education on religiosity in China. Different from the popular view in the U.S. that science and religion belong to separate areas, the science-religion-conflict discourse is well integrated into the Chinese education system. In the early 20th century in China, progressive intellectuals launched the May Fourth Movement (1919) as well as the companion New Culture Movement in the mid-1910s and 1920s as an endeavor for cultural renewal. Two signature slogans of these movements were "Mr. De (Mr. Democracy)" and "Mr. Sai (Mr. Science)". In the "Mr. Science" discourse, science, especially natural and applied sciences, was portrayed as knowledge that was rational and progressive and that was the promise for a modern and prosperous nation, while religion was connected to ignorance, backwardness, superstition and a barrier to modernity and development. These intellectuals argued that national rejuvenation was impossible until religions (or superstitious beliefs) were replaced by modern sciences.[1] Such intellectual discourse had a profound influence over subsequent social thought in the country. According to a recent survey about the spiritual life of Chinese residents, about 67 per cent of respondents agreed that people should only believe in science and not in any religion. The influence of the religion–science-conflict discourse, through the promotion of official propaganda, is particularly strong in the contemporary higher education context (Ji 2015). Based on this reasoning, we hypothesized that *natural/applied science education would be negatively associated with religiosity among university students in China* (H1).

Further, the other explanatory mechanism mentioned above, that dynamic campus ministries help preserve the religious plausibility in spite of the science education, may be less effective in the Chinese context. Although some religious activists have been conducting underground missionary work on campus, the Chinese government has prohibited proselytization activities by religious organizations (even legally sanctioned religious organizations) on campuses. Therefore, these proselytization activities in China's universities may be less vibrant and effective than their counterparts in the U.S. and thus might not be able to offset the secularizing effect of the science education.

3. The CPC's Political Indoctrination

Mandatory political indoctrination with anti-religious content is a unique phenomenon in socialist higher education. The CPC has systematically incorporated political indoctrination programs into the higher education system since it assumed national power in the late 1940s. The purpose of political indoctrination is to propagate the Party's ideology and guiding socio-economic principles, as well as to prepare the highly educated to be politically subservient in the future. The content of the political indoctrination is composed of atheism, authoritarianism, and nationalism. The political indoctrination is implemented via two primary mechanisms in colleges: (1) mandatory political education courses and (2) student Party member recruitment. The former targets are all students, while the latter are more focused on elite students.

Mandatory political education courses are built into the higher education curricula. All university students are required to take a series of political education courses in which the Party's ideology is systematically taught.[2] Of course, students vary in their responses to these political indoctrination programs. Some passively resist, some grow aloof or cynical, while others consider the programs useful and necessary. These different responses serve as a good indicator of the students' intellectual stance towards the Party's ideological teachings. Therefore, we hypothesized that *students with a more positive attitude towards the political education courses would be less religious* (H2).

Meanwhile, universities are a primary recruiting ground of the CPC. University CPC recruitment is a highly selective and stringent process.[3] It takes at least two years to attain full membership, during which time applicants must attend a series of special training programs, report to the local CPC branch, take exams, and undergo a probation period. After being recruited, the student members must regularly participate in Party activities to continue their political studies. Given the selection process and dramatically different levels of exposure to the Party's ideology between the CPC students and the non-CPC students, a comparison of their religious plausibility opinions provides an additional

---

[1] Cai Yuanpei, then-president of Peking University and a prominent leader of the New Culture Movement, publicly denounced religion as being outdated and obsolete. He instead preached that religion should be replaced by aesthetic education. Other leaders, such as Hu Shi (a student of John Dewey), took a similar secularist stance and decried religion as being irrelevant in the modern world. Chen Duxiu, another well-known intellectual at that time, argued that to avoid being colonized, traditional Chinese culture must be replaced with science and democracy.

[2] The mandatory political education courses are currently 马克思主义基本原理 (Basic Principles of Marxism), 毛泽东思想和中国特色社会主义理论体系概论 (Mao Zedong Thought and the Theory of Socialism with Chinese Characteristics), 中国近现代史纲要 (Modern History of China), 思想道德修养与法律基础 (Moral and Legal Education), and 形势与政策 (National Condition and Policy). For more detailed information on these courses, see http://www.sxz.edu.cn

[3] The recruitment is a highly selective and stringent process. It was reported that the CPC's acceptance rate in 2014 was on par with the Ivy League—2 million applicants were accepted from a pool of 22 million (McMorrow 2015).

tool for testing the influence of political indoctrination. We hypothesized that *students who are CPC members would be less religious than non-CPC students* (H3).

4. Anti-Christianity Religious Policy of the CPC

Political education courses may have a particular undermining effect on students' perceptions of Christianity, because the CPC's authoritarian and nationalistic teachings often single out Christianity as a potential threat for several reasons. First, Christianity has been historically connected with imperialism and is still suspected by the party of being a tool for infiltration by the West. Second, the CPC's vigilance towards Christianity has escalated via a momentum-gaining intellectual discourse—inspired by the Solidarity movement in Poland and other pro-democratic movements—that associates Christianity with liberal democracy (e.g., Huntington 1993). Last—but not less crucial—the government is very concerned with the mobilizational potential of religious groups. The power of religious groups in mobilizing massive protest movements was an important catalyst for the collapse of some former Eastern European communist regimes. Recently, leaders of some independent churches in China have been active in social movements that aim to achieve political change (Vala 2012). The CPC's hostile attitude towards Christianity is illustrated by the government campaign to remove crosses from church buildings that took place from 2014 to 2015 in Zhejiang Province, the heartland of Chinese Christianity. In fact, such a massive antireligious campaign has rarely happened to other religions since the late 1970s. When it comes to the political indoctrination in the higher education context, top Party leaders in charge of propaganda and ideology have expressed concern about the growing influence of Christianity on campuses and have urged rank-and-file cadres to contain it in colleges (Ifeng 2015; Xinhuanet 2017).

In contrast, other religions are portrayed somewhat positively in CPC's propaganda. The authorities view Buddhism and Daoism as spiritual cures for the social anomie, which is a byproduct of social transformation, as well as forces to counterbalance the rapid growth of Christianity. In particular, the party uses Buddhism as a channel to boost China's "soft power" globally (Johnson 2017a, 2017b, 2018; Laliberté 2011). As for Islam, the authorities do not explicitly frame this religion per se as a disruptive force of national unity, though the party-state has placed serious restrictions on Islamic activities in the northwestern provinces. For example, about the violent incidents related to some Muslims, the official media emphasized that it was a handful of terrorists and separatists who were to blame, while the majority of Chinese Muslims were patriotic and peaceful (People's Daily 2014, 2016). The discriminatory religious policy of the CPC may be embodied in the content of the political education courses. It is possible that students who find the political education courses helpful choose to avoid Protestantism and Catholicism, two major types of Christianity in China. Therefore, *the negative association between the positive attitudes towards political education courses and the perceived plausibility of Protestantism and Catholicism stronger than for other religions* (H4).

5. Data and Methods

5.1. Data

The analysis was based on data from the Beijing University Students Religious Attitudes Survey, which is a cross-sectional study of a representative sample of university undergraduate and graduate students enrolled between 2007 and 2010 in universities in Beijing. The survey is a part of the Chinese Spirituality and Society Program, based at the Center on Religion and Chinese Society at Purdue University and funded by the John Templeton Foundation.[4] The primary objective of the study was to collect data about university students' attitudes toward religion, involvement in religious activity,

---

[4]   For more information, see https://www.purdue.edu/crcs/projects/cssp/.

and religious knowledge in order to understand the sociocultural factors influencing college students' religious cognitions, knowledge, and practices. The survey was conducted in April–June 2011.

The study follows a multistage stratified probability design. The primary sampling frame covers all public universities (N = 55) in Beijing. From this frame was selected a stratified sample of 13 universities with probability proportional to size.[5] Universities were stratified by National Department of Education ranking ("985" or "211" project universities, other first-tier universities, and second-tier universities),[6] school type (comprehensive universities, social science and humanities, science and engineering, medical universities, fine arts, and sports universities), and ethnic composition (ethnic minority universities and regular universities). Our sample of universities reflects the diversity of university ranking, school types, and ethnic composition, thus representing not only the universities located in Beijing but also to some degree the higher education sector in China. The secondary sampling frame covers all student residential units in each university (in China, the overwhelming majority of students live in residential units assigned by the university). One student was randomly selected for interviewing in each randomly selected room from the sampled residential unit. In total, 1876 university students were successfully interviewed (response rate = 93.8%). After a list-wise deletion of observations that had missing data, the final analytical sample sizes varied across models with different dependent variables (ranging from 1669 to 1736).

Here we first present the descriptive statistics (Table 1). Then, we present the fitted logistic regression models for the perceived plausibility of the five major religions and for religious behavior among college students, and the estimated linear regression models for a supernatural belief score. Estimated coefficients and associated standard errors for all predicting variables are presented (Table 2). All analyses were weighted by the sampling weights to account for the complex multistage cluster sampling design. We used listwise deletion to address the missing values and so that the regression results presented were based on observations with available data on all variables included in the models.

Table 1. Descriptive Statistics.

	Mean	Standard Deviation	Min	Max
Outcome Variables				
Buddhism plausibility	0.378	0.485	0	1
Daoism plausibility	0.213	0.410	0	1
Protestantism plausibility	0.188	0.390	0	1
Catholicism plausibility	0.092	0.289	0	1
Islam plausibility	0.076	0.265	0	1
Worshipping behavior	0.729	0.444	0	1
Supernatural Belief	0.000	1.000	−2.552	3.071
Independent Variables				
Science/engineering/medical area of study	0.440	0.497	0	1
Evaluation of political education courses	2.500	1.029	1	5
CPC membership	0.283	0.451	0	1

[5] The 13 universities are Peking University, Tsinghua University, Renmin University of China, Minzu University of China, China University of Political Science and Law, China University of Geoscience, Beijing University of Post and Telecommunication, Beijing University of Chemical Technology, Capital Medical University, Beijing Film Academy, Beijing University of Civil Engineering and Architecture, Capital Normal University, and University of International Relations.
[6] Universities in mainland China could be divided into two broad types: first tier (一本) and second tier (二本). Among the universities classified as part of the first tier, some have been selected for the so-called "985" project or "211" project, and these are regarded as elite higher education institutions. In 2017, the "985" and "211" projects were replaced with the "Double First-Rate" project (双一流).

Table 1. *Cont.*

	Mean	Standard Deviation	Min	Max
Covariates				
Age	22.428	2.904	12	41
Women	0.471	0.499	0	1
Sense of control	6.771	1.630	1	10
Urban origin	0.654	0.476	0	1
Have contacted a Buddhist missionary	0.073	0.260	0	1
Have contacted a Daoist missionary	0.008	0.089	0	1
Have contacted a Protestant missionary	0.551	0.498	0	1
Have contacted a Catholic missionary	0.079	0.270	0	1
Have contacted an Islamist missionary	0.049	0.216	0	1
Have contacted missionary of any religion	0.661	0.473	0	1
Father's occupation				
Managerial/Professional	0.422	0.494	0	1
Administrative staff	0.098	0.297	0	1
Manual labor	0.420	0.494	0	1
Other	0.060	0.238	0	1

Source: Beijing College Students' Religious Attitudes Survey 2011.

Table 2. Regression Model Coefficients for the Perceived Plausibility of Five Religions, Religious Behavior, and Supernatural Belief of College Students in Beijing.

	Buddhism Plausibility	Daoism Plausibility	Protestantism Plausibility	Catholicism Plausibility	Islam Plausibility	Religious Behavior	Supernatural Belief
Science and Engineering Area of Study	−0.130 (0.113)	0.008 (0.135)	−0.387 ** (0.147)	−0.391 * (0.198)	−0.675 ** (0.217)	−0.208 (0.123)	−0.200 *** (0.052)
Positive Towards Political Education	−0.036 (0.055)	−0.073 (0.066)	−0.252 *** (0.076)	−0.219 * (0.098)	−0.048 (0.104)	−0.036 (0.061)	−0.024 (0.026)
CPC Membership	0.116 (0.130)	0.088 (0.154)	−0.020 (0.162)	−0.017 (0.204)	−0.153 (0.235)	0.203 (0.149)	−0.073 (0.058)
Age	0.032 (0.027)	0.044 (0.031)	0.034 (0.032)	0.094 * (0.038)	0.138 *** (0.036)	−0.025 (0.028)	−0.007 (0.013)
Female	0.534 *** (0.112)	0.059 (0.132)	0.635 *** (0.143)	0.862 *** (0.194)	0.580 ** (0.204)	0.368 ** (0.123)	0.314 *** (0.051)
Sense of Control	−0.039 (0.033)	0.025 (0.038)	−0.057 (0.041)	−0.015 (0.051)	−0.044 (0.061)	−0.050 (0.037)	−0.089 *** (0.016)
Postgraduates	−0.350 * (0.171)	−0.480 * (0.201)	−0.139 (0.210)	−0.371 (0.266)	−0.852 ** (0.303)	0.139 (0.193)	0.035 (0.077)
Urban Origin	0.070 (0.137)	−0.091 (0.156)	0.045 (0.175)	0.143 (0.245)	−0.121 (0.245)	−0.173 (0.146)	0.180 ** (0.063)
Have Contacted Missionaries of This Religion	0.563 ** (0.216)	0.727 (0.635)	0.153 (0.136)	0.141 (0.318)	0.879 * (0.343)		
Have Contacted Missionaries of Any Religion						0.045 (0.123)	0.114 * (0.051)
Father's Occupation							
Managerial/Professional (reference group)							
Administrative staff	−0.322 (0.193)	−0.208 (0.232)	−0.394 (0.259)	−0.095 (0.331)	0.090 (0.352)	−0.165 (0.202)	−0.089 (0.087)
Manual labor	−0.110 (0.138)	−0.127 (0.159)	−0.026 (0.174)	−0.239 (0.246)	−0.071 (0.257)	−0.047 (0.148)	−0.069 (0.062)
Other	−0.058 (0.230)	0.073 (0.265)	0.509 * (0.254)	0.567 (0.309)	0.435 (0.360)	−0.072 (0.250)	0.062 (0.096)
Constant	−0.931 (0.662)	−2.039 ** (0.765)	−1.430 (0.797)	−4.033 *** (1.030)	−4.947 *** (0.999)	1.947 ** (0.687)	0.641 * (0.313)
N	1701	1679	1680	1669	1677	1717	1736

Standard errors in parentheses. * $p < 0.05$, ** $p < 0.01$, *** $p < 0.001$. Source: Beijing College Students' Religious Attitudes Survey 2011.

5.2. Dependent Variables

The perceived plausibility of the five major religions—Protestantism, Catholicism, Buddhism, Daoism, and Islam—constitute the five dependent variables in this analysis. Each dependent variable was measured with a single survey question: "Regardless of whether you go to church or temple, do you believe in [the religion]?" Original choices provided were: "do not believe", "do not believe very much", "somewhat believe", and "believe". Due to the gradations of the answers and the ambiguity of religious identity in Chinese society, we think that these questions actually measure respondents' perceived plausibility of a specific religion, rather than actual religious belief or identity. To validate the claim, we found that when students were later asked about their religious identity, around 72 per cent of those who chose "somewhat believe" or "believe" Buddhism reported having no religious identity. Additionally, for the other religions, such figures remained rather stable at around 70 per cent. To take into account the potential qualitative differences between "believe" and "not believe", we recoded these variables dichotomously, with 1 representing "somewhat believe or believe" and 0 otherwise.

Religious behavior was measured by the question, "In the past year, did you worship divinities in any of the following places: religious site; cemetery, or ancestry hall; home; work place; or other place." We coded this as a dummy variable in which students who worshipped in any one of these places were 1 and otherwise 0. About 70 per cent of the students reported having worshipping behavior.

We constructed a **supernatural belief** factor score from the five items through principle-component analysis. Scholars of religion in the Chinese context have pointed out that although many Chinese do not hold an exclusive and clear religious identity, they may believe in the existence of ghosts, gods, or demons and follow spiritual or superstitious practices such as fortune-telling and Fengshui. To measure students' supernatural beliefs, we used five items from a question in the survey, "What is your opinion on these arguments? (1) There is a supernatural force; (2) Humans have a soul; (3) Fortune-telling and Fengshui are effective; (4) Astrology is important for one's life; and (5) Everything is determined by fate." The original five choices ranged from "strongly agree" to "strongly disagree". The Cronbach's alpha of these five items was 0.751. Factor analysis revealed one factor that we referred to as a belief in supernatural forces. The eigenvalue of the supernatural belief factor was more than 50 per cent of the total, and the factor loading of the five items was between 0.7379 and 0.6355.

5.3. Key Independent Variables

Science education was measured as a dummy variable that took the value of 1 if the student was studying natural sciences/engineering/medical sciences and 0 otherwise. In the "otherwise" category, more than 98 per cent of the students were studying Social Sciences or Humanities and the rest were studying Fine Arts or Sports.

We examined two independent variables related to political indoctrination: **CPC membership** and **attitude towards political education courses**. CPC membership was measured with the question, "What is your political affiliation?" (1 = formal or probationary member; 0 = otherwise). Students were asked how much they agreed with the statement that "political education courses are beneficial". Responses were coded along a 5-point scale ranging from "absolutely do not agree" to "absolutely agree" and were used to measure students' receptiveness toward political education.

5.4. Control Variables

We controlled for some basic characteristics of the students: gender (woman = 1, man = 0), age (measured in years), urban-rural origin (urban = 1, rural = 0), and level of program enrolled in (postgraduate = 1, undergraduate = 0). We also controlled for the sense of control over one's own life based on the question, "How much do you think you can control your own life?" Responses were coded on a 10-point scale ranging from 1 (no control at all) to 10 (complete control). Father's occupation was used as a proxy for students' socio-economic status, which consisted of four occupational categories: managerial or professional (reference group), administrative staff, manual labor, and other. In addition, we constructed a dichotomous variable to indicate whether students had contacted religious missionaries or not (have contacted = 1, have not contacted = 0).

6. Results

The descriptive statistics are presented in Table 1. The respondents who viewed Buddhism as plausible were more than a third of the sample, one percentage higher than for any other religion. Buddhism appeared more authentic to university students than the other religions. For Daoism and Protestantism, the proportion of the respondents who reported them as plausible was about 21 and 19 per cent, respectively. The numbers of students with a positive perception of Daoism and Protestantism were close. The percentages of Catholicism and Islam were the lowest among the five religions, about 9 and 8 per cent, respectively. About 73 per cent of the students reported having worshipping behavior. CPC members were 28 per cent of all respondents. Students studying science/engineering/medicine comprised 44 per cent of the sample.

Table 2 reports the estimated coefficients and associated standard error for the perceived plausibility of the five religions, religious behavior, and belief in supernatural forces. We first looked at the results for those studying natural sciences/engineering. There were significant differences between students who were studying natural sciences/engineering and those who were studying other disciplines in terms of the plausibility of Protestantism, of Catholicism, and of Islam. Students with a sciences/engineering/medical background were 32.1 per cent (1-exp[−0.387]), 32.4 per cent (1-exp[−0.391]), and 49.1 per cent (1-exp[−0.675]) less likely than those studying in other areas to perceive Protestantism, Catholicism, and Islam as plausible, respectively. However, regarding the plausibility of Buddhism and Daoism, there were no significant differences between the two groups of students.

As for religious behavior, this did not relate to those studying natural sciences/engineering. There were no significant differences among students from different academic backgrounds regarding the likelihood of worshipping divinities. However, in terms of supernatural belief, we found that students with a science/engineering background were 18.1 per cent (1-exp[−0.200]) less likely to support this belief than those studying in other areas. Thus, we found some support for Hypothesis 1, which posited that students studying natural sciences/engineering were less religious than other students. Although science education was related to lower levels of perceived plausibility of Protestantism, Catholicism, and Islam and to supernatural belief, it was not significantly associated with perception of Buddhism and Daoism or with worshipping behavior.

Here, we discuss the findings on political indoctrination. The first measurement of political indoctrination was students' attitudes towards political education. Evaluation of the university political education program was significantly related to the perceived plausibility of Protestantism and Catholicism. Students who spoke highly of the political education courses were 22.3 per cent (1-exp[−0.252]) and 19.7 per cent (1-exp[−0.219]) less likely to report Protestantism and Catholicism, respectively, as being plausible. On the other hand, evaluation of political education programs was not associated with the perceived plausibility of Buddhism, Daoism, or Islam. Moreover, we found that evaluation of political education was not related to religious behavior or supernatural belief. Therefore, a positive attitude towards political education was only related to the perceived plausibility of Protestantism and Catholicism, while not being associated with other indicators of students' religiosity. These findings do not support Hypothesis 2, which posits a negative association between the evaluation of political education courses and all religiosity indicators of college students. Instead, we found that Hypothesis 4, which expects that the political education course mainly affects the perceived plausibility of Protestantism and Catholicism, was supported by the statistical evidence.

As the second measurement of political indoctrination, CPC membership was found not to be related to any indicator of students' religiosity. It seems that students who were CPC members were not less religious than others who did not obtain CPC membership. These findings were not supportive of Hypothesis 3, which posited a negative association between CPC membership and students' religiosity.

Among the control variables, age was not positively related to the indicators of religiosity except for the perceived plausibility of Catholicism and Islam. Female students were more likely to have a positive perception of the plausibility of all the religions except for Daoism and were more likely to worship divinities and to support supernatural belief. Postgraduate students were less likely to consider Buddhism, Daoism, and Islam as being plausible than were undergraduates, but there were no significant differences between postgraduates and undergraduates on other religious indicators. In addition, the only difference between students from urban and rural backgrounds was that students from cities were more likely to support supernatural belief. The father's occupation, indicating a student's social and economic status, was not found to be consistently associated with a student's religiosity. Additionally, there was no significant association between the sense of control over one's life and any indicators of religiosity except for supernatural belief.

7. Conclusions and Discussion

This study examined how two components of higher education in China—science education and political indoctrination—influenced the religiosity of college students, using a cross-sectional analytic sample of about 1700 college students in Beijing. We found that, first, students studying natural sciences/engineering were less likely than those studying in other areas to perceive Protestantism, Catholicism, and Islam as plausible and to have a supernatural belief. This partially supports our hypothesis that science education would be negatively associated with students' religiosity.

Why did science education not weaken the perceived plausibility of Buddhism and Daoism? This may be because Buddhism and Daoism are widely perceived to be part of popular culture. Today, many Buddhist and Daoist activities are still carried out in the name of traditional culture (Yang 2006). It is very possible that Buddhism and Daoism are treated by college students as a combination of philosophical thoughts, ethical teachings, and health practices. Since they are perceived as part of traditional culture, therefore, the two religions may not be perceived of as in a head-on conflict with science by students studying science.

Similarly, the nonsignificant association between science education and religious behavior may be due to the fact that some worshipping activities are viewed as cultural, touristic, or habitual. For example, quite a few religious sites in mainland China, especially Buddhist and Daoist temples, have recently been reconstructed as tourist sites. When Chinese tourists visit these temples, it is a common practice for them to burn incense or to bow to the gods. Additionally, visiting ancestors' tombs during the Qingming Festival, in which offering sacrifices and bowing are indispensable elements, is a regular family activity for many Chinese. People usually conduct this ritualistic worshipping activity for family cohesion and for mourning departed relatives, without necessarily believing in the existence of the ancestors' souls.

Another finding of the present study is that the positive evaluation of political education courses was related to low levels of the perceived plausibility of Protestantism and Catholicism. However, the evaluation of political education courses was not related to how students perceived Buddhism, Daoism, or Islam, or to their religious behavior and supernatural belief. It seems that the Party's political indoctrination particularly threatens the Christian faith. As we articulated in the hypothesis-developing section, due to Christianity's international connections and strong mobilization capacity, the leadership of the CPC is alert to the growth of Christianity in China and are taking measures to contain its burgeoning influence in colleges. Therefore, the content of the political education courses may be particularly hostile to Protestantism and Catholicism.

CPC's membership, which is the other measurement of political indoctrination, was found not to be related to the perceived plausibility of religions, religious behavior, or supernatural belief. This may be because many students join the CPC for material interests. CPC membership is often a prerequisite for getting a job at a public institution or a state-owned enterprise. In many cases, it is the material interests, rather than ideological passion, that motivate students to join the party. These student members motivated by material interests may in fact be indifferent to the official propaganda. This finding echoes one study that found that many CPC members were engaged in some kind of religious activity (Yang 2015).

Our findings have rich implications for the literature. So far, only a few studies have examined the association between education and religion in former/current socialist countries. The results from these studies are confusing: One study found that the negative effect of higher education on religion was stronger in communist countries (Sacerdote and Glaeser 2001), whereas another showed that the secularizing effect of higher education did not vary between communist and non-communist countries (Schwadel 2015). Other studies found that higher education was positively related to religiosity in China (Wang and Uecker 2017; Xie et al. 2017). These studies often used a single indicator—that is, the educational level—to represent the influences of higher education. Our research improves on these studies in two ways and helps address the inconsistency problem in these past works. First, we distinguished between science education and political education courses. The findings showed that science education and political education courses had different influences on students' religiosity. Second, we accounted for different religiosity dimensions. We found that science education and political education courses were negatively related to the perceived plausibility of Protestantism and Catholicism and to supernatural belief. In other words, our research suggests that higher education in China does change students' religiosity, though the effects of higher education vary among the types of education and among the religious dimensions.

Moreover, our findings provide more nuances for the debate on the secularizing effects of higher education. Most research that has debated whether higher education reduces religiosity has been conducted in the U.S. or Europe, where the dominant religion, either Protestantism or Catholicism, is highly institutionalized and well separated from other social areas (e.g., Hill 2009, 2011; Mayrl and Uecker 2011; McFarland et al. 2011; Reimer 2010; Schwadel 2011). However, in the present research, science education was found not to result in a lower plausibility level for Buddhism and Daoism. As we explained earlier, it may be that the values, practices, and beliefs of Buddhism and Daoism are merged in popular culture. In contrast, the acquisition of scientific knowledge was a weakening factor in the religious plausibility of Protestantism and Catholicism, a finding in-line with previous research in the U.S. that argued for the secularizing effect of science education. Therefore, our findings suggest that, in China, the effects of science education in this regard differ between "Western" religions and "traditional" religions.

There are several limitations in this study. The sample only covered college students in Beijing, the capital of China, where the political indoctrination programs might be more seriously implemented and so might have a stronger influence than in other cities with a looser political environment. If a national sample becomes available in the future, it is necessary to re-examine the findings from this study on a nationwide scale. In addition, this study is based on cross-sectional survey data with the inherent disadvantage of causal inference. The model results show statistical correlations instead of a causal relationship. It is possible that students who are inclined towards religion/supernatural belief will self-select into humanities/social sciences disciplines. Similarly, some students who agree with scientism are more likely to choose to major in natural sciences/engineering. Thus, the negative association between science education and some religious dimensions may be partly due to this selection mechanism. Further research could take into account this selection processes when longitudinal data on education and religion in China become available.

Our study contributes to the knowledge on education and religion, even though some limitations remain. First, we found that science education and political indoctrination had different influences on students' religiosity. This finding helped open the "black box" of how higher education influences religiosity in an antireligious context. Second, the findings in this study suggest that science education in college has a limited effect on the perceived plausibility of religions whose values and practices have become part of popular culture. This provides more nuances to the secularization debate around higher education and religion. Third, our findings show that students who agreed with the content of political education courses reported lower levels of perceived religious plausibility of Christianity. This finding implies a discriminatory religious policy on the part of the CPC towards certain religions.

Author Contributions: Conceptualization, M.L. and Y.L.; methodology, M.L.; formal analysis, M.L. and Y.L.; investigation, F.Y.; resources, F.Y.; data curation, M.L.; writing—original draft preparation, M.L. and Y.L.; writing—review and editing, M.L., Y.L. and F.Y.

Funding: This research received no external funding.

Conflicts of Interest: The authors declare no conflict of interest.

References

Caplovitz, David. 1977. *Religious Drop Outs: Apostasy among College Graduates*. Newcastle upon Tyne: SAGE.

Cherry, Conrad, Betty A. DeBerg, and Amanda Porterfield. 2001. *Religion on Campus: What Religion Really Means to Today's Undergraduates*. Chapel Hill: University of North Carolina Press.

Comte, Auguste. 2015. *A General View of Positivism*. Whitefish: Kessinger Publishing. First published 1865.

Ecklund, Elaine Howard, and Jerry Z. Park. 2009. Conflict between Religion and Science among Academic Scientists? *Journal for the Scientific Study of Religion* 48: 276–92. [CrossRef]

Evans, John H., and Michael S. Evans. 2008. Religion and Science: Beyond the Epistemological Conflict Narrative. *Annual Review of Sociology* 34: 87–105. [CrossRef]

Gross, Neil, and Solon Simmons. 2009. The Religiosity of American College and University Professors. *Sociology of Religion* 70: 101–29. [CrossRef]

Halman, Loek, and Veerle Draulans. 2006. How Secular Is Europe? *The British Journal of Sociology* 57: 263–88. [CrossRef] [PubMed]

Hill, Jonathan P. 2009. Higher Education as Moral Community: Institutional Influences on Religious Participation during College. *Journal for the Scientific Study of Religion* 48: 515–34. [CrossRef]

Hill, Jonathan P. 2011. Faith and Understanding: Specifying the Impact of Higher Education on Religious Belief. *Journal for the Scientific Study of Religion* 50: 533–51. [CrossRef]

Hunter, James Davison. 1983. *American Evangelicalism: Conservative Religion and the Quandary of Modernity*. New Brunswick: Rutgers University Press.

Huntington, Samuel P. 1993. *The Third Wave: Democratization in the Late Twentieth Century*. Norman: University of Oklahoma Press.

Ifeng. 2015. Diyu Liyong Zongjiao dui Gaoxiao Jinxing Shentou He Fangfan Xiaoyuan Chuanjiao (Resisting Religious Infiltration in Universities and Campus Ministry), 24 November. Available online: http://news.ifeng.com/a/20151124/46375631_0.shtml (accessed on 17 May 2018).

Ji, Mason. 2015. Science and Technology in Modern China: A Historical and Strategic Perspective on State Power. *The Yale Review of International Studies*. Available online: http://yris.yira.org/essays/1551 (accessed on 2 May 2018).

Johnson, Daniel Carson. 1997. Formal Education vs. Religious Belief: Soliciting New Evidence with Multinomial Logit Modeling. *Journal for the Scientific Study of Religion* 36: 231–46. [CrossRef]

Johnson, Ian. 2017a. *The Souls of China: The Return of Religion after Mao*. New York: Knopf Doubleday.

Johnson, Ian. 2017b. Is a Buddhist Group Changing China? Or Is China Changing It? *The New York Times*, June 24. Available online: https://www.nytimes.com/2017/06/24/world/asia/china-buddhism-fo-guang-shan.html (accessed on 17 May 2018).

Johnson, Ian. 2018. What a Buddhist Monk Taught Xi Jinping. *The New York Times*. January 20. Available online: https://www.nytimes.com/2017/03/24/opinion/sunday/chinas-communists-embrace-religion.html (accessed on 17 May 2018).

Laliberté, André. 2011. Religion and the State in China: The Limits of Institutionalization. *Journal of Current Chinese Affairs* 40: 3–15.

Lehman, Edward C., and Donald W. Shriver. 1968. Academic Discipline as Predictive of Faculty Religiosity. *Social Forces* 47: 171–82. [CrossRef]

Mayrl, Damon, and Jeremy E. Uecker. 2011. Higher Education and Religious Liberalization among Young Adults. *Social Forces* 90: 181–208. [CrossRef] [PubMed]

McFarland, Michael J., Bradley R. E. Wright, and David L. Weakliem. 2011. Educational Attainment and Religiosity: Exploring Variations by Religious Tradition. *Sociology of Religion* 72: 166–88. [CrossRef]

McMorrow, R. W. 2015. Membership in the Communist Party of China: Who Is Being Admitted and How? *JSTOR Daily*. December 19. Available online: https://daily.jstor.org/communist-party-of-china/ (accessed on 17 May 2018).

O'Brien, Timothy L., and Shiri Noy. 2015. Traditional, Modern, and Post-Secular Perspectives on Science and Religion in the United States. *American Sociological Review* 80: 92–115. [CrossRef]

People's Daily. 2014. Yisilanjiao Bu Zhuzhang Baoli Kongbu (Islam Is Not Equal to Violent Terriorism). *People's Daily*. November 8. Available online: http://opinion.people.com.cn/n/2014/0811/c1003-25438524.html (accessed on 2 May 2018).

People's Daily. 2016. Ruhe Renshi He Kandai Xinjiang Zongjiao Yu Jiduan Zhuyi (How to View Religion and Extremism in Xinjiang). *People's Daily*. June 3. Available online: http://opinion.people.com.cn/n1/2016/0603/c1003-28408089.html (accessed on 2 May 2018).

Reimer, Sam. 2010. Higher Education and Theological Liberalism: Revisiting the Old Issue. *Sociology of Religion* 71: 393–408. [CrossRef]

Ruiter, Stijn, and Frank van Tubergen. 2009. Religious Attendance in Cross-National Perspective: A Multilevel Analysis of 60 Countries. *American Journal of Sociology* 115: 863–95. [CrossRef]

Sacerdote, Bruce, and Edward L. Glaeser. 2001. Education and Religion. Working Paper 8080. Cambridge, MA, USA: National Bureau of Economic Research.

Scheitle, Christopher P. 2011. U.S. College Students' Perception of Religion and Science: Conflict, Collaboration, or Independence? A Research Note. *Journal for the Scientific Study of Religion* 50: 175–86. [CrossRef]

Schwadel, Philip. 2011. The Effects of Education on Americans' Religious Practices, Beliefs, and Affiliations. *Review of Religious Research* 53: 161–82. [CrossRef]

Schwadel, Philip. 2015. Explaining Cross-National Variation in the Effect of Higher Education on Religiosity. *Journal for the Scientific Study of Religion* 54: 402–18. [CrossRef]

Stark, Rodney, and Roger Finke. 2000. *Acts of Faith: Explaining the Human Side of Religion*. Berkeley: University of California Press.

Uecker, Jeremy E., Mark D. Regnerus, and Margaret L. Vaaler. 2007. Losing My Religion: The Social Sources of Religious Decline in Early Adulthood. *Social Forces* 85: 1667–92. [CrossRef]

Vala, Carsten T. 2012. Protestant Christianity and Civil Society in Authoritarian China. The Impact of Official Churches and Unregistered "Urban Churches" on Civil Society Development in China in the 2000s. *China Perspectives* 2012: 43–52.

Wang, Xiuhua, and Jeremy E. Uecker. 2017. Education, Religious Commitment, and Religious Tolerance in Contemporary China. *Review of Religious Research* 59: 157–82. [CrossRef]

Weber, Max. 1993. *The Sociology of Religion*. Boston: Beacon Press. First published 1922.

Xie, Ying, Yunping Tong, and Fenggang Yang. 2017. Does Ideological Education in China Suppress Trust in Religion and Foster Trust in Government. *Religions* 8: 94. [CrossRef]

Xinhuanet. 2017. Guanche Luoshi Zhongyang Guanyu Zongjiao Gongzuo Zhongda Juece Bushu Jingyan Jiaoliuhui Zhaokai (A Conference on the Implementation of the Party's Decision on Religious Works). *Xinhuanet*. September 11. Available online: http://www.xinhuanet.com/politics/2017-09/11/c_1121645261.htm (accessed on 17 May 2018).

Yang, Fenggang. 2006. The Red, Black, and Grey Markets of Religion in China. *Sociological Quarterly* 47: 93–122. [CrossRef]

Yang, Fenggang. 2015. The Other Chinese Miracle. *Association of Religion Data Archives*. December 1. Available online: http://globalplus.thearda.com/globalplus-religion-in-china/ (accessed on 2 May 2018).

religions

MDPI

Article

The Gendered Space of the "Oriental Vatican"—Zi-ka-wei, the French Jesuits and the Evolution of Papal Diplomacy

Wei Mo [1,2]

[1]   Centre for Studies in Religion and Society, University of Victoria, 3800 Finnerty Road,
      Victoria, BC V8P 5C2, Canada; weimo@uvic.ca
[2]   College of Humanities and Communications, Shanghai Normal University, No.100 Guilin Rd.,
      Shanghai 200234, China

Received: 3 August 2018; Accepted: 11 September 2018; Published: 14 September 2018

Abstract: In a global context, the story of the Jesuit compound in Shanghai, since its establishment by French Jesuits in 1847, reflected not only conflicts between rival powers in Europe but also the fight for their interests in the Eastern world. The female Catholic orders at the east bank of Zi-ka-wei compound provided a unique window approaching the complexity. The Pope, who was stuck without legal status in the Vatican after 1861, was also seeking the chance to save the authority of the Church in the face of questions regarding the extent of his temporal power and the status of Rome in the context of Italian unification. As in the Reformation, a break-through in the east seemed to offer a solution for losses in Europe. However, the Jesuits to the East in the late 19th century were not only troops working and fighting on behalf of the Pope; their identities under the French Protectorate added complexity to an already complicated story involving not just the Church, but the course of world history. Locating the Jesuit-affiliated women and children hospice in the French Concession but outside the Zi-ka-wei compound was a result of how different conflicts played themselves out.

Keywords: Jesuits; French Protectorate; female orders; Zi-ka-wei; Roman Question

1. Introduction

This paper has four objectives. First, it seeks to explain the site selection of a major Jesuit compound in Shanghai after the Jesuits' restoration and return to China in the new nineteenth century global context. Second, it analyzes the compound's carefully planned layout, which was based on gender and the division of various responsibilities. Third, this paper highlights the connection between the French Religious Protectorate in China and the prosperity of the Catholic compound and illustrates that the decline in French power and instability in Europe provided the Pope with more responsibilities for the Catholic mission's agenda in China. Fourth, the paper analyzes how a particular female Catholic institution came to be located where it was.

From the map of Zi-ka-wei (Xu Jia Hui, 徐家匯) Area in 1937 (Figure 1), we can see before us a mature and complete Catholic compound with fully functioning institutions under Jesuit leadership. Associated with the Jesuits in the compound were female religious of the Helpers of the Holy Souls, the Présentadines, the Josephines and the Discalced Carmelite Nuns. The name of this area, Zi-ka-wei, is a Romanized spelling of the pronunciation of Xu Jia Hui in Shanghai dialect. Such a completed compound was a symbol of the gendered organization of Chinese Catholicism had, since its establishment in the mid-19th century. A Chinese Catholic constituency, made up of survivors of several decades of the court repression, was an unalloyed blessing for the Church. Zi-ka-wei stood as a model, showing that a uniform structure for the Chinese Catholic church was not a distant prospect.

Yet, while the Pope tried to restructure the missions, another European power—the French—usurped the Pope's supervisory role over the whole of Catholicism in China.

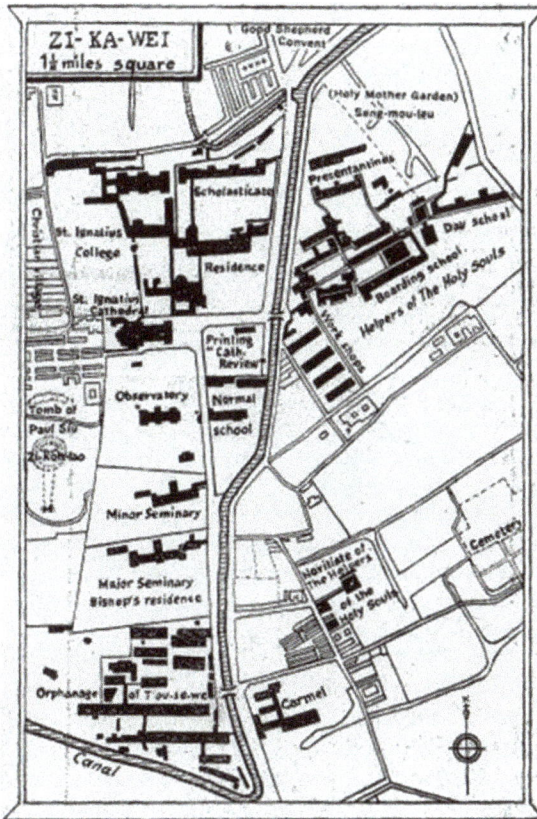

Figure 1. Map of Zi-ka-wei, see (Song 2005).

In a global context, the story of the Jesuit compound over the next century reflected not only conflicts between rival powers in Europe but also the fight for their interests in the Eastern world. The Pope, who was stuck without legal status in the Vatican after 1861, was also seeking the chance to save the authority of the Church in the face of questions regarding the extent of his temporal power and the status of Rome in the context of Italian unification. As in the Reformation, a break-through in the east seemed to offer a solution for losses in Europe. However, the Jesuits to the East in the late 19th century were not only troops working and fighting on behalf of the Pope; their identities under the French Protectorate added complexity to an already complicated story involving not just the Church, but the course of world history.

Those missionaries who arrived in the 1930s praised the magnificence of the Zi-ka-wei compound as the "Oriental Vatican". There are various ways to approach this issue; here I want to throw light on the gendered layout of this Catholic institution by examining the political and diplomatic developments that were taking place. In particular, I want to consider the reason the Hospice of the Sisters of the Good Shepherd (善牧院) was not situated inside Jesuit Zi-ka-wei compound.

2. Site Selection and Structure of the Jesuit Compound in Shanghai

The building of the Catholic compound in Zi-ka-wei by the "New Jesuits"[1] of the order's Paris Province[2] began in 1847.[3] At this time, there were already Catholic communities in other parts of Shanghai, such as those anchored in the Jingyi Tang (敬一堂) and St. Joseph Cathedral, both in the Chinese in the Qing-controlled parts of the city (華界). The French Jesuits could have established a compound based on one of those; however, they were determined to construct an independent compound from scratch, without reliance on the local community. Moreover, the Jesuits would never take a risk on such a huge project without initially having detailed plans that met their specific purposes. Their thoroughgoing selection of an appropriate site finally settled on the southwest end of Zi-ka-wei, the suburban area of Shanghai. The reasons for their selection were multifold, but can be generalized into five major points.

The first and most superficial reason was stated in their official claim of the necessity of a new residence. They argued that the humidity of the former compound, situated in the rural area, Hengtang of Qingpu County (青浦縣橫塘), discomforted the majority of the Jesuits from France. Their inability to the dampness in the old place motivated their expansion outwards.

Secondly, they felt that the new site should have convenient access to the central part of the city and especially to the French Concession. With the help of the natural rivers and artificial canals, Zi-ka-wei took advantage of its geographical features for the purpose of city access. Thus, "Hui" (匯, which represents the confluence of multiple waterways) was also retained in the name of the delta place and the compound.

More importantly, however, the fact that there was a remnant Catholic population in this specific local area was decisive. The Xu clan, a strong local Catholic family, had been residing there since the 16th century because their famous ancestor Xu Guangqi (徐光啓, 1562–1633), who had been a native of Shanghai, was buried in Zi-ka-wei where his Catholic descendants kept the tomb. Xu Guangqi, who had been a Grand Secretary (文淵閣大學士) in the Ming (明) court, was a significant helper and promoter of Matteo Ricci (利瑪竇, 1553–1610) and the first of the Jesuit "generation of Giants"[4] Therefore, the words "Xu Jia" (徐家, which literally means the Xu's family) was also kept in the name of the Catholic compound, indicating the family's pride at on being descended from the very first group of converts.[5]

Fourth: related to the previous point, was the fact that the Jesuits intended to make the new compound the scientific centre of the Jiang-nan religion. Xu Guangqi himself had used the site of the new compound for agriculture experiment that formed a base for his major agricultural treatise *the Nongzhengquanshu* or "Complete treatise on agricultural administration" (《農政全書》). In addition, Xu Guangqi himself had extensive mathematical and astronomical research interests and initiated a major translation project in these area. Such interests made the Zi-ka-wei site highly suitable for the

---

[1] The Jesuits had been suppressed globally by the papal brief *Dominus ac Redemptor* (21 July, 1773). After seven decades, the order was restored. To designate the two generations before and after the restoration, the term "New Jesuit" was invented, but it most often refers to those who worked after the restoration in particular. See the entry term "China" (Worcester 2017, p. 164).

[2] As a territorial division of the Catholic Church in apostolic vicariates or perfectures in the 19th century, Jesuits ultimately served in nine different areas, led by Shanghai staffed by French Jesuits of the Paris province. See (Gernet 1985, p. 17).

[3] It took some time after the restoration of the Society of Jesus in 1814 before New Jesuits were sent to China. After multiple requests by Chinese Christians, the first three French Jesuits led by Claude Gotteland (南格祿, 1803–1856) finally arrived in China in 1842. They arrived in Hengtang at first and built their residence and 5 years later, they were able to move into the central part of Shanghai. It was in 1847 that construction on the Jesuit Residence in Zi-ka-wei was started.

[4] "Generation of Giants" was a specified term for the first generation of Jesuits who worked in China from 1582 to 1775, see (Dunne 1962).

[5] On the relationship between the New Jesuits and the remnant old communities of Catholics who had survived since the eighteenth century, "Given the relative paucity of European personnel, it is important to note that the number of Catholic faithful, in spite of the periodic persecutions, had increased by about 100,000 by the middle of the nineteenth century. At the same time, priestly duties were performed primarily by the Chinese clergy. As a matter of fact, Chinese Catholics had developed their own patterns of church life." See (d'Elia 1927, p. 50).

New Jesuit scientific centre including in particular the astronomical Observatory and the Museum of Natural History then were planned for construction.

Fifthly and perhaps the most critically, the relatively low cost of land in this suburb, to some extent ensured the scale and potential expansion of the compound both immediately and into the future. Certainly, the donation of land by the local Catholics also mitigated the burden for the Church. At the same time, the "official" contribution from the French side was more imperial. The Sino-French treaty (Treaty of Huangpu 《黃埔條約》, 1844) allowed the French to establish churches, hospices, schools, and cemeteries in five designated ports, including Shanghai and Tianjin, which were already opened for foreign residence, trade, and naval vessels by the previous British treaties. The French were granted in their own treaty immunity from prosecution by Chinese authorities (extra-territoriality, or more precisely, consular jurisdiction)[6]. Despite numerous occurances in the 1840s and 1850s of missionaries going outside the designated areas, French authorities never attempted to enforce restrictions on the missionaries[7]. The continuing pattern of the emerging French Religious Protectorate over Roman Catholics (as laid out in the French Treaty of Tianjin[8] 《天津條約》, 1858 and the Sino-French Convention of Beijing[9] 《北京條約》, 1860) helped the missionaries to overstep the boundaries of where they were permitted to travel. The Protectorate prioritized the land used for French religious orders at a lower price. The diplomatic and military muscle of the French was what the French Jesuits were desperate for.

French Jesuit-run Jiang-nan, covering two provinces and including Shanghai centered by Zi-ka-wei, had by far the largest investments (6,924,303 gold dollars, or about seventy million French francs)- over three and a half times the next in line. Its expenses were also high, because of its size and its many priests and costly institutions. The selection of Zi-ka-wei as the centre of the Jesuit presence in China, and perhaps even in the whole of East Asia, was acceptable by all sides in the mid-late 19th century.

3. The Compound and Protectorate under the Sino-French Conventions

The practice based on the treaties was critical in holding together the transnational pretensions of the French Religious Protectorate. When venturing beyond the five major ports, all the Catholic missionaries[10] were formally presented to the Chinese world as protégés of the French state. Increasingly, French authorities called on the missions to establish more schools where the French language and French learning would be taught. They were also encouraged to found more hospitals, which the missions would manage but which would not be staffed only with religious personnel, as a way of displaying French science to China. Zi-ka-wei under the supervision and leadership of French Jesuits was the most vivid example of the expansion of Catholic missionary interests in the Qing (清) Empire.

---

[6] Like the British and Americans, the French were supposed to be confined to the environs of these five treaty ports. However, the French treaty specified that, if a French person violated this restriction and "proceeded far into the interior", they should be conducted unharmed to the French consul in the nearest treaty port. Although it made no mention of missionaries, they were the object of interest here. See (China. Hai guan zong shui wu si shu 1917, pp. 771–813).

[7] Restrictions embodied in a formal Sino-Franco treaty and agreed to in discussion about a Chinese toleration pronouncement. See (Gernet 1985, p. 83).

[8] Under the Treaty of Tianjin, special passports were issued as envisioned in Articles 8 and 13. See Tableau des Traité, Conventions et arrangements divers, relatifs au Protectorat de La Franc sur les chrétientés en Chine. 10 May 1900, file box 59. Archives Diplomatiques de Nantes, documents of the French legation in Beijing. Paris and (Cannone 1987, p. 116).

[9] The Beijing Convention, another Franco-Chinese treaty, was imposed in 1860 under the threat of military continued occupation of the imperial capital, additions were made that opened the door to endless complications and conflict. Article 6 of the convention treated Christians and their religion. Part of the reason that the article led to so much controversy was that it treated property, never an easy topic. Another part of the problem was the ambiguity engendered by differing texts. The French and Chinese version of Article 6 of the Beijing Convention were conspicuously divergent in phraseology and even in content.

[10] Missionaries as Italian, Belgian, German, Austrian, Spanish, Portuguese, Dutch, and Irish, as well as French.

Reviewing the whole structure from the map, the Zi-ka-wei compound was generally divided by the Zhaojia Canal (肇嘉), which operated as the central axis between the west and east banks. The layout was strictly arranged according to the division of responsibilities by gender. The west bank was lined up from the top to the bottom with St. Ignace College, the Scholasticate, the Jesuit residence, the Zi-ka-wei library, the St. Ignatius Cathedral, the astronomical Observatory, the Museum of Natural History, the Major and Minor Seminaries and the T'ou-sè-wè Orphanage[11] (土山灣孤兒院). All of these institutions were without exception operated by and for male members of the compound, while the east side was totally reserved for female members from the Carmelite Convent, the Notre Dame complex and the Hospice of the Sisters of the Good Shepherd. Most of the supporting staff were French missionaries. By virtue of their pivotal position under French power, the political fact of being French was the most prominent asset in the Zi-ka-wei compound. How curious it was that France, which was such a model of modern nationalism, should have sponsored in China such a subversion of the sacred relationship of citizen and the country. Although French power in China was a source of contention with other states, which openly complained to the Pope especially during the peak decades (1840s–1914) of French power, the response from the Vatican was one of indifference. Between the Pope and the French there was "a sort of tacit mandate" entrusting the defense of Catholic interests in China to France. The long official French memo continued:

> Apart from that, [there is] no right, no strict obligation in the basis of our protectorate. Nothing binds Catholic missionaries to our operation. If all, from whatever countries they hail, have gave up to now resorted to French protection, it is because this protection was the best to be offered them, without distinction of nationalities, strongly enough organized to be efficacious with the Chinese authorities and constituting an assemblage of advantages substantial enough to connect the missionaries to it. Thus our protectorate became a tradition, and the beneficiaries have never had reason to complain about it.[12]

In the 1930s, a grand Catholic compound was "honored" as the "Oriental Vatican"[13] frequently. In addition, the following reports from the Church followed this trend without any hesitation. Interestingly, however, a more accurate comparison might have been between the Vatican and either Goa,[14] the entry point of Jesuits in India that developed into the Jesuits' mission centre in 16th century Asia, or Macau,[15] the long serving base of operation for the missions in China and Japan during 17th and 18th century. What, then, was the intention behind the compliment? An inconspicuous institution, the Hospice of the Sisters of the Good Shepherd, standing atop the east bank of the compound, might offer an explanation as the Hospice itself was also established as a refraction of a trend in global history.

---

[11] Tòou-sè-wè was also a Romanized spelling of the pronunciation in Shanghai dialect.

[12] Crise de notre Protectorat religieux en Chine (1886–1892). Archives Diplomatiques de Nantes, documents of the French legation in Beijing, file box 59, which states "The memorandum is not dated. Internal evidence suggests that it was written about 1898. Since one German-staffed vicariate had already departed from the French Protectorate, the reference to 'all' missionaries was not exact." Quoted in (Young 2013, p. 42).

[13] See (Xiao 1997, p. 45).

[14] Goa was the beginning point of the early Jesuits as they expanded into the Indian subcontinent, and later it was the seat of the first Jesuit province to be established in Asia. Francis Xavier led the way in 1542 at the request of the Portuguese king, under whose patronage (the Padroado) the Pope had entrusted the mission. Jesuits ministered to the native population in Goa and its environs, quickly becoming a base for missions throughout India. See (Pfister 1932, pp. 95–102).

[15] Many notable Jesuits spent time in Macau. This territory was established by the Portuguese in 1557 for the purpose of exploration and trade in China. Despite its small size, its prime location on a tip of a peninsula on the southern Chinese coastline facilitated rapid population growth. Most early inhabitants were Portuguese merchants and their families; they were rapidly joined by various religious orders, including the Jesuits. The Christian population more than doubled, from 400 to 1000, in the first twenty-five years of the settlement's existence. A Jesuit residence was built in 1565 and Jesuit official visitor Alessandro Valignano (範禮安, 1539–1606) arrived in 1577. Ten months spent awaiting favorable weather for sailing to Japan allowed him time to observe, evaluate and establish the policy of cultural accommodation. Michele Ruggieri (羅明堅, 1543–1607) arrived in Macau two years later, and Matteo Ricci in 1583. They began studying the Chinese language and preparing for their historic mission work there. See (Brockey 2007).

4. Female Orders in Zi-ka-wei as an Echo of Catholic Evangelistic Energy

Within Catholicism, groups of women, renouncing marriage and living either with their birth-family or in small self-organized groups, formed communities centered on a chapel, taught children prayers and doctrine, helped the sick and the dying, baptized babies, and cared for their local chapel. Such women became known in China as Virgins (tongzhennü 童貞女). They would eventually be found in most parts of the country, though with considerable local variation. These women attracted the attention of the missionaries, Jesuits mainly, who were reestablishing themselves in Jiang-nan area (south of the Yangtze River, 江南地區) after the Opium Wars.[16]

The formal rules for women's social behavior could be extremely restrictive in late imperial and under the Republic of China. Female leadership or presence at any mixed-gender setting outside the family could be tarred with the brush of potential sexual promiscuity. Yet it is also the case that leadership roles for Chinese women in religious practice were not unheard of. Female spirit mediums and shamans were common in folk religious practice among the Chinese. Nonetheless, the returning Jesuits were distinctly hostile to the fact that they found women exercising leadership in remnant Catholic communities from the strong Catholic tradition of male supremacy in the Church matters. It would seem that this initial hostility of the returning missionaries toward this assertiveness by Catholic women in the Jiang-nan arose as much as anything from an anxiety about the difficulty of controlling these hidden Catholic groups. French missionaries asserted their authority over the Virgins without abolishing the practice. Already in the 18th century, they had rules, approved by Rome, for the work and living circumstances of these women. It was in part the evident departures from those rules in Jiang-nan that alarmed the returning Jesuits. One tactic was to reorganize the Virgins in conventual religious congregations, with various designations: the Présentadines (Association of the Presentation of Blessed Virgin, 貞女獻堂會), the Josephines (若瑟會), and so on.

As we have seen, the east bank of the Catholic Compound in Zi-ka-wei was designated for female religious congregations. The Notre Dame complex, under the management of the Helpers of the Holy Souls (Auxiliatrices des âmes du Purgatoire, 拯望會), who were French sisters invited by the Jesuits from Paris, had the most popularity and fame. When the Jesuits had just launched their plan of establishing the Zi-ka-wei compound, the Helpers were their first option for taking on lead administration over the indigenous Catholic female orders, whose service and training were less organized but more practical for local residents. The Notre Dame complex was initiated in 1855 under the leadership of the Helpers and grew gradually by increasing the number of affiliated institutions with comprehensive divisions and different emphases[17]. The achievements of the Virgins movement[18] were a valuable addition to Catholic evangelizing efforts. A Jesuit missionary expressed his appreciation of the female institutions:

> The Virgins, because of their instruction, are especially in ascendancy. These fine girls, who have renounced marriage to serve the cause of religion and have spent years studying, render us immense services. Chinese women, who never engage in studies, look on them as oracles. In the Catholic communities where they [the Virgins] sojourn, they train girls, preach, catechize, lead prayers, prepare the ille [sic] for death, keep the church clean, etc.

---

[16] Wrote the chronicler of the Jesuits' return to Jiang-nan: "In more than one village, a Virgin had usurped the functions of administrator. Almost everywhere they led the chanting of prayers at the church, gave pious readings, and admonished delinquents." See (La Servière 1925). The English translation was quoted from (Young 2013, p. 20).

[17] Some of the unmarried Jiang-nan laywomen were encouraged to organise themselves into an indigenous religious association. Virgins of the Presentation did not take the vows and were under the authority of the French mission superior to instruct and form the girls. The French sisters took charge of girl orphans and pupils at Notre Dame. In this context, it can be argued that the Virgins were coming into contact and working with foreign sisters and becoming attracted to a life in a communal religious environment. See (Tiedemann 2010, pp. 587–99).

[18] Direct Catholic evangelization among women continued to be undertaken by the "institutes of virgins", namely unwed Chinese Catholic women who had dedicated their lives to God and the mission, as well as by the emerging diocesan-level Chinese sisterhood. See (Tiedemann 2010, pp. 319–21).

They are generally from the thirties to forty years old. They always have with them one or two orphans, who follow them. We give to one Virgin the equivalent of eight fr. per month. With that they have to feed themselves.[19]

In addition to the European missionary sisters, the first group of nuns arrived in 1869. In that year, French Discalced Carmelite Nuns established their convent at the opposite side of Tòu-sè-wè across the Canal. In contrast to the Virgins and the Helpers, the nuns led rather more cloistered lives and were primarily involved in the contemplative apostolate. Curiously, the Hospice of the Sisters of the Good Shepherd was settled half a century later in 1933 and located at the rim of far north end of the whole compound.

This new institution relatively distant from the core part of the compound would become a window to disclose bigger trends in international relations as well as in mission strategy. I will turn now to consider some of those larger developments in Europe and in China.

5. The Pope's Absence in Global Instabilities, and the Fall of Ecclesiastical France

By the year 1870, the Notre Dame complex was running successfully under the Virgins and the Carmelite Sisters. Yet this year was also a turning point in global history. The Franco-Prussian War (1870–1871) resulted in the collapse of the Second French Empire and in the formation of both the French Third Republic and the German Empire[20]. The unification of Italy occurred in the same year, due to Rome and the Papal States losing the protection and force of French troops since 1861 who were engaged with the Prussian Army. The dispute regarding the "temporal power" of the Pope and the status of Rome as a civil territory in the context of Italian Resorgimento (Italian unification) was named the Roman Question (Italian: Questione romana)[21]. In China, the Tianjin Massacre (Tianjin Church Incident 天津教案) took place, becoming one of the most important anti-Catholic incidents of the late Qing dynasty, involving attacks on French Catholic priests and nuns, violent belligerence from French diplomats, and armed foreign intervention in Tianjin.

Before 1870, Catholics in France were a major financial supporter of the global growth of Catholic missions in the 19th century. Although there were funding branches throughout various European countries, from 1822–1872, two-thirds of all funds for global Catholic mission work came from French contributions. The rate of departures of Catholic missionaries from France steadily increased from

---

[19] R.G. Tiederman indicates that the Catholic Virgins were generally supported by their families, implying a certain affluence, but that others might support themselves by labor, like textile production, or might receive mission subsidies. See (Menegon 2009, pp. 332–42).

[20] With the French garrison gone, widespread public demonstrations demanded that the Italian government take Rome. But Rome remained under French protection on paper, therefore an attack would still have been regarded as an act of war against the French Empire. Furthermore, although Prussia was at war with France, it had gone to war in an uneasy alliance with the Catholic South German states that it had fought against (alongside Italy) just four years earlier. It was only after the surrender of Napoleon and his army at the Battle of Sedan the situation changed radically. The French Emperor was deposed and forced into exile. The best French units had been captured by the Germans, who quickly followed up their success at Sedan by marching on Paris. Faced with a pressing need to defend its capital with its remaining forces, the new French government was clearly not in a military position to retaliate against Italy. In any event, the new government was far less sympathetic to the Holy See and did not possess the political will to protect the Pope's position. Finally, with the French government on a more democratic footing and the seemingly harsh German peace terms becoming public knowledge, Italian public opinion shifted sharply away from the German side in favour of France. With that development, the prospect of a conflict on the Italian peninsula provoking foreign intervention all but vanished. See (Howard 1991, p. 123).

[21] The capture of Rome (Italian: Presa di Roma) on 20 September 1870 was the final event of the long process of Italian unification known as the Risorgimento, marking both the final defeat of the Papal States under Pope Pius IX and the unification of the Italian peninsula under King Victor Emmanuel II of the House of Savoy. The capture of Rome ended the approximate 1116-year reign (AD 754 to 1870) of the Papal States under the Holy See and is today widely memorialized throughout Italy with the street name in virtually every town of any size. As nationalism swept the Italian Peninsula in the 19th century, efforts to unify Italy were blocked in part by the Papal States, which ran through the middle of the peninsula and included the ancient capital of Rome. The Papal States were able to fend off efforts to conquer them largely through the pope's influence over the leaders of stronger European powers such as France and Austria. When Rome was eventually taken, the Italian government reportedly intended to let the pope keep the part of Rome west of the Tiber called the Leonine City as a small remaining Papal State, but Pius IX refused. One week after entering Rome, the Italian troops had taken the entire city save for the Apostolic Palace; the inhabitants of the city then voted to join Italy. See (Schapiro 1921, p. 160).

1830 on, including priests, brothers, and members of female religious orders. In China, where French missionaries had already been a substantial fraction, the French soon became a strong majority of all Catholic missionaries—as much as seventy percent or more. When, in 1870, the first Vatican Council defined papal infallibility and affirmed the immediate jurisdiction of the pope throughout the Catholic Church, anticlerical zeal was stoked in France and elsewhere. The Franco-Prussian War saw the capture of Napoleon III himself by Prussian forces and later his departure into exile. In Paris, the short-lived Commune seemed for a time to revive the Terror of 1793–1794 and its violent anticlericalism. In May 1871 the archbishop of Paris was executed, as were five Jesuits. The establishment of the Third Republic, with its deal of a muscular laïcité, would lead, in 1880, to a decree dissolving the Society of Jesus in France. Of the nearly 3000 French Jesuits at the time, approximately a third were young Jesuits in formation. For them, houses of studies were established outside France, on the English island of Jersey, and in Belgium and Spain. In France, some of the Jesuit colleges continued to function with Jesuit staffing, but with ownership of property and governance of the institutions legally conferred on diocesan priests or laity.

From 1880 to 1914, most French Jesuits took a dim view of the French Republic and pessimistic view of the modern world. Many longed for restoration of the French monarchy. However, Pope Leo XIII (1878–1903) called for French Catholics to accept a republican form of civil government, a call that fell on largely deaf ears, Jesuit and others. In his 1891 encyclical *Rerum novarum*[22], Leo appealed for fair wages and humane working conditions for workers, for the natural right of workers to unionize to be respected, and for the state to intervene in the ceremony to protect workers from unfair treatment. Action Populaire, founded by Jesuits in 1903 in Reims, echoed Leo's response to the Industrial Revolution, but many French Jesuits sided with the wealthy elite, not with the poor and workers. When the Jewish military officer Alfred Dreyfus[23] (1859–1935) was accused of treason, more than a few French Jesuits embraced a tirade of anti-Semitic polemics[24]. The French 1901 law on associations made it very difficult for a religious order to function in France; the Society of Jesus became one of many French orders living and working in exile[25].

However, the failure of the French in the war with Prussia and the unification of Italy sparked the entry of both Germany and Italy into competition for the role of Catholic protection, while the constant stream of Church Incidents definitively weakened the French for the rest of the century and beyond. The French Catholic compound of Zi-ka-wei as the centre of Catholicism in China quietly moved to prevent upheaval. The expansion that took place remained within the inner structure of the existing layout, however.

The spring of 1900 inflamed China and grabbed the world's attention, due to the Boxer Rebellion[26], which led to the intervention of eight-foreign powers (八國聯軍). The climactic events of the Boxer

---

[22] *Rerum novarum* (from its opening words, with the direct translation of the Latin meaning "of the new things"), or *Rights and Duties of Capital and Labor*, was an encyclical issued by Pope Leo XIII on 15 May 1891. It was an open letter, passed to all Catholic Patriarchs, Primates, Archbishops and bishops, that addressed the condition of the working classes. It discussed the relationships and mutual duties between labor and capital, as well as government and its citizens. Of primary concern was the need for some amelioration of "The misery and wretchedness pressing so unjustly on the majority of the working class." It supported the rights of labor to form unions, rejected socialism and unrestricted capitalism, whilst affirming the right to private property. See (Molony and Thompson 2006, pp. 148–49).

[23] Alfred Dreyfus was a French Jewish artillery officer whose trial and conviction in 1894 on charges of treason became one of the tensest political dramas in modern French history with a wide echo in all Europe. Known today as the Dreyfus Affair, the incident eventually ended with Dreyfus's complete exoneration.

[24] See the entry "France" (Worcester 2017, p. 310).

[25] The big crisis in the relations with the new Republic came already in 1880. They weren't exactly forbidden to be Jesuits, but they also not recognized as a legal association. Perhaps most significantly, they were banned from teaching and their educational institutions were abolished. Many therefore went abroad to work, and those that stayed just had the status of private citizens. A particular interesting point was that in the 1878 nearly one third of all Jesuits were French, and an even larger proportion of Jesuit missionaries were French. See (Lacouture 1991, p. 250).

[26] Recent scholarship has preferred the term Boxer Uprising (leaving open the question of the relationship between the movement and the government), or the Boxer War (at its climax, there was a war between the Qing court and an assemblage of eight allied countries). See (Waley-Cohen 2006; Brook and Blue 1999).

summer overwhelmed the French Religious Protectorate. It had already been somewhat battered even before the Boxers: by the German defection, by vociferous Italian discontent with a French-run system, by possible undermining from other "spheres of influence" (could French protection of Catholics persist in areas of the country where some other foreign power claimed priority in all things?)[27], and by doubts within the French establishment regarding the legality of it all. One of the consequences of the Boxer Uprising was the sustained critical evaluation of the missionary enterprise. Would the limits of French protection, so evident in the Boxer Rebellion, vitiate its future in the eyes of its crucial constituency, the Catholic missionaries?

Following the Boxer Rebellion, Émile Combes, an anti-clericalist and a French statesman as a former member of a leftist cabinet, began pushing an anti-clerical agenda and guided the initial steps towards the full legal separation of church and state of France, which was finally passed in the year 1905. Would the French Protectorate survive the Separation Law of 1905?[28] The French consul-general in Shanghai warned against the possible consequences of weakening officialdom in both ends of the Protectorate. When the tensions between France and the Vatican were served since the beginning of the 20th century, the foreign minister instructed his representative in China that French rights in China were based on treaties and that it remained no change in existing instructions.[29] As an echo to this political blow, the French Religious Protectorate in China was challenged by both Germany and Italy. At the same time, France persisted in trying to assert its Religious Protectorate and in seeking the adherence to it of the Catholic bishops, whose foreign nationality was essential to the Protectorate's operations and usefulness. French authorities in China also continued to press Chinese officials for the protection of Catholic missions and the punishment of anyone who inflicted injury on the missions. The new bishop in Beijing assured the Vatican in early 1906 that the French minister in China was instructed by Paris to continue protection for all Catholic missionaries and their work, in accordance with France's traditional policy.[30] However, the French system was under challenge, as Catholic voices for a new dispensation became more audible. In addition, at this point until the 1911 Revolution (辛亥革命), which resulted in the overthrown of the Qing and the establishment of the Republic of China, the violence that had targeted Chinese Christians meant the protectorate's intervention with the Chinese authorities was no longer salient. On the eve of the 1911 Revolution and in its immediate aftermath, although the French legation reaffirmed its consular instruction that "France was still continuing to assume the protection of Catholic missions in China, without discriminating by nationality"[31], missionaries faced danger to their persons and property most often due to more general social disorder and the prevalence of banditry.

Not long thereafter, the assassination of Archduke Franz Ferdinand of Austria, heir to the throne of Austria-Hungary, by Yugoslav nationalist Gavrilo Princip in Sarajevo on 28 June 1914 triggered World War I. The assassination set off a diplomatic crisis when Austria-Hungary delivered an ultimatum to the Kingdom of Serbia and, as a result, entangled international alliances, formed over the previous decades, were invoked. Within weeks the major powers were at war, and the conflict soon spread around the world. The war drew in all the world's great economic powers, assembled in two opposing alliances: The Allies (based on the Triple Entente of the Russian Empire, the French Third Republic, and the Greater Britain) versus the Central Powers of Germany and Austria-Hungary. Although Italy

---

[27] Pichon, 3 June 1899: "the creation of spheres of influence inevitably runs counter to [the protection of missions] . . . It will become less and less easy to give indications to the Chinese government of possible military interventions on our part to bring justice to our protégé." *Documents diplomatiques francaus (1871–1914)*, 1st series, vol. 16, p. 336. The English translation was quoted in (Young 2013, p. 79).

[28] Louis Ratard (acting concul-general) to Delcassé, Shanghai, 27 July 1901: Archives du Ministère des Affairs Etrangères, n.s. 327.

[29] Delcassé to French ambassador in Constantinople and the French ministers in Beijing and Cairo (n.d): Archives du Ministère des Affairs Etrangères, n.s. 312.

[30] S. Jarlin to Gotti (Propaganda perfect), Beijing, 13 February 1906: Pro A, vol. 490, p. 237r.

[31] Beauvais (consul in Guangzhou) to Conty (minister in Beijing), #75, Guangzhou, 20 March 1913: Archives Diplomatiques de Nantes, documents of the French legation in Beijing, file box 59.

had been a member of the Triple Alliance alongside Germany and Austria-Hungary, it did not join the Central Powers, but entered on the side of the Entente powers. Following the war, during the Paris Peace Conference of 1919, the Big Four victorious powers (Britain, France, the United States and Italy) imposed their terms in a series of treaties. In this context, the Roman Question became a problem that every side would like to make use to impede Italian benefits.

6. A Solutions from China? The Refraction of Europe in Zi-ka-wei

The same year, the Church devised a new strategy to separate the Congregation of the Oriental Churches from the former Congregation de Propaganda Fide. Through this separation, the Pope was attempting to solve the Roman Question through altering its path in "the East"; interest in the "Eastern world" may become a bargaining chip in the ownership of Rome. However, a papal pronouncement on Catholic missions in November 1919 was surely prompted by a variety of circumstances. At the same time, an ever-louder voice for change was emerging from the China mission field. Moreover, there was the particular effect of the European war; the wartime circumstances highlighted the fragility of dependence on foreign powers for the future of Catholicism in the non-western world. More particularly, the reliance of so many Catholic missions on France looked increasingly foolhardy, given French opposition to change and French exhaustion from the war. In addition, most importantly, the Pope was motivated to find in the missions a vehicle for a greater insertion of the Vatican into the world affairs.

Pope Benedict XV (1914–1922) embarked on a comprehensive reorientation of mission work. He endeavored to change the prevailing situation in the mission fields, against which the Popes had been struggling for several decades. Particularly, the Pope was determined to weaken the close ties between foreign national interests and Catholic missionary interests, to liberate the mission from the burden of colonialism and to focus once again on the supra-nationality of the Church and its mission[32]. On 30 November 1919, the Pope issued the Apostolic Letter (Lettre apostolique) *Maximum illud* (《夫至大》, the Chinese name of the Letter came from the first three words)[33]. As Belgian scholar Claude Soetens discusses, the papal letter particularly targets China[34]. Two major points from the letter focus on the primary responsibilities of those in charge of the missions, stating that those responsibilities are raising and training a clergy recruited from the native population. The letter points out that this has long been papal policy:

> Yet, notwithstanding the Roman Pontiff's insistence, it is sad to think that there are still countries where the Catholic faith has been preached for several centuries, but where you will find no indigenous clergy, except for an inferior kind . . . nations which for many centuries have come under the salutary influence of the Gospel and the Church, and have yet been able to yield neither bishops to rule them, nor priests to direct them. Therefore, to all appearances, the methods used in various places to train a clergy for the missions have up to now been defective and distorted.[35]

The Pope excoriates any tendency to serve the "earthly glory and power" of one's own country over the "divine task" of spreading the gospel:

> Suppose the missionaries then to be in any way preoccupied with worldly interests, and, instead of acting in everything like an apostolic man, to appear to further the interests of his own country, people will at once suspect his intentions, and may be led to believe that the Christian religion is the exclusive property of some foreign nation; that adhesion to this religion implies submission to a foreign country and the loss of one's own national dignity.

---

[32] See (Tiedemann 2010, pp. 571–86).
[33] See (Benedict XV 1919).
[34] See (Soetens 1997).
[35] See (Cummins 2016, p. 97).

From the time of the Opium War, the Jesuits were trying to have Lazarists removed. In response, Rome's vigorous proactive approach was to a considerable extent inspired by a small group of outspoken foreign missionaries and Chinese priests who came together since 1900 around the Lazarists Antonio Cotta (汤作霖) and Vincent Lebbe (雷鳴遠). French diplomats in China were alerted to the Propaganda Fidei's moves regarding Cotta and Lebbe. The French minister suggested that the government in Paris take advantage of the pressure it put upon a congregation with its motherhouse in France to exile Cotta from China, and that the Belgian government be "mobilized" to persuade the Vatican to remove Lebbe. They both had in his view collaborated in the effort to break the French protectorate and to indigenize China's Catholic Church, and their work brought the condition of the church in China to the attention of the Vatican.

In this situation, the new pope, Pius XI, decided to intervene by naming an Aposolic delegate who would visit China with papal authority behind him. The appointment went to Celso Constantini (剛恒毅, 1876–1958) in November 1922, a few months after the plan to dispatch an apostolic delegate was put into effect. Constantini wasted no time in dealing with crucial issues[36], among which the elimination of the French Protectorate carried the most tension. Constantini's first assignment was to accomplish a nationwide meeting of Catholic leadership. He proceeded to do so and he chose Zi-ka-wei, Shanghai for "The First Chinese Council", recorded as the Primum Concilium Sinense, to take place in mid-May 1924. Indigenization of the Chinese Catholic church still had a long way to go, but Constantini persisted in the Vatican's agenda, as long as he was supported from Rome[37].

1929 was the year of the Lateran Pacts. After a sixty-year standoff, the Vatican reconciled with the Italian state. By then, after several years of the Church encouraging the indigenization policy an increasing number of local clergymen were working in Zi-ka-wei compound with less French color and ethnicity. The multiple institutions in Zi-ka-wei were not as functional as they had been before 1900, however, because they were now not supported materially either by the Vatican or by France.

This was the time in which when the Hospice of the Sisters of the Good Shepherd mentioned at the beginning of this paper was founded. By 1930, the Catholic compound was no longer being expanded by the French, whether they were French Jesuits or from other French orders. Yet the Sisters as a French female order arrived in Shanghai at this sensitive point. The Hospice aimed at educating the prostitutes who were misbehaving and protecting homeless females from being mistreated. As an institution run by a female religious order, it should have been situated in an appropriate part of the concentrated complex. Nevertheless, the location of the Hospice was at the far end of the Zhaojia Canal, or to be more specific, in the territory of the French Concession instead of within the scope of Zi-ka-wei, though it was still on the east side of the River.

7. Concluding Remarks

The French Protectorate had an array of significant opponents, including various foreign powers, the Chinese officials and the Pope. In contemplating the French Religious Protectorate and the character of the Catholic compound in Zi-ka-wei Shanghai in the 19th and early 20th centuries, some features stand out. One was that the pact between Catholic missions and representatives of the French government in China was never formally specified. It was a product of French arms and diplomacy with a primary task of preventing the Vatican from establishing any similar organization. The protectorate was generally popular in France during the mission's history, however. It was another feature of the Protectorate that it depended on a foreign Catholic episcopate to justify the interventions. Another noteworthy feature of this drama was the tension of the conflict between the defenders of the status quo and the reformers. This time which was which was difficult to define in the ever-changing

---

[36] The crucial issues were namely: (1) the reduction of tension between foreign and Chinese Priests; (2) the phased transfer of mission territory to the Chinese clergy; and (3) the elimination of the French Protectorate. See (Tiedemann 2010, pp. 571–86).
[37] See (Wu 2018, pp. 165–87).

diplomatic background. The position of France in the contemporary China was constructed from the mid-19th century onward due to the measure out of Catholic, especially the Jesuits, appeals for help, which formed the occasions for extending France's influence as a leading foreign power in the contemporary context.

The reception of the French Protectorate in early 20th century was more complicated. Conflicts of the status quo inside the missions gained volume. In the first instance, the French Protectorate contributed to the embitterment of Sino-foreign relations. In addition, the various calls for the Catholic church to distance itself from French policy evoked distinct compaign by French officials and by the Vatican, which led to the new Hospice slight locationally separation from the female religious sector of the Zi-ka-wei compound.

The compliment towards Zi-ka-wei in the 1930s as an "Oriental Vatican" was a consequence under the scheme of the Vatican. As a key foundation of the Catholic Church in the Far East, Zi-ka-wei, if it were marked as belonging to the Vatican, would extend the power of the Pope. The question arises: was doing so an attempt to solve the Roman Question through exerting the influence of the Vatican in Asia?

The practical function of the Hospice never ended, even during the Cultural Revolution (1966–1976): based on its original purpose, it was eventually transformed into a hospital for women and infants only. My aim has been to provide a new perspective for the study of female Catholic religious and social philanthropy in Shanghai by placing it in the context of post-Opium War Jesuit strategy at Zi-ka-wei.

Funding: China State Scholarship No. 201708310074; Malatesta Scholarship of 2017 sponsored by Ricci Institute, University of San Francisco.

Conflicts of Interest: The author declares no conflict of interest.

References

Benedict XV. 1919. *Maximum Illud: Apostolic Letter on the Propagation of the Faith throughout the World*. Translated by Thomas J. M., and Burke S.J.. Available online: https://www.svdcuria.org/public/mission/docs/encycl/mi-en.htm (accessed on 15 January 2011).

Brockey, Liam Matthew. 2007. *Journey to the East: The Jesuit Mission to China, 1570–1724*. Cambridge: Belknap Press of Harvard University.

Brook, Timothy, and Gregory Blue. 1999. *China and Historical Capitalism: Genealogies of Sinological Knowledge*. Cambridge: Cambridge Univerisity Press.

Cannone, Domenico. 1987. *Lèvangelizzazione della provincia cinese del Ho-non nella seconda metà del secolo XIX*. Naples: Pontificio Instituto Missioni Estere.

China. Hai guan zong shui wu si shu. 1917. *Treaties, Conventions, etc., between China and Foreign States*; Shanghai: Statistical Department of the Inspectorate General of Customs.

Cummins, J. S. 2016. *Christianity and Missions, 1450–1800*. New York: Routledge.

d'Elia, Pasquale M. 1927. *Catholic Native Episcopacy in China: Being an Outline of the Formation and Growth of the Chinese Catholic Clergy, 1300–1926*. Shanghai: Tòu-Sè-Wè Press, p. 50.

Dunne, George H. 1962. *Generation of Giants: The Story of the Jesuits in China in the Last Decades of the Ming Dynasty*. Notre Dame: University of Notre Dame Press.

Gernet, Jacques. 1985. *China and the Christian Impact*. Translated by Janet Lloyd. Cambridge: Cambridge University Press.

Howard, Michael. 1991. *The Franco-Prussian War: The German Invasion of France 1870–1871*. New York: Routledge.

La Servière, Joseph de. 1925. *La nouvelle mission de Kiang-nan (1840–1922)*. [The new Jiang-nan mission (1840–1922)]. Shanghai: Impromerie de la Mission, Orphelinat de T'ou-sè-wè, Zi-ka-wei.

Lacouture, Jean. 1991. *Jésuites: Une multibiographie: Les Conquérants*. Paris: Seuil.

Menegon, Eugenio. 2009. *Ancestors, Virgins, and Friars: Christianity as a Local Religion in Late Imperial China*. Cambridge: Harvard University Asia Center.

Molony, John, and David Thompson. 2006. Christian Social Thought. In *World Christianities c. 1815–c.1914. Cambridge History of Christianity. Vol.8*. Edited by Sheridan Gilley and Brian Stanley. Cambridge: Cambridge University Press.

Pfister, Louis. 1932. *Notices biographiques ET bibilographiques sur les Jésuites de l'ancienne mission de Chine, 1552–1773*. Shanghai: Imprimerie de la Mission Catholique, vol. I.

Schapiro, J. Salwyn. 1921. *Modern and Contemporary European History (1815–1921)*. Cambridge: The Riverside Press.

Soetens, Claude. 1997. *LÈglise catholique en Chine au XXe siècle*. Paris: Editions Beauchesne, pp. 104–5.

Song, Haojie, ed. 2005. *Zikawei History [历史上的徐家汇]*. Shanghai: Shanghai Culture Publishing House.

Tiedemann, R. G. 2010. *Handbook of Christianity in China*. Leiden: Brill Publisher, vol. 2.

Waley-Cohen, Joanna. 2006. *Culture of War in China: Empire and the Military under the Qing Dynasty*. New York: St. Martin's Press.

Worcester, Thomas, ed. 2017. *The Cambirdge Encyclopedia of the Jesuits*. Cambridge: Cambridge University Press.

Wu, Albert. 2018. In the shadow of empire: Josef Schmidlin and Protestant–Catholic Ecumenism before the Second World War. *Journal of Global History* 13: 165–87. [CrossRef]

Xiao, Yihua, ed. 1997. *Record of Xuhui District*. Shanghai: Shanghai Academy of Social Science Press.

Young, Ernest P. 2013. *Ecclesiastical Colony: China's Catholic Church and the French Religious Protectorate*. New York: Oxford University Press.

religions

MDPI

Article

Geopolitics and Identity-Making in US Diasporic Chinese Churches

Shirley Lung

The Department of Sociology, The Johns Hopkins University, Baltimore, MD 21218, USA; slung1@jhu.edu

Received: 16 September 2018; Accepted: 11 December 2018; Published: 24 December 2018

Abstract: Using ethnographic and interview data, my paper analyzes how geopolitical relationships manifest at the community level in Chinese America. Responding to Lien Pei-Te's call to meaningfully disaggregate among the commonly "lumped together Chinese Americans", I draw upon the experiences of specific groups of Chinese immigrants to the US, post-1949 migrants to Taiwan, pre-1949 migrants to Taiwan, and the People's Republic of China (PRC) Chinese, in order to understand how boundary drawing occurs in their various communities but also consider how the act of being "lumped together" itself in the US context complicates identity formation. The year 1949 marks the communist victory in the PRC as well as the inaugural year of the Kuomingdang (KMT)-led Republic of China (ROC) in Taiwan. Carved out of these historical events, the contemporary social relations among these groups persist after their migration to the US, but they manifest differently in various domains of practice, including religious ones. As political relationships among states reorganizes their social relations, the religious site offers what Carolyn Chen calls a "moral vocabulary" to articulate, contemplate, and, in some cases, justify these divides. Even within a Christian context, messages of inclusivity are not universal but redefined according to the political and social contexts. By not assigning a singular definition to Christian thought, my paper makes way for a theorization of an intersectional Christian identity.

Keywords: Chinese Diaspora; Sinophone; geopolitics; Christianity

1. Introduction

With China's rise in the global order combined with the continuing push for Taiwanese independence,[1] questions of who counts as Taiwanese and who counts as Chinese have come to the forefront, even affecting areas outside of distinct political arenas. As these fraught geopolitical relationships evolve, the meanings attached to these subethnic identifications not only retain their historical saliency but also continue to manifest in present-day forms. In other words, being Chinese today builds upon its historical meanings but simultaneously changes as new meanings seeking precedence are circulated according to various political agendas. While scholars of Asian American Studies have highlighted these groups previously (e.g., Chen 2008; Lien 2010; Hsu 2000; Yang 1999), few have identified how they have structured different aspects of social and political life in the years since their emergence, demonstrating that they do more than simply mark moments of migration. In other words, the politics of Chineseness do not only encompass political views or positions but also engage the broader historical question of how individuals came to be and continue to become Chinese itself. Nonetheless, many works primarily rely upon the broader Chinese label within their analytical frameworks and fail to attend to what Wang (2013) calls "less obvious" forms of segmentation within

---

[1] Recent 2018 elections have brought the Kuomingdang (KMT) back into power, so it is uncertain how Taiwan's position on independence will change in the future.

Chinese America that would highlight these historical dimensions, like clan divides, geographic and linguistic origins, and political party affiliations in China or Taiwan. Often originating from China and Taiwan, these forms of segmentation tend to be neglected in Asian American Studies in favor of ones that are more legible in North American academia like gender, nativity status, and social class (Wang 2013). Other scholars of the Chinese diaspora have not only identified the significance of these types of social organizations in Southeast Asia and mostly other non-US locations but also established some kind of commonality or linkage, however contested, among diasporic Chinese (Amrith 2011; Duara 1997; Kuo 2014; Wang 2000, 2013a; Zhou and Liu 2016). Similarly, my paper envisions Chinese America as a part of the greater Chinese diaspora and, thus, highlights this transnational dimension of being Chinese American.

Observing these less-visible segments and their intersections not only forward the Asian American scholarship but also reveal how the process of meaning-making changes over time within Chinese America. As a result, my study examines the Chinese American community in terms of identities produced after 1949 and how combinations of emergent and residual meanings[2] attached to these identities continue to redefine relationships within the community. Specifically, I explore the Taiwanese (American) identity internally as well as relative to that of the People's Republic of China (PRC) Chinese. Within the North American sociological literature as well as the public forum, the Taiwanese people and Taiwanese Americans are commonly associated with a definition of Chineseness that centers the PRC Chinese while viewing Taiwan, Hong Kong, and sometimes Singapore, as added-on satellites or "ethnic supplements" (Chow 2013; Tu 2013; Wang 2013a). By not exploring these places individually, we not only overlook how domestic and international forces shape these groups but also how they engage with dominant renderings that they institutionally encounter in their daily lives.

As such, my paper analyzes the politics of identity formation at the intersection of geopolitics, religion, and US immigration among Taiwanese and PRC Chinese Christians. Building upon Wang's (2013) "structure of dual domination", my paper examines how "domestic politics and bilateral relations between the US and China" (p. 176) as well as Taiwan shape these post-1949 identities and manifest at the community level after migration to the US. Taiwan or the Republic of China's (ROC) status remains increasingly precarious today as China's President Xi takes a hardline stance toward Taipei. Furthermore, President Trump's America continues to be unpredictable and drastic in policymaking toward both the PRC and the ROC. These external and internal social processes affect identity-making within these Christian communities and, thus, the contested contours of being Taiwanese, Chinese, American, and Christian. As these boundaries are fluid, immigrant communities will be affected in both large and small ways by these geopolitical relationships, making my study a timely topic.

My research questions are twofold. First, what is the relationship between geopolitics and the ways in which diasporic Chinese Christian communities organize themselves in the US? Implicit within this first question is a second one: what is the role of the US and broader American Evangelical culture in fashioning these narratives of ethnic or cultural identity?

Responding to Pei-Te Lien's (2010) call to meaningfully disaggregate among the commonly "lumped together Chinese Americans," I argue that disaggregation by post-1949 identities can contribute new theoretical and conceptual frameworks for understanding contemporary Chinese America. Post-1949 identities refer to those forged after the 1949 victory of the Communist Party of China and the subsequent establishment of the PRC as well as the inaugural year of the Kuomingtang

---

[2] Originating from Williams (1977) seminal work *Marxism and Literature*, concepts of dominant, residual, and emergent nuance what he calls an "epochal" representation of history in which periods transition from one to another without attention to the "determinate dominant features" at play (p. 121). By highlighting the interrelations and the internal dynamics of new stages or periods, the residual and the emergent can offer insight into the workings of the dominant.

(KMT)-led ROC.[3] Specifically, I look at the diasporic Chinese of three subethnic groups: those of *waishengren* (those who fled to Taiwan after the communist victory and are sometimes known as second-generation mainlanders), *benshengren* (those who migrated to Taiwan prior to the communist victory), and PRC Chinese (those who remained in mainland China after the communist victory).[4] As noted, my paper emphasizes the complexity of the Taiwanese American experience, relative to that of PRC Chinese Americans who take a secondary role. Like that of Shih's (2013a) Sinophone Studies among other critics of the Chinese diaspora, my project aims to "decouple Chineseness and China [in order to bring] to the fore a critical perspectivalism and an interpretive positionality that are essential in our reconceptualization of 'diaspora' in the twenty first century" (Tsai 2013). However, unlike Shih, I do not do away with diaspora altogether. Instead, my rendering of diaspora attempts to recuperate the concept by centering the *huaren* identity rather than any kind of Chinese state, a framework akin to Tu's (1994, 2013) notion of "cultural China".

I conducted approximately ten months of ethnographic research and in-depth interviews at a majority Taiwanese Christian church, now known as Maryland Evangelical Church (MEC), and a majority mainland Chinese Christian church, now known as Maryland Baptist Church (MBC),[5] as well as interviewed other diasporic Chinese whom MEC and MBC congregants introduced to me. Through ethnography at relatively homogenous churches, I understand why some groups worship together while others worship apart, building on the literature on cosmopolitan or diverse immigrant churches[6]. Interrogating both the experiences of those minority and majority members of both churches gives insight not only into who congregants choose to worship with but, more importantly, which communities they experience what Levitt and Schiller (2004) call "ways of belonging" with as opposed to merely "ways of being".

Based on my ethnography and interview data, I find that Christian messages from the leadership are overwhelmingly inclusive and encourage members to pattern themselves after God's irrational and "reckless" love, to embrace all members of the Chinese diaspora and not fragment along subethnic lines.[7] However, interviews and informal conversations with churchgoers show that both subethnic groups of Taiwanese construct their identity against a PRC Chinese other as well as a broader white American or "foreigner" other.[8] Using what Chen (2008) calls their "moral vocabularies" to articulate these differences, Taiwanese congregants complicate and redefine what it means to be "inclusive" and "decent" Christians. Their anxieties about a strong China manifest through their fear of "hordes" of PRC Chinese immigrants "taking over" their church and changing worship practices. Pointing to commonly circulated stereotypes of materialism and desires for social status, Taiwanese congregants simultaneously sympathize with, but also distance themselves from, PRC Chinese immigrants. As a result, I argue that contemporary and historical geopolitical relationships among Taiwan, China, and the US inform the ongoing construction of self and other and that at the site of religion, the language of the Gospel provides a way to make sense of and justify those boundaries. In other words,

---

[3]   1949 represents the Communist victory in mainland China, setting in motion the emergence of these identifications of interest, while 1965 marks not only the establishment of Immigration Act and Nationality Act but also the time period when multiculturalism becomes a political aspiration for many immigrants.

[4]   In 1949, Chiang Kai-Shek, the leader of the KMT, fled to Taiwan with approximately two million soldiers, bureaucrats, their families, as well as art from the imperial palace as a result of losing the Chinese Civil War with the communists (Hsu 2015; Lien 2010). As a result, 1949 is commonly noted as the date of arrival in Taiwan, but people were fleeing during the entirety of the Chinese Civil War (1946–1949).

[5]   Names of churches and individuals are pseudonyms. While MBC is Baptist in name and history, its current practices as well as identification by leadership remain non-denominational, independent, and Evangelical in nature like most Chinese churches. For more information on characteristics of Chinese churches, see Yang (1999).

[6]   Both MEC and MBC are short distances from several other diasporic Chinese churches, demonstrating the existence of an array of choices.

[7]   Sermon, 12 November 2017, 3 June 2018.

[8]   Here, I employ the language used by my informants when describing predominantly white, middle-class Americans. Typically, my informants characterize them as either *meiguoren* or *waiguoren*, "Americans" or "foreigners" respectively. They perceive this group as representing America at large as well as the one in which they compare and contrast themselves with.

messages of inclusivity and transcendence of worldly relations are neither universal nor fixed but redefined according to political and social contexts. By not assigning a singular definition to Christian thought, my paper makes way for multiple interpretations and more importantly, a theorization of an intersectional Christian identity.

2. Theory

2.1. Labeling the Chinese Diaspora

While Asian American Studies in the social sciences have disaggregated Asian American communities by nativity status, gender, educational attainment, and to some extent, social class (e.g., Hirshman and Wong 1984; Sakamoto and Furuichi 2002; Zeng and Xie 2004), less obvious forms of segmentation like by clan divides and linguistic groups have been neglected. Moreover, when analyzing the Chinese diaspora in the US, it is important to interrogate presentist assumptions about China or Asia at large instead of drawing conclusions based upon generally unpacked concepts of "American", "Asian", or "Chinese". Indeed, historian McKeown (2001) notes that the process of unpacking these labels is an integral part of "conceptualizing a diaspora" itself. Similarly, commenting on Chinese literary studies, Chow (2013) notes that the label of Chinese is "untheorized and taken for granted" so when analyses are built upon "this unproblematized, because assumed, notion of Chineseness", "an entire theory of ethnicity becomes embedded (without ever being articulated as such) in the putative claims" (pp. 42, 51). Indeed, US scholarship on immigration and, in particular, assimilation build sophisticated theories on the process without questioning notions of Asianness or Chineseness and how these categories have been constructed across time (e.g., Alba and Nee 2003; Kao and Tienda 1995; Kasinitz 2008; Portes and Rumbaut 2001; Zhou and Portes 1993; Lee and Zhou 2015). While probing the multiple meanings of being Chinese or Asian may be beyond the scope of their studies, observing and analyzing how Chinese Americans identify may answer or deepen answers to general questions of gender relations, social class status, among other stratifications. As Chow (2013) notes, unpacking "what constitutes the ethnic label itself" remains the last frontier.

Scholars of diaspora have long debated the intricacies of Chineseness, contributing transnational frameworks. By bringing this perspective to bear on the Asian American experience, we can discover new "ways of being and belonging" within these communities and move beyond what Ang (2001) calls "American centered" approaches. Chow (2013) asserts that, until recently, what are commonly known as Chinese communities oftentimes referred to themselves by their "subprovincial identities" as opposed to a broader Chinese label, demonstrating that being Chinese is a relatively modern notion that is deceptively straightforward. Being Chinese in American implicitly centers the PRC while tacking on Taiwan, Hong Kong, and sometimes Singapore as other majority Han Chinese societies. As such, this definition smooths over various inconsistencies under a guise of objectivity. Studying the Chinese and overseas Chinese or *Huaqiao* in San Francisco, Shanghai, Singapore, and Hong Kong, Wang (2013a) questions the meaningfulness of distinguishing between Chinese in Shanghai, for instance, compared to their overseas counterparts in Singapore. By pointing to the degree of accuracy and implicit racism in counting Chinese by blood and descent, his research casts doubt on neat delineations between Chinese and their diaspora

Concepts of the Chinese diaspora or overseas Chinese are diverse and range from more *zhongguo*-based models like that of Chan (2018) who describes diaspora as serving "to unify a fragmented time and space, a means through which the homeland-nation can be constituted and reconstituted" (p. 11) to those that reject the notion of diaspora altogether like Shih Shu-Mei. Contrasting the approaches of many recent works, Chan brings the center back to China, forwarding a one-China thesis that emphasizes the contested Chinese identity as a result of postwar geopolitics. On the other side is Shih Shu-Mei (Shih 2013a), who decries diaspora as "a euphemism that covers up the systematic and widespread violence against native peoples that accompanied the settlement of imperial subjects" (p. 3). Shih's anxieties about the homogenizing effect tying Chineseness to China after centuries have passed as well as those on an assumed "cultural dependence" or "political loyalty" to the Chinese state by Han Chinese migrants everywhere are legitimate. By using the Sinophone in reference to the multiple Sinitic languages spoken around the world, Shih attempts to get rid of the center and periphery framework by reminding us that "the center is always already the margin (Tsai 2013). Amrith (2011) echoes this view as he questions how methodological nationalism underlies debates of center and periphery. He describes researchers being "too quick to project into the past the modern world of nation-states with strict controls over movement into and out of their territories", elaborating that "borders did not pre-date mobility". In other words, transnationalism is the historical norm, not the exception.

While my analysis is informed by both Shih and Chan, I retain the use of diaspora while opting to sever the link between an ethnic Chineseness and a contemporary political loyalty or cultural dependence on the Chinese state. Conceptually, diaspora remains salient in my study because the ancestral homeland for Taiwanese and PRC Chinese immigrants in the US is China, but the PRC is only one source for the making of Chineseness in the US. The core or center of Chineseness in my rendering of diaspora is the *huaren* identity or a general sense of Chineseness, one that changes across time and space.[9] Like Ang (2001), I pair diaspora with the idea of "Chineseness" because the paradigm is "necessarily unstable" and "anti-essentialist". In this way, diaspora embodies the in-betweenness of transnational spaces as it resists centering dominant narratives of Han-ness or politically driven notions of "Chineseness". In other words, diaspora destabilizes both popular notions of "Chineseness" forwarded by the ROC and the PRC as well as the orientalism of the West because it allows for multiple and simultaneous "Chinese" and "Taiwanese" identities without prioritizing any single one.

Because it takes place in the US, my study is careful to recognize what Peggy Levitt and her colleagues (Levitt and Lamba-Nieves 2011) call "an American-inflected version" of Taiwan and China in circulation. Culturally "anchored" by the US, the version of Taiwan and China produced in the US may resemble but not align with that of people still living there. Levitt's notion of inflection complements the local nature of the Sinophone because Sinophone culture is place-based and thus, a key part of where it is created. "Sinophone American culture is American culture" (Shih 2013a, p. 7). The importance of the US context is located precisely where it is unseen. When particular attributes of diasporic Chinese appear racially fixed and distinctly un-American, it emphasizes how embedded the process of racialization is and drives us to question these ostensibly hard boundaries between Chinese and American. Shih's Sinophone further unsteadies the binary of ethnic preservation and assimilation that took place in early migration scholarship, asking why the eating of certain foods or celebration of certain holidays are necessarily Chinese and not American. Thus, a deeper dive into all aspects of identity-making within these diasporic Chinese communities provides us with answers not only to how this process is negotiated between diasporas and their homelands but also unearths the American inflection inherent in Chinese America.

Similarly, scholars of race caution against making arguments without questioning the labels and categories employed. While race may be "socially constructed", its "social reality" is made material because individuals believe it is true (Bonilla-Silva 2003). Ethnicity and race are not fixed categories but rather ones that have become "taken-for-granted" and "normalized" through racialization processes that are historically contextualized (Chen and Jeung 2012; Jeung 2005; Omi and Winant 2014). By showing that the decisions made by immigrants are subject to "the racial identity typically imposed on them by white outsiders" (Chou and Feagin 2014, p. 16), we can direct our

---

9 Yang (1999) highlights the different ways of saying Chinese in Mandarin: *zhongguoren* means people who are citizens of the Chinese state; *huaren* is broader in meaning and refers to those who are of Chinese descent and living outside of China; *huayi* refers exclusively to those who are of Chinese descent, especially the second-generation. Depending upon the political climate, the specific Chinese identity of members of diaspora may change. For more information on being *hua* or generally Han, see Shih (2013b), Chow (1997), and Carrerio (2012).

attention to how immigrants forge their identities under these conditions rather than emphasizing their agency in choice-making.

2.2. Geopolitics and the Taiwanese Identity

Yang (2000) notes that the Taiwanese are "not a homogenous people", pointing to the "host of subcultural, language, and sociopolitical differences" within the people (p. 99). In his study of Chinese churches in Houston and Washington, D.C., Yang (1999, 2002) writes that many early members were from Taiwan, Hong Kong, and areas of Southeast Asia, while mainland Chinese began arriving during the 1980s when the US "switched its formal diplomatic relations from the ROC to the PRC". As a result of their different migration histories and country-of-origin experiences, these diasporic Chinese groups may not always relate to each other as a single group. Thus, in various situations, diasporic Chinese may more closely identify with their regional or subethnic identifications rather than simply being generally Chinese. It is important to recognize when they deploy their Chinese identities as opposed to their subethnic groups.

My paper highlights the salience of these internal divides that began with the return of Taiwan to China in 1945 after fifty years of Japanese colonization continues to this day. Hsiau A-chin (Hsiau 2013) writes that under KMT rule, the relationship between the *benshengren* or local Taiwanese[10] and *waishengren* or "people from another province" quickly became strained. As Chiang Kai-shek and KMT or Nationalists saw being in Taiwan as a temporary stop on their way to retake the mainland, they claimed their government to represent "free China" or only legitimate Chinese government. During this period of martial law, commonly known as the White Terror, (1949–1987), the KMT promoted mainland Chinse cultural values and ideas at the expense of the local culture, effectively minoritizing the majority. Philips (1999, p. 276) writes of the ambivalence that the local Taiwanese felt upon decolonization and reintegration into China: "where did they fit in the nation of China? What was their place in the Nationalist state?" To them, the chaotic and brutal way that the Nationalists governed was simply a less competent form of colonization (ibid.). After the return of Taiwan, local Taiwanese, at least among the Han Taiwanese, imagined that they could simply become Chinese again, but the blatant corruption within the KMT government and military as well as authoritarian practices ultimately dispelled those hopes (Brown 2004, p. 9).

Violent encounters like the February 28 Incident in 1947 or the Kaohsiung Incident in 1979 color the relationship between the state and citizens, complicating internal divides. Furthermore, while the KMT deemed that local Taiwanese were corrupted or degraded by Japanese colonization, during Japanese colonization itself, anticolonial movements were spearheaded by the local Taiwanese, and prominent writers of the time even envisioned themselves as part of the greater Chinese literary traditional (Hsiau 2013). These ardently anticolonialist local Taiwanese writers, like Chen Shaoting, affirmed their Chineseness and nationalized their literature by highlighting its unique anti-Japanese perspectives (ibid.). This kind of affirmation of Chineseness would later be picked up by the early political challengers to KMT rule in the late 1960s, forwarding a reformist program. During the 1970s, intellectuals and activists of both *waishengren* and *benshengren* background began to explore the dynamics of a Taiwanese identity apart from China, anticipating the democratization movement and cultural indigenization or "Taiwanization" that would come in the following decades (Hsiau 2013).

Today's KMT, known as the pan-blue coalition, no longer espouses the "oppose communism and restore the country" platform it held well into the 1970s, but rather supports status-quo cross-strait

---

[10] It should be noted that the term "local Taiwanese" refers to earlier waves of Han Chinese immigrants, specifically those who arrived prior to 1895 when the Japanese colonial government stopped immigration from China (Brown 2004, p. 9). Shu-Mei Shih Shih (2013a, p. 12) notes that "immigrants from China arrived on the island of Taiwan beginning in the seventeenth century and proceeded to colonize the aboriginal Austronesian peoples, even though they had previously been subjected to Dutch colonialism, and later to Japanese colonialism, followed by a new regime from China after WWII". Brown (2004, p. 8) also highlights that prior to Japanese colonization, Han Taiwanese did not consider themselves to be a unified group. Hoklo, a regional variety of Han Chinese, also refers to local Taiwanese and *benshengren*, a term coined during the 1980s (ibid.).

relations between mainland China and Taiwan and opposes Taiwanese independence. While the *waishengren* and their descendants were the original followers of the Nationalists, this group has also developed a sense of Taiwaneseness that separates them from their PRC Chinese counterparts and may no longer support today's KMT. Some have learned Hokkien, the language commonly called "Taiwanese" by pro-independence proponents, and have intermarried with the local Taiwanese. Indeed, today's *waishengren* have started to embrace being "from Taiwan" if not being "Taiwanese" itself (Brown 2004). Nevertheless, this does not mean that tensions fostered have disappeared. During the White Terror, *waishengren* were largely excluded from small- and medium-sized businesses owned by the local Taiwanese while *benshengren* were excluded from positions of power in the government (Brown 2004, p. 10). These historical events are not soon forgotten, and so, these labels continue to articulate themselves in contemporary society. However, these post-1949 identities do not stand still but rather take on new meanings with political and social developments. In the historical memory of those who experienced martial law and migrated to the US shortly after, these labels.

The production of these *waishengren* and *benshengren* identities reveals the significance of states and institutions in shaping identity formation. Criticizing the gaps left by both the loyalist (used in China and Taiwan) as well as the assimilationist paradigms (used in the US), Wang (2013) formulates the structure of dual domination to describe how domestic US policies and US relationships with the home countries of Asian American immigrants jointly affect the social organization of Asian American communities. He notes that China "will continue to have a profound influence over the identity formation of Chinese Americans and Chinese overseas in a shrinking world and in an age of instant global communication and transnational migration of capital and labor" (p. 175). Thus, not only do Chinese Americans experience racism and exclusion in the US but they also are subject to what he calls "the extraterritorial domination" of the Chinese and Taiwanese governments. Both China and Taiwan have historically inspired loyalty within their overseas populations (Shih 2013b; Wang 2013a, 2013).

In his study on early twentieth century Chinese Nationalist factions, Duara (1997) writes that these political parties relied upon "older, pre-national or non-territorial discourses of community such as Confucian culturalism or Han racism" or "primordialist narratives of belonging and rootedness" emerge in later narratives of identity with the explicit purpose of rallying support for each group's particular cause. Similarly, Chow (2013) highlights that both the KMT and the Chinese Communist Party (CCP) have appropriated a "historical master narrative" that emphasizes the "national humiliation" (*guochi*) of China at the hands of western powers from the late Qing to the Republican period. Currently, this fabricated "collective memory" is the official view of Chinese history in the PRC. These examples demonstrate how states mobilize notions of Chineseness and forge a collective Chineseness to forward their political aims, competing for the loyalties of overseas populations.

These geopolitical relationships among Taiwan, China, and the US manifest within Chinese communities. Wang (2013) describes these communities as a litmus test of sorts because "they lay bare the practice of imperialism, racism, extraterritorialism and political opportunism in Chinese politics and in American democracy and the complicity played by intellectuals on both sides of the Pacific in their history writing". In short, tensions in Asia cannot be contained to that region and the individuals living that region. As a result, the ever-changing relationships among Taiwan, China, and the US affect the boundary drawing delimiting the many "simultaneous" identities of contemporary Chinese America (Duara 1997, 2003; Levitt and Schiller 2004). We can see the articulations of these boundaries across various areas of social life and domains of practice, including religious ones.

Today, cross-strait relations between Taiwan and China are deteriorating. Specifically, the historic phone call between US President Donald Trump and Taiwan President Tsai Ing-wen, leader of the

Democratic Progressive Party (DPP) or the pan-green coalition,[11] have muddied the waters. While the PRC has maintained the "one China Policy", which is supported by the US and formerly supported by Taiwan (Brown 2004), it has taken a hardline stance since Tsai's election in 2016 by freezing diplomatic relations and has acted to restrict mainland Chinese tourism in Taiwan (Smith 2016) and demand that US airlines designate Taoyuan Airport in Taiwan as "Chinese Taipei" (Wee 2018). Taiwanese immigrants among other diasporic Chinese are affected by these political changes as they reconstruct the boundaries of their identities.

2.3. Christian Frame of Mind

A space uniquely both intimate and inclusive, the social context of religious organization is an apt site to examine these modern articulations of historical cleavages that create identities. As political relationships among nations spur present-day logics of regrouping, it is important to investigate how religious sites, as represented by church leaders and influential congregants, respond and shape them. With rituals and worship practices aimed at creating close connections within both immediate and broader (imagined) communities, the religious context reveals its particular vision of inclusivity and thus the type of Christianity it practices through interpretations of the Bible, lessons embedded within sermons, as well as "real world" events of interest. As such, rather than applying a universal definition of Christian values to my framework of identity formation, I instead opt to understand their Christian framing. Specifically, I do not assume a definition of inclusivity but rather how congregants interpret inclusivity, decency, or other commonly cited values. Levitt (2013) defines religion "not as a packageable, stable set of beliefs and practices rooted in a particular bounded time and space, but as a contingent clustering of diverse elements that come together within to-be-determined spaces riddled by power and interests" (p. 160). Thus, religion, like ethnicity and other markers of identity, is affixed with characteristics rather than pre-packaged. As a result, it is necessary to consider various forms of religion, not simply what is readily recognizable or legible popularly (Levitt 2013; Edgell 2012; Bender and Klassen 2010).

In order to productively conceptualize religion, it is necessary to explore the contingency of the religious form especially when in encounters with "power and interests like geopolitical relationships. What happens when Christian values like inclusivity meet with potential political divisiveness? How do definitions of these values then change with shifting powers and interests, especially those that mobilize ethnicity? These questions make ethnicity-based congregations an ideal site to explore the impact of geopolitics at a community level. As congregants differently articulate their post-1949 identities according to the political climate, their attitudes toward who should be included in their congregation and who counts as one of them also changes. By examining the way that they justify or implement these boundaries and re-curate, in a sense, their congregation, we can probe what being Christian means to them and how that identity intersects with and integrates with their ethnic identities.

Chen (2008) shows that becoming Christian in effect means becoming a "new person" as one gains "new moral vocabularies, institutional structures, and ethical traditions that reconstruct community, identity, and self in the United States" (p. 5). Chen stresses that religious conversion not only alters the core of one's identity but also includes a "systematic reordering of personal meanings" (pp. 42, 61). Not only does this Christian frame of mind allow for re-interpretations of difficult experiences that are part and parcel of migration, but also extends to rethinking social inequality and racial hierarchies. Becoming Christian entails and implies a shift in value system, which is articulated with new moral vocabularies to regard social phenomenon such as racism or other forms of discrimination. In fact, the ideas of inclusion and exclusion, constructions of insiders and outsiders, are themselves transformed in the process. The Christian frame of mind, a result of personal transformation, cannot be limited,

---

[11] Founded in 1986, the DPP is the opposition party to the KMT. It has supported Taiwanese Independence from China and a distinct Taiwanese identity separate from that of PRC Chinese.

bounded, or universalized. Commonly invoked values of tolerance, inclusion, and love among others require deep scrutiny so that we can understand how they materialize across various contexts.

Such reorientations recall deeper familial-type relationships that Weber (2009) identifies as a "new social community", a "universalist brotherhood" that effectively competes with and devalues natural sibling, matrimonial, and other worldly bonds. Weber elaborates that committing to religious communities means the acceptance of both an "in-group morality" as well as an "out-group morality" and a prioritization of the former, especially in transactional relationships (pp. 329–30). For insiders, the principle of "simple reciprocity" applied and the wealthy or those with means are obligated to help others in need without concern for profit or repayment, while outsiders were excluded from such reciprocity (ibid.). For Weber, religious norms operate according to its own logics and, most importantly, applies in all aspects of one's life, not simply during church activities. Religious frames may complement or oppose secular value systems and laws of the world. In the event of clashes, the degree to which Christian ones take precedence over others remains personal and thus, individualized.

According to the Pilot National Asian American Political Survey (PNAAPS)[12], over half of Asian Americans have a religious identity (Lien and Carnes 2004). They (ibid.) further note that despite being the Asian American group with the lowest religious identification, among Chinese Americans, there is "fast growth of Fujianese, Taiwanese, and college-educated mainland Chinese religious groups; transnational religious contacts" (p. 45). While the survey combines all Taiwanese groups, PRC Chinese, and other subethnic groups into one Chinese category, these trends highlight the importance of religion as a site of social organization among all Chinese American groups. As previous studies on Chinese Americans have shown (e.g., Yang 1999; Chen 2008; Jeung 2005), the context of religious sites differs from those of other secular ethnicity-based organizations. Their voluntary nature, frequent meetings, and their inward focus on the intimate and the sacred make them a fitting site to understand the interrelationships among race, ethnicity, and politics. As Chen (2008) and Yang (1999) point out, the personal stakes are uniquely high for immigrants as they consider metaphysical issues such as their salvation as well as transmitting their religious beliefs to their children (Min 2010).

Within diasporic Chinese churches, issues of inclusion and exclusion are not uncommon. Various sociopolitical differences and viewpoints arise as a result of different migration histories and political loyalties both within the US and abroad. While cosmopolitan congregations may have what Yang (1998) calls a "tenacious unity", more insular ones that are formed based upon narrower definitions of Chineseness have what I call contingent inclusion. This concept builds upon Yang's "tenacious unity" in that minority members may not be overtly excluded from joining the congregation, but their spiritual needs, among others, may be of lower priority or ignored altogether. One example is being subject to often disparaging characterizations or beliefs of the majority group as a condition of their inclusion, one that they can contest at the cost of conflict. Within MEC, conversations surrounding Taiwanese independence as well as negative descriptions of the PRC Chinese and President Xi Jinping's administration are common topics that the minority PRC Chinese churchgoers have to endure. In other words, while they are not excluded from joining or participating in the worship activities, it is still important to emphasize that they do not dictate the culture of the church and may, at times, be marginalized. While they are united by their Christian faith and a general sense of being Chinese, this type of unification does not ensure that everyone in the church is treated equally.

Even though contention within a cosmopolitan Chinese church may ultimately result in a necessary or de facto unity, that within homogenous churches may not be acceptable at all. Yang (1999) notes that when some members of cosmopolitan churches display "divisive tendencies", they are reminded by church leaders that "they are Christians after all, united in the same God, same Christ, and

---

12 Data from PNAAPS was collected from 2000 to 2001 and published in 2004. For more information on this survey, see https://doi.org/10.3886/ICPSR03832.v1.

same Spirit" (p. 173). Depending on who constitutes the majority, different viewpoints are perceived as divisive or political; ones that are generally accepted appear rational or common sense. Unity within a homogenous church may be similarly procured through reminders of a global or universal Christian identity but are instead applied to other sets of behavior. What may have been divisive within cosmopolitan settings, like vocal support for Taiwanese independence, is normalized and even embraced. Within MEC, church leadership and other influential voices may encourage a Chinese identity, but the terms of that identity prioritize being Taiwanese, displayed in either Mandarin accents, political views, or even common childhood activities. In other words, being Chinese is a moving target depending on which group of diasporic Chinese's idea is dominant. Therefore, it is important to recognize the dominant characteristics being circulated so that we can examine who benefits from such a rendering and who is marginalized.

3. Ethnographic Details

Founded by five families who are affectionately and reverently known as "the founding families" approximately twenty years ago, MEC, a majority Taiwanese church[13], holds its main events like Sunday worship services and seasonal holiday celebrations in a small building it rents. Many of these congregants, like the founding families, used to attend more cosmopolitan Chinese churches but ultimately settled on MEC because they felt more comfortable among other Taiwanese. With approximately seventy active members who contribute weekly to monthly offerings in support of church activities, MEC serves a middle-class first-generation Taiwanese American population and their families. Most of the congregants arrived in the US in the 1980s or 1990s for graduate school or as accompanying spouses and later raised families here. As a result, they do contribute resources toward conducting their own English language Sunday school with a rotating teacher selected among Baptized members.[14] While MEC primarily recruits among and serves an immigrant population, there is a growing contingent of the second generation who return sporadically after college.

While MEC is a homogenous church, one issue that reveals internal differences is language. While Sunday worship is currently held in Mandarin with simultaneous English translation by a Baptized member, originally it was in Hokkien or Taiwanese. Because more recent arrivals from Taiwan experienced their education in Mandarin, Taiwanese may no longer be generally understood by both *waishengren* and *benshengren*. To accommodate these later generations, MEC voted to have Mandarin service every other week and, eventually, it became the norm with the added English translation. Recently, it was decided to have one Sunday worship a month that was conducted solely in English, from announcements to sermon. These changes reveal not only the generational differences in educational experiences among Taiwanese immigrants but also how earlier generations attempt to adapt and accommodate later ones. Printed and online materials are all written in traditional Chinese script (adopted by Taiwan) with occasional English translation. Members also send their children to the local Chinese language school with a curriculum that teaches traditional script run by Taiwanese staff as opposed to the local one run by PRC Chinese staff.

I began attending MEC at a point when they were in the middle of a pastor search. For over two years, they had been without a regular pastor and, thus, rotating among four pastors: two white American and two first-generation Taiwanese American men. Depending upon the pastor, the sermon translation would either be in English or Mandarin. From conversations, I have gleaned that the two white American pastors are generally better respected for their Biblical interpretations and messages than the Taiwanese ones. Nevertheless, these feelings do not represent a complete embrace of all white Christians. Prior to the search, the church retained a white pastor who committed significant

---

[13] MEC is evenly split between *waishengren* and *benshengren* congregants with one or two PRC Chinese families at any given time.

[14] Roles in the church from leadership positions like being a deacon to ushers, translators, pianists, and hosts for local small group fellowship meetings are selected among the Baptized individuals and decided months in advance.

church resources toward helping inner-city black youth. After allowing this practice for some time, the leadership informed the pastor that they did not want to continue this type of outreach, resulting in the departure of that pastor. Towards the middle of March 2018, they finally concluded the search and decided upon a Singaporean pastor who has a Taiwanese wife who is also a minister. Through reactions to these various pastors, it was obvious that congregants were most comfortable with leaders of Taiwanese or other overseas Chinese descent but not PRC Chinese. Furthermore, their contingent acceptance of white pastors or friends of the church reveal not only the type of American Evangelical culture they approve of but also how their vision of their church is bounded. A fruitful venue for future research on ethnicity-based churches would be to explore how issues of race emerge and are dealt with in worship practices.

After a recommendation from a Christian student group, I started to attend Bible study, Sunday worship, and joint activities with area churches at MBC in November 2017. MBC represents a secondary site in my project and allows me to compare and contrast experiences within different kinds of homogenous Chinese churches. Compared to MEC, MBC is much smaller in scale with approximately twenty active members and caters primarily to PRC Chinese graduate students or young professionals, which contributes to a quick turnover in members. The printed material circulated by MBC is also written in simplified Chinese script (adopted by the PRC). Finally, because there are no second-generation members, apart from myself, Sunday services are conducted entirely in Mandarin without any translation.

They also have an informal daycare for children, but there is no formal Sunday school because the children are too young. They conduct their activities in a church rented from a predominantly white congregation Unlike MEC which has a rotating and formally elected deacon's board, the leadership of MBC is comprised of a *waishengren* couple who have been in the US since the early 1990s. Both middle-class professionals, this couple encountered Christianity in Taiwan but did not become very devout until coming to the US for their graduate education. Having attended primarily cosmopolitan Chinese churches, they know of MEC but encourage their congregation toward activities hosted by mainly PRC Chinese organizations. The relationship between the leadership and the congregants takes on more of a teacher-student or mentor-mentee dynamic as opposed to one of equals, as demonstrated by MEC.

3.1. Internal Divisions within Taiwanese

For congregants at MEC and MBC, maintaining strict in-group and out-group moralities solely according to one's religious status remains a struggle as these post-1949 identifications threaten religious unity. During a conversation with Thomas, a deacon from MEC who identifies as *benshengren* and specifically "native Taiwanese", he told me a story about one of his *waishengren* church friends who was born in Taiwan:

> [My friend] is a second generation in Taiwan, meaning his dad came with the military. He told me this, which I never thought about it. When I was growing up in Taiwan, my mom would say, oh, they are the other province people [*waishengren*], so she does look down on them. For us, it was just a thing, we didn't care much, because mom can tell me he's from the other province all she wants, but you still tell me to call him, 'grandpa.' So, what's the difference? Not until I was at the church [in another state], there's this gentleman who told me, 'please help me understand this. People from Taiwan don't view me as Taiwanese. People from China also don't view me as from China. What am I? I'm not ABC [American Born Chinese], I'm not born here. I'm nothing.' To me, I think it is different and it is difficult.

Thomas describes himself as not caring about the difference between *waishengren* and *benshengren* despite his mother's condescension. He even goes as far as to note that he would respect all elders in the same way even if they are not *benshengren*. However, after I mention that another self-identified *benshengren* congregant told me that she felt both groups were interchangeable as "one Taiwan" and "from the same island", Thomas noted that *waishengren* are Taiwanese only when "politically speaking" and elaborated,

> To say that we're all Taiwanese, that is a very ... she did it with a lot of consciousness, to say that. What I do think is that if you consciously say something, it doesn't necessarily mean what's in your heart. Because you just said something politically correct. But that of course is a big blanket statement too.

While Thomas did not directly disagree with the other congregant, he demonstrated that the "one Taiwan" view was a popular one to say aloud but belied deeper, more divisive feelings, perhaps even for himself. While citizenship status and political identity may be clear-cut, Thomas wavers on who has the right to claim a cultural Taiwaneseness, an assertation that simultaneously suggests and questions an authentic Taiwaneseness beyond membership in the polity. While he remains sympathetic to his church friend, access to this cultural Taiwaneseness appears to be nevertheless selective and reserved for those unaffiliated with the KMT. Consistently referring to *waishengren* as "those who came with the KMT", Thomas reveals that the aspect of the *waishengren* identity that remains most salient for him is the historical relationship with the KMT despite the fact that not all *waishengren* were willing members and suffered through not-infrequent purges. The boundaries of Taiwaneseness go beyond the mere demarcation of arriving before or after 1949, but rather, draw upon what Ang (2014) calls an "inherent exclusivity". Simply put, in order for one to be Taiwanese, others cannot be Taiwanese. Far from fixed, these shifting boundaries of ethnic and cultural identifications are sourced from both historical constructions of what it means to be Taiwanese and informed by contemporary revisions. As such, while Thomas' generation may not care about this divide or relate to it in the same way as that of his parents, the fact that he does not wholesale accept a "one Taiwan" view reveals that historical and current geopolitical relationships manifest at the community level.

Similarly, Rebecca, a self-identified *waishengren* from MEC, highlights how these internal divides have changed over time. While she felt that she would relate to any immigrant who "shared the same values" whether they are "Jewish or Italian", she did identify some important factors for making friends and establishing close relationships with other Taiwanese. Like many *waishengren* in the US, Rebecca adheres to the practice of telling others that she is from Taiwan rather than Taiwanese:

> I think that I'm Chinese American, if I had to be more specific, I would say that I'm Chinese but from Taiwan. As a kid, I would feel like I'm Chinese but not Taiwanese, but after being in the US for so many years, and we don't like the Communist system so I'll explain more and say that that I'm from Taiwan.[15]

Here, Rebecca identifies how the process of migration and becoming a minority within the US has led her to become more specific with her identity. As a member of the minority but historically politically dominant *waishengren* group, Rebecca felt that in Taiwan, she did not relate to *benshengren* and that she equates being Taiwanese with the *benshengren* identity. Thus, even though she was born in Taiwan, she does not call herself "Taiwanese" or *taiwanren*, a term mobilized by pro-independence supporters. However, while before she would simply say that she is a Chinese person, she now has expanded her explanation to include that she is from Taiwan, and thus, implies that she is not PRC Chinese. As she and her husband do not support the Chinese Communists or the CCP, she does not want to be conflated with them by the ambiguous label "Chinese". For Rebecca, being PRC Chinese is associated with Communism and Xi's regime. As her evolution of identification shows, Rebecca's ways of thinking about herself have changed according to the political events around her.

After I asked her if she relates to other immigrants from Taiwan, she said that,

---

[15] While this interview with Rebecca is mainly translated from Mandarin, here she uses the more ambiguous English word "Chinese" rather than *huaren* or *zhongguoren* so I am not sure how she is identifying as Chinese, whether it is politically, culturally, historically or a combination of all three.

Of course. I relate to those who came from Taiwan. We spent our childhoods in Taiwan, raised in the same educational system, and we eat the same foods. Of course, we would feel a close connection, but [laughs] if I meet those who are very pro-independence [*taidu*] . . . if they have a lot of bias, then I will feel uncomfortable. I won't be able to identify with them. I've once met some Taiwanese [*taiwanren*]. I don't hate them, and I don't hate anyone. In the 1970s, those pro-independence people really despised us so-called *waishengren*. I've once met this Taiwanese person who told me, 'oh now, I can talk to you people who only speak Mandarin [*Guoyu*].' She said that before she never spoke with people who speak Mandarin [laughs]. The fact that she had that kind of comment, I felt it was so ridiculous. These kinds of people, I won't like so much; I won't feel that I can recognize them.[16]

Rebecca reminisces about her childhood in Taiwan and recalls the 1970s as a time when she felt the full force of the disdain that pro-independence Taiwanese aimed at post-1949 immigrants. It is important to show that Rebecca conflates Taiwanese (*taiwanren*), pro-independence supporters, and *benshengren* at various points in our conversation, displaying how these three identities and simultaneous political stances are interrelated, even though nowadays there are also *waishengren* pro-independence groups in Taiwan. While these internal divides are still very much active in today's Taiwan and its US diaspora, Rebecca's story regarding the *benshengren* she met at a church retreat reveals not only the past prejudice harbored but also that those prejudiced, however "ridiculous" they may have been, are no longer articulated in the same way. Similar to how Rebecca has embraced being from Taiwan more in the US than she did in Taiwan itself, that person no longer feels the difference between *waishengren* and *benshengren* to be so unbridgeable in the US. It is also important to point out the role of language in *waishengren* and *benshengren* relations. *Benshengren* typically speak Hokkien,[17] a language or dialect that has been dubbed Taiwanese by those who support Taiwanese independence while *waishengren* generally speak Mandarin or *Guoyu*. Thus, the politics of language are actively at play in contours of Taiwanese identity.

In addition to language differences, another defining difference is perception of migration to Taiwan. MBC is led by a *waishengren* couple but the congregation is mainly comprised of PRC Chinese. During an early visit, Ellen, one of the leaders, drove me back to my house. While we discussed my previous religious experiences, she also asked where my parents are from. After I told her that my parents are *waishengren*, she nodded and said, "they are like me". Later, during another meal, she elaborated upon the *waishengren* and *benshengren* difference, noting that *benshengren* are also immigrants from China to Taiwan, they merely came earlier. For Ellen, it was frustrating that *benshengren* had more "legitimacy" to being Taiwanese simply because of earlier migration and that *waishengren* have been referred to as "second generation mainlanders".

Another attitude among *waishengren* members is an embrace of being from Taiwan and even knowing Taiwanese themselves. One MEC member, Seth, another self-identified *waishengren* who was born in Kaohsiung, a known "green" city in southern Taiwan with DPP and pro-independence supporters. When Seth interpreted one of my follow-up questions to suggest that he was not Taiwanese because of his *waishengren* background, he highlighted that he spoke Taiwanese outside the home with his friends and that he was comfortable with the language. He further noted that he considers himself to be "Chinese in America" in a strict "race or ethnicity" sense. His daughter, a second-generation Asian American, will refer to him and his wife as "Taiwanese", he believes "his ancestors are from China, so it's not the same". However, "politically, [he] is from Taiwan" and not China as they are separate countries. Similar to Rebecca, Seth attempts to affirm his Taiwaneseness through language proficiency. Nevertheless, this connection relies upon a definition of Taiwaneseness that centers *benshengren* and

---

[16] I have provided the relevant Mandarin terms that Rebecca used in the interview in italics.
[17] Hokkien is a general language spoken in the southern region of mainland China as well as among many diasporic Chinese in Taiwan, Southeast Asia, and other places. While each version of Hokkien is unique to its particular region, they are not mutually unintelligible.

potentially the pro-independence movement. The liminality of the *waishengren* identity especially in changing national contexts merits further research.

In a church with both *waishengren* and *benshengren*, DPP and KMT supporters, hardline anti- and pro-independence proponents as well as the apathetic, Taiwanese congregants have found a unity that is not necessarily "tenacious" or tenuous even, but rather one based upon native-place identity, the nostalgia of cuisine and childhood, that is animated not only by migration but by a common difference. In other words, together, they forge a Taiwanese identity that does not necessarily root itself in the struggle for Taiwanese independence or the ideologies of any singular political party in Taiwan but rather one that reflects the political and linguistic diversity of Taiwan.

3.2. A PRC Chinese Other

Initially from attending Sunday worship, weekly fellowship meetings, sporting events, celebrations, and other official activities, I did not hear about conflict or contention within the group. However, as I became embedded in the congregation, I began to receive invitations to informal activities from congregants who viewed me in a parental manner because of my proximity in age to their own children. It was from these late-night conversations in the car when they would give me rides back to campus or over dinner that I learned of disagreements among leadership. One particularly contentious issue was the inclusion of PRC Chinese within the congregation. One of my close contacts in the church told me about a PRC Chinese congregant whom she suspected was only using the church to gain permanent residency in the US. She did not feel like his motivations were "pure", linking his PRC background to her disdain. On the leadership level, some board members have left the church entirely over disagreements over congregation composition.

As one of the East Asian "tigers" or economic "miracles", Taiwan's growth in GDP and recognition as a developed state makes its mark discursively as Taiwanese are widely considered to be "open-minded" and "thoughtful" while PRC Chinese are represented as "materialistic" and "status-seeking". Variations of these stereotypes circulate in MEC with even one non-Chinese visitor remarking upon the difference between immigrants from China and Taiwan is that mainlanders have different values that disregard the family and focus solely on acquiring material possessions. When these Taiwanese congregants describe the facets of their identity, they draw upon not only what being Taiwanese means but also what it is not. Pointing to growing tensions between China and Taiwan, both *waishengren* and *benshengren* congregants have expressed fears and anxieties of an increasingly powerful and invasive PRC alongside assertions of dissimilarities with PRC Chinese.

During an MEC retreat workshop on being Christian in the workplace, a Taiwanese former member shared a story about a frustrating colleague. As a lawyer, she primarily makes money through billable hours, and her colleague from Peking University, "full of degrees" advised her to work slower so that she can earn more money. She felt "so annoyed" by this colleague among other colleagues from China who are "obsessed with money". She noted that during one assignment, she needed only fifteen minutes to complete it, but this colleague told her to simply rush it. Fed up, she announced to him that he had a personality that's "likely to be struck by lightning". In a safe space with other Taiwanese, she felt that she could share her experience without judgement in an effort to find a Christian resolution to her problem. In her rendering of the situation, she focused on his PRC Chinese identity as the root of his materialism and desire to get rich rather than any other markers, demonstrating the strength of these stereotypes.

Another variation of this stereotype is materialism aligned with notions of moral depravity. At the same MEC retreat, the husband of a Taiwanese member struck up a conversation with me outside of the cabins. Hailing from Hong Kong, another East Asian "tiger", he finds affinity with Taiwanese, an attitude is common among Cantonese immigrants I have interviewed and met through church activities. An employee of the US government, he describes how PRC Chinese tourists like to visit old US battleships and scrape off paint with keys so that China can more easily get water-proofing technology. He described them as "stealing our technology doing the type of things we can't even imagine". With the "we" and "us" referring to the US, he simultaneously highlights our commonality as American, rather than Chinese, and others the PRC Chinese by casting them as foreign and inscrutable agents of the government. For him, their identity is inseparable from Chinese politics and the agenda of Xi's government. He further notes that they "are all about moving up and making money" and that they do not consider their "moral development" or interpersonal relationships. For him, the reason for their lack of morality is the fact that "they make so much money that they have a *fuerdai* or rich second-generation problem". Thus, not only are the PRC Chinese spying for Xi, but they are also mindlessly pursuing wealth within attention to something greater than themselves.

This idea of a difference in moral beliefs also emerges in discussion of worship practices. Sally, a PRC Chinese member of MEC, is from Fujian, a southern province in China, and grew up in a working-class family. She immigrated to the US at the age of 8. Having attended predominantly white, Evangelical churches, cosmopolitan Chinese churches, and now MEC, she has had a variety of religious experiences. When I asked her about how Taiwanese Americans worship, she said that they base their churches around a Taiwanese identity and that "Chinese people" worship differently. Furthermore, after I asked her why she chooses to worship in a homogenous Taiwanese church as opposed to a cosmopolitan Chinese church, she noted,

> I'm probably not the first Chinese person in our church but we had another couple who was Chinese and they came here and they're much older than me so they're more influenced by their Chinese culture. I think there are still differences [between PRC Chinese and Taiwanese] in how they communicate about things and their perspective of things and that's why they're no longer here [at MEC] . . . I have to admit that the Taiwanese people are more influenced by their western culture because they were dominated during a certain period by Americans, right? So, they're all a little bit more open-minded yet they still have the Chinese tradition. That's why I like it so much. The Chinese people are a little bit more closed-minded. They're still stuck in that close-knit traditional Asian culture even though they know that they can think a little bit more freely but I think it's ingrained in them and it's hard for them to separate themselves.

Sally also implies that living under the PRC government has impeded the ability of the PRC Chinese to think freely and most importantly, their ability to be open to an ideal hybrid Chinese-western culture, like that of the Taiwanese. Sally positively associates being "western" or "open-minded" with the Taiwanese whereas the PRC Chinese are unfortunately bound by their traditional ways. For her, it is precisely getting this "western" influence without having to go an American church that makes her stay at MEC, a church where she is not only a minority but also where she is subjected to stereotypes of PRC Chinese.

When I asked her about specific examples of Chinese and Taiwanese having different interpretations of the Gospel, she noted that,

> That's my biggest worry, when you interpret the Bible, there's no way that you can separate yourself completely from your background, your perspective. You'll always use your perspective to interpret the Bible, so therefore, you're always influencing the interpretation. It may not be what it was actually intended to be.

> **SL:** Do you have any examples of Chinese and Taiwanese people interpreting the Bible differently?

> **Sally:** I think some Asian people, Chinese people, take the Bible verse very literally. The Bible says this, that's all we can do. Taiwanese people may step outside the box a little bit and say maybe it could be this. I get it if you have a strict interpretation but it goes back to my perspective that you're only using your own perspective to interpret.

Sally identifies an accurate or intentional meaning of the Bible and then, elaborates on her fear that certain perspectives may obscure the real meanings. Not only do certain loaded readings of the Bible worry Sally but some interpretations and perspectives are indeed better than others. Sally emphasizes the rigidity of how PRC Chinese people think through their strict interpretations and, again, refers back to the Taiwanese being more "open-minded" than their PRC Chinese counterparts.

These stereotypes in circulation also affect church selection and, more specifically, whether to become a minority member or a majority member of a congregation. I asked Thomas how he and his wife, also a *benshengren*, decided to worship at MEC, he told me the factors that were most important to him:

> Before we moved here, I was on the internet looking up Chinese churches because my wife feels more comfortable being in a Chinese church speaking the Chinese language. In fact, she feels more comfortable being with other Taiwanese people. To make it even further, she [wanted] to spend more time with Taiwanese young couples. Now, that could be Christian or not Christian. We start off with Chinese churches [in this area] and we had a list of 6-7 churches. [...] The last church on my list to visit was the very one that I'm at today. Because [the name] says [Taiwanese] on it, I knew it had a close relationship with the Taiwanese Presbyterian Church [PCT]. The two are closely related; one is like a cousin of the other. The [PCT] has some Taiwan politics because in the development of Taiwan's history, there was so much oppression for religious freedom so the [PCT] was the dominant Christian group in Taiwan so they wanted to fight for religious freedom. So, they declared that they want freedom, independence from the KMT. Then, it became a thing for the [PCT] to constantly talk about independence. To me growing up, that's my knowledge of the [PCT]; it's about Taiwan being independent. To me, growing up, that has nothing to do with God. Although now that you know the history, you can see why they did that, but nonetheless, that distorted what church ought to be doing. Their political agenda is based on wanting religious freedom. But then, their religious freedom can lead to a political freedom as well, which distorted the whole point of this. [...] I didn't want to come to visit this church because I'm afraid that there are these politics involved. But the first couple churches that we visited, it's all filled with people from China. And my wife was like, well, [shakes head]. She wasn't too happy so I told her, what are your expectations for seeing young Taiwan families, it's slim. I told her, we either burst our little bubble and we start to mingle with people from China, or let's go visit that church at the bottom of our list.

While church selection may seem fairly straightforward, Thomas' answer meandered into a short political history, demonstrating how narratives of ethnicity espoused by political parties ultimately permeate into these diasporic communities. For both Thomas and his wife, the *waishengren* or *benshengren* status ceased to matter when confronted with "[mingling] with people from China". As an immigrant from Taiwan, Thomas' worldview prior to conversion continues to inform the way he organizes the social domains of his life after his conversion. In other words, like all Christians, Thomas enacts that identity according to the contexts in which he was socialized. While the company he worships with matters, the practices themselves should not be affected by "political agendas". At face value, Thomas' engagement with Christianity may seem selective, but I argue that it is precisely this selectivity that defines the Christian frame of mind; it does not mean an uncritical or unconditional embrace or inclusivity across all areas of stratification. For Thomas, worshipping in the company of his peers is within the limits of being Christian but devoting time toward forwarding political goals unaffected by religious ones is not legitimate.

3.3. Coming Together in Church

The Christian frame of mind fosters the contingent inclusion within MEC. Indeed, even one of the white American pastors, John, is keenly aware of potential conflict between Taiwanese and PRC Chinese, commonly preaching against divisiveness and forwarding examples from his own experience:

[. . .] One of my good Taiwanese friends up in [city name] said, 'This church is not for the mainland Chinese. We are from Taiwan!' [laughter]. If you feel that kind of prejudice my friends, you're going to have to overcome it if you're going to be obedient to God. No place in this kingdom for harboring resentment and prejudice.

Pastor John's anecdote demonstrates Christianity's potential to mend political rifts that impact Chinese immigrants. Indeed, his hope and directive is that it is precisely that salve for political problems. While congregants understand his perspective, he somewhat misses theirs. One congregant, Hugo, mentioned that Pastor John's lessons are "very interesting" but everyone is here because "they want to worship with other Taiwanese". Hugo's view shows that while there is a Christian need to serve the community, this church should prioritize the spiritual needs of the members they serve.

Similarly, Seth later mentions that he does not relate to immigrants from the PRC unless they are at church where he relies on a pan-Chinese identity to make friends. For Seth, Chinese is merely a racial/ethnic label, one that denotes his ancestors, rather than one that defines him. Even though his parents are from China, he does not relate to that identity politically as they are "separate countries and places". Only when he is in church does he default to a pan-Chinese identity in order to remain friendly but apart from that, he does not consider other Chinese immigrants to have a similar migration experience. Indeed, during my time at MEC, I have witnessed baptisms of PRC Chinese members and even offers of transportation to international students from the PRC. Nevertheless, it is the fact that MEC's vision is not about building a cosmopolitan church but rather a space for Taiwanese Christians and minority members to worship. Thus, while there may not be animosity or hostility, PRC Chinese and their experiences are not central to practices.

Charles, a self-identified *benshengren* who opposes Taiwanese independence and its divisive reverberations in other areas of social life, has always attended cosmopolitan Chinese churches before coming to MEC. He and his wife, also *benshengren*, wanted "to try something new" and join a smaller size church, so they came to MEC where they quickly became integrated into the community and eventually, the leadership. He explicitly tells me that he will not be "political" in the interview. However, despite his best efforts, questions of Taiwanese identity and church life ultimately draw him towards elaborating on his views. After I ask him about his opinion of MEC, he replies,

[. . .] We have arguments about stuff. Like should we buy a church or not; we've accumulated a lot of money at this point. Of course, I know who thinks yes and who thinks no, but they're all my friends, all good brothers and sisters, I don't want to go into that kind of debate. Whether or not our church [laughs] need to get some more [PRC Chinese] people. Church should be separate from that Taiwanese independence ideology. I start to realize that some of the important people at church associate with Taiwanese independence ideology. At least they don't have very obvious actions to support their ideology. Right now, I think I'm okay; they just talk about it, not really strong ideology. [pause]. We just need to continue to do what we've been doing, consistently seeking God's wisdom.

Charles reveals that PRC Chinese recruitment is a hotly contested topic among the leadership and that some members are indeed very pro-Taiwanese independence, something leaves him uncomfortable. For him, these two topics go hand-in-hand as political moves that would negatively affect the worship practices at MEC. He attempts to overcome these divisions by appealing to "God's wisdom" and seeing everyone first and foremost as "good brothers and sisters". For Charles, Christianity not only has a reparative effect, but it also becomes a way to maintain that tenacious unity. However, it is important to attend to Charles' stance on what that unity looks like and the kind of status quo that he supports. For Charles, if contained within the realm of talk and not action, the "Taiwanese independence ideology" is acceptable even if it may alienate potential PRC Chinese recruits or current members. While Charles appears sympathetic toward PRC Chinese and supportive of a pan-Chinese congregation, he still harbors fears of Xi's spies in Chinese American congregations and does not act in actually recruiting PRC Chinese members.

Similarly, Thomas who prefers to worship with Taiwanese over PRC Chinese and strongly identifies with being Taiwanese perceives being Christian as compatible with these views. A self-identified devout Christian who reads the Bible every day and consistently gives time toward evangelizing efforts, he tells me that everything filters through his Christian frame of mind. It is his lens for interpreting the world. He reveals his strategy for forming friendships:

> Because of my understanding of the Gospel, today could be the last day of the universe. To me, I feel like it is extremely critical to tell people who Jesus is and I talk about Jesus passionately. I do want to encourage people to talk about Jesus passionately. The people I spend a lot of time with often end up [being] people I'm trying to encourage and trying to challenge to have a personal relationship with Jesus, want to share the love that God has for them with others. Our friends often end up [as] people we care about and we want to share this part of our life with them. So, my friends, I have a purpose with my friends. I want to share this very important thing with my friends and it's hard for me—it's actually hard to be my friend, I'm a very unfriendly person [laughs]. Because I want to tell you about Jesus. And if you don't like Jesus and you get offended by Jesus, then you probably don't want to be my friend, I guess.

By devoting his time to converting others, Thomas' intimate relationships are with seekers of Jesus, something he considers to be a "critical" task based upon his interpretation of the Gospel. By investing in the salvation of others, Thomas conforms to what Weber calls "in-group" and "out-group" morality. He reserves his friendships and his resources for those who are not "offended" by Jesus, implying that hardline nonbelievers are removing themselves from his message and what it has to offer. For Thomas, being Christian means that he needs to be engaged in the work of conversion but the particular seekers he spends time with are up to his discretion. Like Charles, he can maintain his political stances but still continue to proselytize; they are not at odds with each other.

4. Conclusions

Lachmann (2013) writes that, "sociology can help us understand what is most significant and consequential about our contemporary world only when it is historical sociology" (p. 4). The objective of my paper is to disaggregate among Chinese Christians in America who are commonly seen as a single sometimes racial, sometimes cultural, group by the examination of a Taiwanese (American) case. By attending to the historical circumstances of these identities of interest, I hope to "interrogate" those labels by placing them in their proper moment of emergence and addressing their various transformations over time and over space. I also demonstrate how these labels are fixed and instead continue to shift with contemporary geopolitics as a major influence over the direction of those shifts.

Empirically, my paper builds upon previous scholarship on immigrant churches (Chafetz and Ebaugh 2000; Ebaugh and Chafetz 2002; Warner and Wittner 1998) and diasporic Chinese churches that have established concepts of Sinicizing religion (Yang 1998, 1999, 2002), transformative aspect of religious conversion (Chen 2005, 2008), and racialization processes at work within religious contexts (Jeung 2005; Chen and Jeung 2012). Engaging with their findings and frameworks, my paper shows how the Chinese Christian community has established itself over time as well as how it contends with geopolitical tensions that continue to transform its language and logic of being Christian. In a day and age when cross-strait relations between China and Taiwan are in decline, Taiwanese American Christians construct their identities against a PRC Chinese other as well as a white American other. Their "moral vocabularies", in turn, justify the ways they draw the boundaries of being Chinese, Taiwanese, and American.

Funding: This research was partly funded by the Johns Hopkins East Asian Studies.

Conflicts of Interest: The author declares no conflicts of interest.

References

Alba, Richard, and Victor Nee. 2003. *Remaking the American Mainstream: Assimilation and Contemporary Immigration.* Cambridge: Harvard University Press.

Amrith, Sunil. 2011. *Migration and Diaspora in Modern Asia (New Approaches to Asian History).* Cambridge: Cambridge University Press.

Ang, Ien. 2001. *On Not Speaking Chinese: Living between Asia and the West.* Hove: Psychology Press.

Ang, Ien. 2014. Beyond Chinese groupism: Chinese Australians between assimilation, multiculturalism and diaspora. *Ethnic and Racial Studies* 37: 1184–96. [CrossRef]

Bender, Courtney, and Pamela E. Klassen, eds. 2010. *After Pluralism: Reimagining Religious Engagement.* New York: Columbia University Press.

Bonilla-Silva, Eduardo. 2003. *Racism Without Racists: Color-blind Racism and the Persistence of Racial Inequality in the United States.* Lanham: Rowman & Littlefield Publishers.

Brown, Melissa J. 2004. *Is Taiwan Chinese? The Impact of Culture, Power, and Migration on Changing Identities.* Berkeley: University of California Press, vol. 2.

Carrerio, Kevin. 2012. "Recentering China: the Cantonese In and Beyond the Han". In *Critical Han Studies: The History, Representation, and Identity of China's Majority.* Edited by Thomas S. Mullaney, James Patrick Leibold and Stephan Gros. Berkeley: University of California Press.

Chafetz, Janet S., and Helen R. Ebaugh. 2000. *Religion and the New Immigrants: Continuities and Adaptations in Immigrant Congregations.* Lanham: Altamira Press.

Chan, Shelly. 2018. *Diaspora's Homeland.* Durham: Duke University Press.

Chen, Carolyn. 2005. A self of one's own: Taiwanese immigrant women and religious conversion. *Gender & Society* 19: 336–57.

Chen, Carolyn. 2008. *Getting Saved in America.* Princeton: Princeton University Press.

Chen, Carolyn, and Russell Jeung, eds. 2012. *Sustaining Faith Traditions: Race, Ethnicity, and Religion among the Latino and Asian American Second Generation.* New York: NYU Press.

Chou, Rosalind S., and Joe R. Feagin. 2014. *The Myth of the Model Minority: Asian Americans facing Racism.* Boulder: Paradigm Publishers.

Chow, Kai-wing. 1997. "Imaging Boundaries of Blood: Zhang Binglin and the Invention of the Han 'Race' in Modern China". In *The Construction of Racial Identities in China and Japan: Historical and Contemporary Perspectives.* Edited by Frank Dikötter. Honolulu: University of Hawaii Press.

Chow, Rey. 2013. On Chineseness as a Theoretical Problem. In *Sinophone Studies: A Critical Reader.* Edited by Shu-Mei Shih. New York: Columbia University Press.

Duara, Prasenjit. 1997. Transnationalism and the predicament of sovereignty: China, 1900–1945. *The American Historical Review* 102: 1030–51. [CrossRef]

Duara, Prasenjit. 2003. Nationalists among transnationals: Overseas Chinese and the idea of China, 1900–1911. In *Ungrounded Empires.* Abingdon: Routledge, pp. 49–60.

Ebaugh, Helen R., and Janet Chafetz. 2002. *Religion across Borders: Transnational Religious Networks.* Walnut Creek: Altamira.

Edgell, Penny. 2012. A Cultural Sociology of Religion: New Directions. *Annual Review of Sociology* 38: 247–65. [CrossRef]

Hirshman, Charles, and Morrison G. Wong. 1984. Socioeconomic Gains of Asian Americans. *American Journal of Sociology* 90: 584–607.

Hsiau, A-Chin. 2013. The Emergence of De-exile: Cultural Politics and the Postwar Generation in Taiwan. *Oriens Extremus* 52: 173–214.

Hsu, Madeline Y. 2000. *Dreaming of Gold, Dreaming of Home: Transnationalism and Migration between the United States and South China, 1882–1943.* Palo Alto: Stanford University Press.

Hsu, Madeline Y. 2015. *The Good Immigrants: How the Yellow Peril Became the Model Minority.* Princeton: Princeton University Press.

Jeung, Russell. 2005. *Faithful Generations: Race and New Asian American Churches.* New Brunswick: Rutgers University Press.

Kao, Grace, and Marta Tienda. 1995. Optimism and achievement: The educational performance of immigrant youth. *Social Science Quarterly* 79: 1–19.

Kasinitz, Philip. 2008. *Inheriting the City: The Children of Immigrants Come of Age.* New York: Russell Sage Foundation.

Kuo, Huei-Ying. 2014. *Networks beyond Empires: Chinese Business and Nationalism in the Hong Kong-Singapore Corridor, 1914–1941.* Leiden: Brill.

Lachmann, Richard. 2013. *What is Historical Sociology?* Cambridge: Polity.

Lee, Jennifer, and Minv Zhou. 2015. *The Asian American Achievement Paradox.* New York: Russell Sage Foundation.

Levitt, Peggy. 2013. Religion on the Move: Mapping Global Cultural Production and Consumption. In *Religion on the Edge: De-centering and Re-centering the Sociology of Religion.* Edited by Courtney Bender. Oxford: Oxford University Press.

Levitt, Peggy, and Nina Glick Schiller. 2004. Conceptualizing simultaneity: A transnational social field perspective on society. *International Migration Review* 38: 1002–39. [CrossRef]

Levitt, Peggy, and Deepak Lamba-Nieves. 2011. Social remittances revisited. *Journal of Ethnic and Migration Studies* 37: 1–22. [CrossRef]

Lien, Pei-te. 2010. Pre-emigration socialization, transnational ties, and political participation across the pacific: A comparison among immigrants from China, Taiwan, and Hong Kong. *Journal of East Asian Studies* 10: 453–82. [CrossRef]

Lien, Pei-Te, and Tony Carnes. 2004. The Religious Demography of Asian American Boundary Crossing. In *Asian American Religions: The Making and Remaking of Borders and Boundaries.* Edited by Tony Carnes and Fenggang Yang. New York: New York University Press.

McKeown, Adam. 2001. *Chinese Migrant Networks and Cultural Change: Peru, Chicago, and Hawaii 1900–1936.* Chicago: University of Chicago Press.

Min, Pyong Gap. 2010. *Preserving Ethnicity through Religion in America: Korean Protestants and Indian Hindus across Generations.* New York: NYU Press.

Omi, Michael, and Howard Winant. 2014. *Racial Formation in the United States: From the 1960s to the 1990s.* New York: Routledge.

Philips, Steven. 1999. Between Assimilation and Independence: Taiwanese Poliitcal Aspirations Under Nationalist Chinese Rule, 1945–1948. In *Taiwan: A New History.* Edited by Murray A. Rubinstein. Armonk: M.E. Sharpe.

Portes, Alejandro, and Reuben G. Rumbaut. 2001. *Legacies: The Story of the Immigrant Second Generation.* Berkeley: University of California Press.

Sakamoto, Arthur, and Satomi Furuichi. 2002. The wages of native-born Asian Americans at the end of the 20th century. *Asian American Policy Review* 10: 17–30.

Shih, Shu-mei. 2013a. Introduction: What is Sinophone Studies? In *Sinophone Studies: A Critical Reader.* Edited by Shu-Mei Shih. New York: Columbia University Press.

Shih, Shu-mei. 2013b. Against Diaspora: The Sinophone as Places of Cultural Production. In *Sinophone Studies: A Critical Reader.* Edited by Shu-Mei Shih. New York: Columbia University Press.

Smith, Nicola. 2016. China is Using Tourism to Hit Taiwan Where it really Hurts. *Time.* November 17. Available online: http://time.com/4574290/china-taiwan-tourism-tourists/ (accessed on 10 November 2018).

Tsai, Chien-hsin. 2013. Issues and Controversies. In *Sinophone Studies: A Critical Reader.* Edited by Shu-Mei Shih. New York: Columbia University Press.

Tu, Wei-ming, ed. 1994. *The Living Tree: The Changing Meaning of Being Chinese Today.* Palo Alto: Stanford University Press.

Tu, Wei-ming. 2013. Cultural China: The Periphery as Center. In *Sinophone Studies: A Critical Reader.* Edited by Shu-Mei Shih. New York: Columbia University Press.

Wang, Gungwu. 2000. *The Chinese Overseas: From Earthbound China to the Quest for Autonomy.* Cambridge.: Harvard University Press.

Wang, Ling-chi. 2013. The Structure of Dual Domination: Toward a Paradigm for the Study of the Chinese Diaspora in the United States. In *Sinophone Studies: A Critical Reader.* Edited by Shu-Mei Shih. New York: Columbia University Press.

Wang, Gungwu. 2013a. Chineseness: The Dilemmas of Place and Practice. In *Sinophone Studies: A Critical Reader.* Edited by Shu-Mei Shih. New York: Columbia University Press.

Warner, R. Stephen, and Judith G. Wittner. 1998. *Gatherings in Diaspora: Religious Communities and the New Immigration.* Philadelphia: Temple University Press.

Weber, Max. 2009. Religious Rejections of the World and their Directions. In *Max Weber: Essays in Sociology*. Edited by Hans Heinrich Gerth and C. Wright Mills. Milton Park, Abingdon and Oxon: Routledge.

Wee, Sui-Lee. 2018. Giving into China, U.S. Airlines Drop Taiwan (in Name at Least). *The New York Times*. July 25. Available online: https://www.nytimes.com/2018/07/25/business/taiwan-american-airlines-china.html (accessed on 10 November 2018).

Williams, Raymond. 1977. *Marxism and Literature*. Oxford: Oxford University Press.

Yang, Fenggang. 1998. Tenacious unity in a contentious community: Cultural and religious dynamics in a Chinese Christian church. In *Gatherings in Diaspora: Religious Communities and the New Immigration*. Philadelphia: Temple University Press, pp. 333–61.

Yang, Fenggang. 1999. *Chinese Christians in America. Conversion, Assimilation, and Adhesive Identities*. University Park: Pennsylvania State University Press.

Yang, Fenggang. 2000. The Chinese Gospel Church: The Sinicization of Christianity. In *Religion and the New Immigrants: Continuities and Adaptations in Immigrant Congregations*. Edited by Helen Rose Ebaugh and Janet S. Chafetz. Walnut Creek: Altamira.

Yang, Fenggang. 2002. Chinese Christian Transnationalism: Diverse Networks of a Houston Church. In *Religion Across Borders: Transnational Immigrant Networks*. Edited by Janet S. Chafetz and Helen R. Ebaugh. Walnut Creek: Rowman and Littlefield Publishers.

Zeng, Zhen, and Yu Xie. 2004. Asian-Americans' earnings disadvantage reexamined: The role of place of education. *American Journal of Sociology* 109: 1075–08. [CrossRef]

Zhou, Min, and Hong Liu. 2016. Homeland Engagement and Host-Society Integration: A Comparative Study of New Chinese Immigrants in the United States and Singapore. *International Journal of Comparative Sociology* 57: 30–52. [CrossRef]

Zhou, Min, and Alejandro Portes. 1993. The New Second Generation: Segmented Assimilation and its variants among Post-1965 Immigrant Youth. *Annals of the American Academy of Political and Social Sciences* 530: 74–98.

religions   MDPI

Article

Sacred Secularities: Ritual and Social Engagement in a Global Buddhist China

Jens Reinke

East Asian Institute, Leipzig University, Augustusplatz 10, 04109 Leipzig, Germany; jens.reinke@uni-leipzig.de

Received: 13 September 2018; Accepted: 31 October 2018; Published: 31 October 2018

Abstract: The Taiwanese order Fo Guang Shan is a major representative of *renjian* Buddhism. The order maintains a global network of over 200 temples and practice centers that spans over not only most of the Asian continent, but also includes Oceania, the Americas, Europe and Africa. This article examines how the order negotiates the modern secular/religious divide by considering the example of its flagship diaspora temple Hsi Lai Temple in L.A., California. Particular attention is given to two prevalent religious practices at the temple—ritual and social engagements—that are often associated with the 'religious' and the 'secular' respectively. Based on multi-sited ethnographic fieldwork, the article aims to assess the relationship between the two practices and discusses how they resonate with a new generation of highly educated, affluent Chinese migrants.

Keywords: religiosity; secularity; Global East; Taiwan; China; Fo Guang Shan; diaspora temple

1. Introduction

Surrounded by greenery and build on a quiet hillside in an unincorporated suburban community of Los Angeles County lies a brightly colored Chinese Buddhist temple. This temple, Hsi Lai Temple *xilai si* 西來寺 or 'Coming West Temple' in English, is one of the biggest Chinese temples in the US and serves as the North American headquarters of the modernist Han Buddhist order Fo Guang Shan 佛光山 (Budda's Light Mountain). The Buddhist tradition promoted by Fo Guang Shan is *renjian* 人間or Humanistic Buddhism.[1] It is a modern Buddhist tradition with its roots in late 19th and early 20th century China that has become Buddhist mainstream in Taiwan today (Long 2000). Fo Guang Shan is one of the biggest promoters of this tradition, not only in Taiwan but on a global scale, and while different groups have adapted different interpretations of *renjian* Buddhism, one of the primary characteristics of this modern tradition is a new esteem for society, or, in other words, the sphere of 'the secular'.

'The secular' as a concept is often studied in the context of Western Europe or North America. One example for this approach is Charles Taylor's seminal work 'A Secular Age' (Taylor 2007). In this work, Taylor challenges what he calls the 'subtraction theory' of secularization, understood as a process where religion disappears in order to be replaced by science and rationality. Instead, he links the development of a secular age to increasingly anthropocentric worldviews that arose from the Reformation.

More recently, scholars have included non-Western settings in their considerations (e.g., Dean and van der Veer 2018). In the edited edition, Jose Casanova emphasizes the concurrency of the birth of secularism within Europe and the global colonial encounters of the early modern era

---

[1]   *Renjian fojiao* is often translated by its adherents as "Humanistic Buddhism"; however, in English, the term "humanistic" contains strong connotations of Renaissance humanism. In order to clarify the distinction between the two, I have adopted the romanized Chinese term.

(Casanova 2018). Earlier, Talal Asad has called for the development of an ethnography of the multiple articulations and consequences of secularism in different time space settings (Asad 2003).

Jessica L. Main and Rongdao Lai (2013) have considered the development of modernist Buddhist movements in the light of the modern religious/secular divide. In an attempt to highlight the linkages and continuities between pre- and post-World War II forms of Buddhist social engagements, they provide a revised definition of Socially Engaged Buddhism. Building on Talal Asad, Main and Lai point out that in modern China the secular and religious as political ideologies have been mutually constitutive categories that are imported from the West. Secularization in this context is understood as the "the exercise of power on the part of secular polities to distinguish between the secular and religious in ways that undermine the resources and moral legitimacy of religious actors with the secular" (p. 4). They argue that Socially Engaged Buddhism, including *renjian* Buddhism, constitutes the "mirror image of secularization" since it understands social involvement within the secular sphere of society as essentially religious (p. 4). Thus, more than any particular political agenda, be it prewar nationalism or postwar pacifism, it is social activity in itself as a form of religious practice that constitutes the core of Socially Engaged Buddhism. This new revised definition makes it possible to include, amongst other groups, Chinese and Taiwanese *renjian* Buddhists under the category.

This article examines how Fo Guang Shan negotiates the modern secular/religious divide within the framework of a 'Global China'[2] (consisting of the Peoples Republic of China, Hong Kong, Taiwan, Singapore, the Chinese diasporas in South East Asia and worldwide, and their dynamic interplay). It does so by considering two prevalent religious practices at the Hsi Lai Temple—ritual and social engagements—that are often associated with the 'religious' and the 'secular' respectively. Since Fo Guang Shan is a highly centralized Buddhist order, religious practices are standardized and there is little difference if one conducts them at the headquarters or in the diaspora. Yet what is different overseas, are the temple visitors. While at a Fo Guang Shan temple in Taiwan most visitors are, not surprisingly, Taiwanese. At the diaspora temple we can find people that origin from all parts of the Chinese-speaking world and even beyond. This article primarily focuses on the Hsi Lai Temple and its entanglements with the complex and pluralistic Chinese diaspora of Los Angeles, California. However, material from other field sites, such as Nan Hua Temple in South Africa, is considered too. The article is based on ethnographic fieldwork and interviews conducted at the Hsi Lai Temple in the US and at the Nan Hua Temple in South Africa, but also considers studies on Chinese migration, diaspora and modern Chinese Buddhism.[3]

It is important to note that the notion of 'Chinese' when used in this article does not refer to a single locality (be it the Peoples Republic of China[PRC], Hong Kong, Taiwan, Singapore, or the diasporas of Southeast Asia and worldwide) but to an association with and literacy in a culture that is comprised of (1) origin from certain geographic localities; (2) languages (e.g., Mandarin, Taiwanese, Cantonese etc.); (3) cultural symbols (e.g., Chinese characters); (4) social practices (e.g., like the Mid-Autumn Festival or Lunar New-year) and (5) discourses (e.g., filial piety). For this article, Chineseness is less understood as some kind of ethnic essence but the term refers to an imagined collectivity that allows people at the diasporic temple to use the parlance of "we Chinese". 'Chineseness' is thus applied as a relational concept. When used in this study, the term 'Chinese' is used as an umbrella term that will be specified when needed (PRC Chinese, Taiwanese, Hong Kongese, SEA Chinese, sec. gen. Chinese American, etc.).

---

2   The notion of a Global China is based on Yang Fenggang's conception of the 'Global East' (Yang 2018, p. 795).
3   This article is part of my dissertation research, an ethnographical study of the transnational spread of Fo Guang Shan. The study is integrated in a collaborative research consortium at Leipzig University "Processes of Spatialization under the Global Condition" which is funded by the German Research Foundation (DFG). Methodically, it is based on multi-sited fieldwork in Taiwan, South Africa, USA, China, Hong Kong and Germany. Most data that is presented in the article is based on ethnographic fieldwork and semi-structured interviews collected during a nine-week residence in the US, six of which I stayed full-time at the Hsi Lai Temple, in spring 2018. However, it also considers data from a nine-week fieldwork stay at Nan Hua Temple in autumn 2017.

2. (Re)Discovering the Secular World as a Field for Buddhist Practice

Humanistic or *renjian* Buddhism constitutes one Buddhist answer to the crisis of Han Buddhism perceived by many Chinese at the turn of the 19th century. China's encounter with Western imperial aggression had led the Chinese of the time to search for reasons for the country's defeat. Han Buddhism, like other traditions, was found as a culprit by many Chinese intellectuals of the late 19th and early 20th century. It was criticized as superstitious, world denying, and a hindrance to the modernization and strengthening of Chinese society. Some Buddhist monastics, most notably Taixu 太虛, set off to modernize their tradition (Pittman 2001). Instead of the old 'Buddhism of the forests' *conglin fojiao* 叢林佛教, that was perceived as escapist and withdrawn from society, or a folk Buddhism that was accused of overly focusing on commercialist rituals for the dead, the modernizers aimed to create a Buddhism that emphasizes education and contributes to modern society (Lai 2017). They called it *renjian* Buddhism (*renjian fojiao* 人間佛教), or, in English, Buddhism of the human realm, in reference to the Buddhist cosmological subdivision of the world into six realms: the realm of the gods, the half-gods or *asuras* (Sanskrit), the humans, the animals, the hungry ghosts, and the hells. A similar term for this modernist movement is 'human life Buddhism' (*rensheng fojiao* 人生佛教) emphasizing on the importance Buddhism is to have for the living. In Taiwanese scholarship latter is often associated with Taixu, while the term *renjian* Buddhism is attributed to his student Yinshun 印順 (Jiang 1990; Yang 2006). Marcus Bingenheimer, on the other hand, argues that Taixu has in fact used both terms and both describe the same phenomenon (Bingenheimer 2007). What matters for this study, however, is that both terms stress the realm of the human world over the realms of the gods, hells and ghosts. By doing so, without denying the existence of the other realms, the modernizers highlighted the new emphasis of the tradition on the world, or, in other words, secular society.

Hsing Yun *Xingyun* 星雲, the founder of Fo Guang Shan was a student of Taixu and his order is one of the biggest representatives of the tradition today (Chandler 2004). Fo Guang Shan is involved in many spheres of society. In addition to its transnational temple network that spans not only most of the Asian continent, but also Oceania, the Americas, Europe and Africa, the order maintains a multitude of secular undertakings (Shi 2016). These include educational institutions that range from kindergartens to universities, a myriad of libraries, teahouses, vegetarian restaurants, bookstores, Buddhist art galleries, as well as mobile medical clinics, an orphanage, retirement homes, translation and publishing center, a daily newspaper, a television station and so on (Foguangshan Zongwu Huiyuan Hui 2008, vols. 3–5). Yet despite being involved in such a broad range of fields, the temple space is always at the center of Fo Guang Shan's global endeavors.

The North American headquarters of Fo Guang Shan, Hsi Lai Temple, is in many ways the organization's paragon overseas temple. Completed in 1988 and located in the Los Angeles San Gabriel Valley, the temple is the first Fo Guang Shan temple in the US. Since 1992, Fo Guang Shan lay Buddhists worldwide are organized at the Buddha's Light International Association (BLIA) (guoji foguang hui 佛光). The BLIA, which has received NGO association status by the United Nations Economic and Social Council (ECOSOC) and the Department of Public Information in 2003, has its global headquarters established at Hsi Lai Temple (vol. 6). The Los Angeles regional BLIA chapter is probably the biggest overseas chapter of the organization.[4] While BLIA in the whole of South Africa, for example, has seven regional chapters with altogether about 1000 members, the BLIA regional chapter for the Los Angeles area alone holds 23 subchapters for approximately 1800 members. In the early days of the Hsi Lai Temple the core of its members were mainly Taiwanese, yet over time a significant number of Cantonese speakers from Hong Kong, Southeast Asia and particularly Vietnam joined the organization. More recently, similar to the situation at other Fo Guang Shan temples worldwide, PRC Chinese membership numbers are on the rise. While most leading positions within the BLIA subchapters are still held by Taiwanese Americans and to a slightly lesser degree by

---

[4]   The following section is based on fieldwork data.

Cantonese speakers, some subchapters, particularly from the very affluent coastal areas, already have first generation migrants from the PRC in leading positions. Not to mention that, on the monastic side, the current abbot is a PRC Chinese. The temple attracts visitors of all ethnic and national backgrounds, yet the majority are first generation immigrants who are proficient Mandarin speakers (some additionally speak Hokkien, Hakka or Cantonese). Although many BLIA members have resided in the US for many decades and are thus fluent in English, Mandarin continues to be the main language of communication at the temple. The predominance of Mandarin is to be understood in regard to demographic changes in the Chinese diaspora that have been occurring since the 1960s.

3. Buddhism in the Ethnoburb

The lay Buddhists one encounters at the Hsi Lai Temple belong to a new generation of affluent, highly educated first generation migrants that are marked by a dual orientation towards the civic society of their new home country and the culture of their regions of origin. Earlier forms of modern Chinese migration that occurred in the 19th and early 20th century were characterized by large scale labor migration from the southern coastal provinces (mainly Guangdong and Fujian) of China (Li and Li 2013). These southern Chinese—who migrated to Southeast Asia, the Americas, Australia, and Africa—were often Cantonese (and Hokkien) speakers. Many of them settled in ethnic inner city enclaves, or Chinatowns, some of which can still be found today (Kwong 1996; Lin 1998; Zhou 2010). However, during the middle of the last century, due to international geopolitical and global economic changes in the second half of the 20th century (including the democratization of the Republic of China[ROC] and the political and economic opening of the PRC, in addition to changing national immigration and trade policies in the migration receiving countries, particularly in the United States) the demographics of the Chinese diaspora outside of Asia have changed significantly (Kuhn 2009, chp. 8). While the earlier Chinese labor migrants were often destitute and had received limited education, the Chinese migrants that emigrated after the 1960s possessed a significantly higher socioeconomic background. New migration laws that were legislated during the second half of the last century in the US attracted highly skilled professionals as well as wealthy migrants who were expected to invested money and thereby create employment for local Americans (Li 2011, pp. 35–38). The new laws also created opportunities for family sponsored migrants and low-skill professionals in areas with labor shortage. This resulted in the overseas community becoming more socially stratified, however, many of the new Chinese migrants are highly educated and often wealthy. Wang Gongwu has called this development the "upgrading of Chinese migrants" (Wang 1998). Furthermore, instead of primarily emigrating from the southern Chinese coastal regions, recent Chinese migrants originate from Taiwan, Hong Kong, Southeast Asia, and increasingly from all the different provinces of the PRC. In summary, compared to their predecessors, the socioeconomic backgrounds and geographic and national origins of the new Chinese migrants have become notably more diverse.

The diversification of places of origin and the fact that many of the current generation of first generation migrants from the PRC and Taiwan, but also to a lesser degree Southeast Asia, have received national language education in Mandarin have led to an ongoing process of Mandarin replacing Cantonese as the most common language in the Chinese diaspora.[5] The new spread of Mandarin overseas was accompanied by new modes of settlement. Migrants from Taiwan and Hong Kong were the first who took advantage of the repeal of race-based immigration policies in 1960s and thus represent the vanguard of the new form of Chinese migration. And it was these 'pioneers' from Taiwan that facilitated the construction of Fo Guang Shan's first overseas temples. It is therefore not a coincidence that Hsi Lai Temple is located in a middle class suburban community. Migrating to their new home countries, the new Chinese migrants had also generated new modes of settlement. Instead of settling in the inner city Chinatowns, as their predecessors have done, they moved directly into the

---

5   Mandarin is also called national language *guoyu* 國語 in Chinese.

suburbs. They did so in big numbers and over time created sizable suburban Chinese residential and business clusters. Some of the earlier Chinese migrants too had eventually moved upward on the social ladder and thus could afford to move on from the Chinatowns into the suburbs. Yet, there they represented only a small minority and were expected to assimilate into the mainstream society. In contrast, the new suburban Chinese residential and business clusters were able to generate spaces for cultural institutions, including religious ones, from their regions of origin. In her study on these clusters in the Los Angeles San Gabriel Valley, the US geographer Wei Li has dubbed this new form of settlement, the 'ethnoburb' (Li 2011). In the earlier days, the ethnoburb in the San Gabriel Valley was built by migrants from Taiwan. Later, Hong Kongese and Southeast Asian Chinese also migrated there in increasing numbers. Most recently, from the 2000s on, a rising number arrives from the PRC. There are ethnoburbs not only in Los Angeles, but also in Houston, the San Francisco Bay Area, the suburban New York/New Jersey region, Australia, and New Zealand (Li 2011). Many of these ethnoburbs also host Fo Guang Shan Temples or have Fo Guang Shan temples close by.

It is important to keep in mind the heterogeneous character of the overseas Chinese communities in the US as well as worldwide. The Chinese diasporic experience has generated layered and multiple identities that are constituted by nationality, gender, class and culture, etc. In other words, the Chinese diasporas are what anthropologist Pnina Werbner calls 'complex diasporas' (Werbner 2010). She claims that late modern diasporic discourses are multiple and rather than to fuse, they intersect and can even be contradictory. What connects the new diasporas despite their heterogeneity are the shared "cultural preoccupations, tastes, cuisines, music, sport, poetry, fashion and popular cinema" that are appreciated in geographical regions that exceed singular nation states (p. 76). There might be conflict in the area of origin, yet it is often possible to transcend these tensions in favor of coalitions within the diasporic space (p. 76). This applies to the Hsi Lai Temple too. At the temple, most Taiwanese and PRC Chinese deemphasize the cross-strait tensions between Taiwan and the PRC and instead stress their commonalities by adopting the parlance of 'we are all Chinese'. This unifying rhetoric also reflects a broader trend of developing new forms of social organization in the diaspora: Instead of the earlier strong focus on native place xiang 鄉, new forms of social organizing transcend identities based on home province and even national citizenship of origin (Kuhn 2009, pp. 360–64). Hsi Lai Temple and BLIA L.A. represent one religious example of the newly emerging despatialized, non-particularistic forms of organization in the Chinese diaspora. Fo Guang Shan's new Chinese cosmopolitanism proposes a modern Chinese religiosity, albeit one that is oriented towards social engagements within the secular sphere of society. However, that doesn't mean that there is no space for more traditional religious practices at Hsi Lai or any other of the Fo Guang Shan Temples. On the contrary, rituals like ceremonies for repentance (*chanhui* 懺悔), dharma assemblies (*fahui* 法會), morning and evening services (*zao wan ke* 早晚課), etc., play an important role in Fo Guang Shan *renjian* Buddhism.

4. Navigating the Secular/Religious Divide

One of the aims of the early 20th century *renjian* Buddhists was to correct the overly commercialist ritual practice of the past. The critique was primarily directed against the common practice of some monastics to provide on call ritual services for the deceased for cash. Fo Guang Shan responded to the issue by deemphasizing (yet by no means completely abandoning) rituals for the deceased, stressing the benefits of rituals for the living and using ritual as an occasion to provide Buddhist teachings (Xue 2013). The following section discusses two prevalent forms of religious practice at Fo Guang Shan: ritual and volunteer work. Of course there are also other religious practices conducted at the temple, such as copying sutras, meditation, reciting the name of the Buddha Amitabha, etc., but rituals and volunteering are amongst the most popular and attract the biggest number of people. The former is often associated with the sacred, while the latter conventionally belongs to the sphere of the secular.

Xue Yu argues that the reform of rituals by Fo Guang Shan constitute an important factor for the order's success. He particularly highlights the new focus on pedagogical aims—to teach the Dharma in order to benefit the living—and the revitalization of sacredness achieved through Fo Guang Shan's ritual reform. Not surprisingly, at Hsi Lai Temple rituals occupy an important part of the religious schedule.[6] There are many rituals at the temple, including large scale ones like the Emperor Liang Repentance Service *liang huang bao chan* 梁皇寶懺 and even, on very special occasions, the biggest and most elaborate of the Chinese Buddhist rituals: the Water Land Liberation Service *shui lu fahui*水陸法會. One of the regular rituals at Hsi Lai Temple, one that is conducted monthly, is the Great Compassion Repentance Service *da bei chan fahui* 大悲懺法會. It is praised for cleansing the minds of the devotees and attendance is normally so high that the main shrine is not big enough to hold all the people. Those who do not get one of the popular spots at the feet of the Buddha statues have to make do with a video transmission at a big conference room. The ceremony consists of the introduction and the chanting of the Great Compassion Mantra while seated and while circumambulating through the shrine room. At the end of the ceremony, the names of all the donors are recited and every attendant receives a bottle of water that is blessed through the recitation of the mantra. On its website, the Hsi Lai Temple states:

> Some of the merits often associated with the Great Compassion Mantra are: rebirth into higher realms, meeting beneficial acquaintances, having competent facilities, bountiful food and wealth, gaining great respect, and the opportunity to learn Buddhist teachings. Moreover, those who recite this mantra will not suffer death by starvation, disease, poison, flood, or fire. Water blessed with the Great Compassion Mantra is called the Great Compassion Water, and is taken by devotees for its spiritually cleansing qualities.
>
> (Hsi Lai Temple)

From the quote above we can see that at Fo Guang Shan, rituals are understood to be efficacious means for the production of good merit for oneself but also the deceased, e.g., to prolong one's life or to generate a good rebirth, etc. To attribute the capacity to generate merit to ritual performance is of course not a unique feature of Fo Guang Shan, but common in Chinese Buddhism in general. In fact, even the reformer Taixu, despite his reformist agenda, had still acknowledged the efficacy of Buddhist ritual. In his collected works, he outlines the idea of an ideal *renjian* Buddhist temple. At this model temple, dharma assemblies are conducted in order to create merits for the victims of natural disasters that occur worldwide (Taixu 1998, p. 404). Justin Ritzinger too highlights the compatibility of Taixu's modernist approach with more traditional religious goals by showing how the reformer's reinvention of the Maitreya cult connects utopian sentiments of the time to the traditional quest for Buddhahood (Ritzinger 2017).

At Fo Guang Shan, rituals are thought of as efficacious, yet they are reformed in order to adapt to the needs of contemporary Buddhists. Not only are sermons integrated in the ritual in order to provide an opportunity to learn the Buddhist Dharma, but there are other changes too: Most rituals are conducted at the weekend in order to accommodate the working hours of the disciples. The design of the shrine hall, ritual proceedings and rules of conduct are all standardized, making it is easy for any lay Buddhist of the organization at any global branch temple to orient him or herself immediately. In addition, some of the bigger ceremonies even include elaborate cultural or performance elements, like music or special lightning, etc. Xue states: "Therefore, I would argue that the rituals of Humanistic Buddhism have not necessarily desanctified or secularized Buddhism; rather, they have re-created Buddhist tradition and revitalized the idea of the sacred within, bringing the sacred into daily life of adherents and extending religious practice into the public arena." (Xue, pp. 362–63).

At Hsi Lai, most rituals are conducted at the shrine halls of the temple. Thus, within the temple space we can identify a 'spatial hierarchy of sacredness' with the shrine halls being located at the top. This spatial hierarchy is also reinforced through certain rules. While people can take pictures at most places at the temple, the practice is forbidden inside of the shrine halls. Furthermore, during the rituals

---

6   The following section is based on fieldwork data.

monastics are positioned in the front, followed by lay Buddhists who have taken refuge and the five precepts and who are thus allowed to wear the full ritual dress (*haiqing* 海青 and *manyi* 縵衣) and behind them lay Buddhists who have only taken refuge (and thus only wear a *haiqing* but no *manyi*). In the back come those who wear regular street clothes.

As mentioned above, social engagement and volunteering are seen as forms of religious practice in Fo Guang Shan. During my fieldwork, many monastics have pointed out to me that practices like ritual, meditation, and sutra study are excellent ways to be involved with Buddhism, but what is gained through these practices has to be applied to daily life. This can be practiced best by participating in one of the many volunteer groups at the temple. At Hsi Lai Temple, about 100 volunteers are on duty on an ordinary weekend day. Besides the spaces designated for religious activity, the temple runs a welcome center, a book shop, a dining hall, Chinese-, prep-, and Dharma schools for the young, an orchestra, a teahouse, a publishing house, funeral services and columbarium for the ashes of the deceased, etc. All these endeavors require manpower and support from the laity. Thus, for Fo Guang Shan Buddhists, volunteer work is the primary space of religious practice. The idea that volunteer work is a form of practice that produces merit for the lay practitioner is, of course, a staple of most if not all forms of Asian Buddhism. But while in more traditional settings volunteer work is often understood as practicing the Buddhist virtue of generosity (*dāna* in Sanskrit), Fo Guang Shan Buddhists also see it as a way to also practice Buddhist qualities like compassion, wisdom and non-self. It is in dealing with other people, through the overcoming of possible conflict that one practices Buddhism most efficiently.

In other words, for Fo Guang Shan Buddhists, while still acknowledging a spatial hierarchy of sacredness where the main shrine is located at the center, the sacred is not something that is separated from the secular, but something that has to be actualized within the secular. To volunteer at the temple is not just a way to contribute and thereby practice *dāna*, but the most efficient way to practice the Buddhist path as a whole. Other Socially Engaged Buddhists who perceive social involvement within secular society as religious activity in itself, often do so at the expense of more 'traditional' forms of Buddhist religiosity. This approach may be best represented by another Taiwanese global actor Buddhist, the Tsu Chi Foundation *ciji jijin hui* 慈濟基金會 (Huang 2009). In contrast, Fo Guang Shan reformulates the 'traditional' practices of Chinese Buddhism (particularly ritual, but also study, meditation, chanting, etc.) in a contemporary, accessible manner. The sacred, that can be experienced through the more traditional practices, is then to be actualized through volunteer work in the secular sphere. The religious and secular at Fo Guang Shan are thus not clearly separated nor are they completely merged. They permeate each other and have to be continually actualized.

5. Popularizing Chinese Buddhism for a Global World

What makes this kind of Buddhism—a Buddhism that maintains, albeit in a reformed manner, the traditional ritual practice of Chinese Buddhism but also strongly emphasizes social engagement in society—so popular in the Chinese diaspora? Fo Guang Shan is not the only Buddhist order in Taiwan (or the PRC for that matter) that has tried to develop globally, but it is amongst the most successful. When I asked Taiwanese first generation migrants at Hsi Lai Temple why they chose to join Fo Guang Shan, many stressed the difference between the Fo Guang Shan Temple and the many small (often more folk religious than Buddhist) temples of their youth that can be found everywhere on the island. One interviewee said:

> We had a temple at the corner of the street where I grew up. It was very dark and there was dust everywhere. My grandma always took me there to pray for good luck, but as a child, I was always very afraid. The Fo Guang Shan temples here are very different. They are bright and colorful, very open and welcoming. Also, the Buddhism practiced here is orthodox [*zhengxin* 正信, added by the author] Buddhism.
>
> (Interview conducted in Chinese; Hsi Lai Temple, US; spring 2018)

In my conversations, similar stories came up over and over again. The Fo Guang Shan temple is often described as a very inviting but also orthodox Buddhist space. The emphasized orthodoxy of *renjian* Buddhism is marked by a clear dissociation from folk religion but is also linked to discourses of Protestantism as a modern model religion. Many members of the Taiwanese middle class emigrated between the late 1970s and 1990s. Taiwan during this era was in the process of transitioning from a totalitarian to a democratic society. While these decades also saw the blossoming of (especially but not exclusively modernist *renjian*) Buddhism in Taiwan, the official state ideology of the governing KMT was characterized by hostility towards religion (Goossaert and Palmer 2011, p. 214). The atheist state ideology goes back to the Republican Era in China. In order to modernize the country and to defend it from Western and Japanese aggression, Chinese intellectuals, from the early 20th century on begun to apply Western categories of science, religion, and superstition to their traditions (Hammerstrom 2015). While folk religious traditions until today are often framed in terms of superstition, Buddhists did all they could in order to present Buddhism as a modern religion. They did so by stressing that Buddhism is able to contribute to modern project of nation state building (Goossaert and Palmer 2011, p. 82). The debates went on in Taiwan under the martial law period, when Protestantism and Catholicism were the only religions that received special privileges (e.g., founding universities). Showing that Buddhism was as an orthodox and modern religion that was contributing to society was particularly relevant for those Taiwanese who belonged to the middle class (Madsen 2008), and it was mostly the middle and upper classes that could afford to migrate to places like the US. Many Taiwanese perceived the United States of America as the ultimate modern nation state and Protestantism plays a major role in the public life of the country. Carolyn Chen has shown that for many Taiwanese migrants of this generation becoming American meant becoming religious (Chen 2008). Many times that meant becoming Protestant. In fact, the rate of Protestants within the Taiwanese American community is significantly higher than in Taiwan. Thus, for *renjian* Buddhists, it was and continues to be, very important to show that Buddhism is a modern religion. In this context, notions of orthodoxy fulfill the need of *renjian* Buddhists to differentiate their tradition from discourses linked to folk religion and superstition, while at the same time, involvement in charity and education aim at showing at the compatibility of Buddhism with the modern nation state project. Furthermore, within the Chinese diaspora, a modernist religiosity that is involved in charity and education demonstrates the utility of Buddhists to contribute to their host society. Hsi Lai Temple is involved in countless charities: It provides scholarships to local students, donates food for the homeless, organizes days to clean up the community, etc. Fo Guang Shan has even founded a liberal arts university in the Los Angeles San Gabriel Valley. The school has the lowest tuition for a private university in the whole state of California and provides many scholarships for local students from the lower strata of society. Besides maintaining a university, the temple also runs smaller educational institutions like a Dharma schools for kids, and Chinese language and cultural classes.

In a recent article about Christian influences on *renjian* Buddhism, Yao Yu-Shuang and Richard Gombrich argue that some of the similarities between Fo Guang Shan and Christian social involvements can be explained by conscious imitation while others represent analogous developments that occurred due to similar circumstances (Yao and Gombrich 2018). The development of *renjian* Buddhist social involvements might have been influenced by discourses of Protestantism as a modern model religion, yet they are legitimized with Buddhist language. Fo Guang Shan achieves this less by an elaborate recourse to Buddhist doctrine, but by making Buddhist teachings and culture more accessible. In order to enhance the attractiveness of Chinese Buddhism, the monastic deemphasizes the overtly philosophical and esoteric Chinese Buddhist terminology by expressing Buddhist doctrine in simple everyday language. The focus lies on the applicability of the teachings, yet while doctrinal subtleties are not pressed on the devotees, more advanced study programs, for example at one of the orders' universities, are provided for those who are interested. In addition, Fo Guang Shan has reduced the religious hierarchy between sangha and laity and interaction between the two groups is greatly enhanced. Hsi Lai Temple, for example, holds many cultural activities including book clubs, exhibitions and flower arrangement classes. Through all these activities, which are all led by a monastic, the temple generates a social space where lay Buddhists can meet with monastics, get involved in temple life, and practice their religion. Fo Guang Shan's founder Hsing Yun is a great popularizer of Buddhism. The bright colors and open spaces that characterize Fo Guang Shan temples, as well as the approachability of the monastics all contribute to this accessibility of Fo Guang Shan style Buddhism. This modern Buddhist religiosity does not only resonate with Taiwanese Americans, but attracts Chinese of different geographic origin to Hsi Lai Temple. In addition to the many Hong Kongese and Sino Vietnamese Americans, PRC Chinese come to the temple in increasing numbers. While many just come as occasional visitors to pray to a *bodhisattva* (a being that compassionately refrains from entering nirvana in order to save others and that is often worshipped as a deity in Mahayana Buddhism), attend a Buddhist ritual or enjoy a vegetarian lunch, more and more are joining the BLIA. When I asked a leading monastic at the Hsi Lai temple how to teach Buddhism to the different groups that come to the temple, he said:

> If we are talking about the Humanistic Buddhism as Fo Guang Shan promotes it, its ways and teachings, then Humanistic Buddhism is the same. What is different is that in Taiwan there is Chinese or Taiwanese culture and here it is mixed. It is both, Chinese or Asian and American or Western. We have people from Taiwan, Mainland China, Vietnam, other Asian countries and cultures, but of course also western cultures. There are local Americans and many Mexican Americans and Latinos. They come here very often too. [...] There are differences between Mainland Chinese and Taiwanese Buddhism. However, from the perspective of ordinary lay people no matter form Taiwan or China, who are not practitioners, they do not really know the differences between Humanistic Buddhism and types that are more traditional or *conglin* monasteries. They just come here to worship.
>
> (Interview conducted in English; Hsi Lai Temple, US; spring 2018)

The ethnic and national background of the visitors at Hsi Lai Temple are significantly more diverse than in Taiwan, since visitors are coming from a variety of localities in Asia and in addition include non-Asian Americans. When asked for the specific perspectives on Fo Guang Shan by Taiwanese and Mainland Chinese, this monastic states that there is less of a difference in regard to origin, but more so in terms of the degree of familiarity with (Humanistic) Buddhism. In other words, a BLIA member understands the difference between *renjian* and other forms of Buddhism, but for an ordinary worshipper, no matter from Taiwan or the mainland, these are of minor importance. Of course, it is important to note that for practicing Buddhists, who are not familiar with Fo Guang Shan and who are not BLIA members, the term *renjian* Buddhism might have a different meaning (Ji 2013). There are several different interpretations of *renjian* Buddhism in Taiwan today, but the term is also used in the PRC. Reinvented by Zhao Puchu 趙樸初, *renjian* Buddhism was given a Marxist instead of its earlier Nationalist meaning. Thus in the PRC, the term is closely connected to the political agenda of the CCP.

In the diaspora, Fo Guang Shan is transitioning from a mainly Taiwanese organization to a more pluralistic one, with PRC Chinese representing the second largest group at many temples. A leading BLIA member from South Africa states that most differences between the Taiwanese and the PRC Chinese at the temple are caused by the fact that both groups have migrated at different times.

> The issue with the mainland Chinese is they came here to work or start a business, they work very hard. So time is an issue. They don't have much time to come to the temple and become a volunteer. The Taiwanese before were well established, the economy was good, they already had retirement funds, so they had plenty of time. The new Chinese are all busy working, create a career, and create a living.
>
> (Interview conducted in English; Johannesburg, South Africa; fall 2017)

The majority of Buddhists at Fo Guang Shan temples still comes from Taiwan, especially within the higher ranks of the BLIA. Many have emigrated from Taiwan in the late 1980s and early 1990s and have reached retirement age now. Therefore they have plenty of time to serve as volunteers. However, the demography at the overseas temples is changing. Fo Guang Shan has reacted to development and begun to attract more PRC Chinese. Chinese from the PRC are now the second big group at the temple, followed by Chinese from Southeast Asia and non-Chinese locals. When I conducted fieldwork in South Africa, for example, the presidents of the local BLIA chapters were still all Taiwanese; however, the majority of the common members were already mainland Chinese.

6. Conclusions

For a Buddhist organization to be included in Main and Lai's revised definition of Socially Engaged Buddhism, social involvement within the secular sphere of society has to be understood as essentially religious. This definition also applies to Fo Guang Shan *renjian* Buddhism. Although Fo Guang Shan does incorporate the whole range of 'traditional' forms of Buddhist practice, social engagement is given a special function. Volunteering at or for the temple is not just a way of practicing the Buddhist virtue of generosity, but constitutes a space of Buddhist practice that is linked to modernist projects such as nation state building, social welfare, and education. However, this is not done at the expense of other more traditionally religious forms of cultivation, but in addition to them. Rituals like repentance services or dharma assemblies are amongst the most popular religious activities at Fo Guang Shan temples in Taiwan as well as abroad. Social engagement is not the only modernized Buddhist practice at the temple; in fact, the more 'traditional' Buddhist practices underwent reform too. Through a number of operations—the standardization and reformation of Buddhist ritual, the simplification of Buddhist language, the increase of monastic-lay interaction, the application of culture and performance elements to the propagation of the dharma and the establishment of discourses of orthodoxy—a particularly modern yet genuinely Chinese experience of the sacred is facilitated. This modern and 'easily accessible sacred' is to be actualized within the secular sphere. Volunteer work serves as the primary space of practice for this undertaking. Thereby, the Fo Guang Shan overseas temple achieves to preserve the sacred aura of more traditional forms of Chinese Buddhism. At the same time, it is engaged in the secular society of its respective host countries through its many charitable and educational endeavors.

Fo Guang Shan is a centrally organized Buddhist order and its facilities, activities, and rituals are all standardized. While the temple design and religious practices are thus similar everywhere, the people at the temples are not. At an overseas temple, one encounters a much bigger variety of people: Chinese that origin from a variety of places in Asia as well as non-Chinese. This paper has focused on the former group. Different understandings of Buddhism might play a role for the occasional visitor but they lose their importance with increasing proximity to the order. Thus, for the common BLIA member in the diaspora, origin from a specific locality in Asia plays only a minor role on their outlook on Buddhism. In the diaspora, Fo Guang Shan achieves to establish itself as a religious civic actor that transcends particularistic identities based on local origin. As Dean and van der Veer put it, religions "[...] produce worlds of experience, in which identities can take shape and partial subjectivities can form, often relatively independent of the processes of capture of identity by the confessional nation state" (Dean and van der Veer 2018, p. 6). By not overtly stressing its Taiwanese origin and through the application of the common parlance of 'we are all Chinese', the Fo Guang Shan overseas temples propose a global Buddhist cosmopolitanism that transcends the older province of origin-based particularisms of the Chinese diaspora. Instead, the overseas temple represents a bi-directional cultural orientation that links a global China with the specific host society of a diaspora community.

Funding: This article is part of my dissertation research, an ethnographical study of the transnational spread of Fo Guang Shan. The study is integrated in a collaborative research consortium at Leipzig University "Processes of Spatialization under the Global Condition" which is funded by the German Research Foundation (DFG).

Conflicts of Interest: The author declares no conflict of interest.

References

Asad, Talal. 2003. *Formations of the Secular: Christianity, Islam, Modernity*. Stanford: Stanford University Press, ISBN 978-0804747684.

Bingenheimer, Marcus. 2007. Some Remarks on the Usage of Renjian Fojiao and the Contribution of Venerable Yinshun to Chinese Buddhist Modernism. In *Development and Practice of Humanitarian Buddhism: Interdisciplinary Perspectives*. Edited by Muzhu Xu, Jinhua Chen and Lori Meeks. Hualien: Tzu Chi University Press, pp. 141–62. ISBN 978-986-7625-08-3.

Casanova, Jose. 2018. Asian Catholicism, Interreligious Colonial Encounters and Dynamics of Secularism in Asia. In *The Secular in South, East, and Southeast Asia*. Edited by Kenneth Dean and Peter van der Veer. Cham: Palgrave Macmillan, pp. 13–35. ISBN 978-3319893686.

Chandler, Stuart. 2004. *Establishing a Pure Land on Earth: The Foguang Buddhist Perspective on Modernization and Globalization*. Honolulu: University of Hawai'i Press, ISBN 978-0824827465.

Chen, Carolyn. 2008. *Getting Saved in America: Taiwanese Immigration and Religious Experience*. Princeton: Princeton University Press, ISBN 978-0-691-16466-3.

Dean, Kenneth, and Peter van der Veer, eds. 2018. *The Secular in South, East, and Southeast Asia*. Cham: Palgrave Macmillan, ISBN 978-3319893686.

Foguangshan Zongwu Huiyuan Hui 佛光山宗務委員會, ed. 2008. *Foguangshan Kaishan Sishi Zhou Nian Jinian Tekan* 佛光山開山四十週年紀念特刊, Fo Guang Shan 40th anniversary ed. 10 vols. Gaoxiong 高雄: Foguang wenhua 佛光文化, ISBN 9789574572083.

Goossaert, Vincent, and David A. Palmer. 2011. *The Religious Question in Modern China*. Chicago: University of Chicago Press, ISBN 9780226304168.

Hammerstrom, Erik J. 2015. *The Science of Chinese Buddhism: Early Twentieth-Century Engagements*. New York: Columbia University Press, ISBN 978-0-231-17034-5.

Hsi Lai Temple. Available online: http://www.hsilai.org/en/df/gc.php (accessed on 11 September 2018).

Huang, C. Julia. 2009. *Charisma and Compassion: Cheng Yen and the Buddhist Tzu Chi movement*. Cambridge and London: Harvard University Press, ISBN 978-0674031333.

Ji, Zhe. 2013. Zhao Puchu and His Renjian Buddhism. *The Eastern Buddhist* 44: 35–58.

Jiang, Can-teng 江燦騰. 1990. *Xian dai Zhong guo fo jiao si xiang lun ji (yi)* 現代中國佛教思想論集(一). Taibei 台北: Xin wen feng 新文豐, ISBN 9789571700670.

Kuhn, Philip A. 2009. *Chinese among Others: Emigration in Modern Times*. Lanham, Boulder and New York: Rowman & Littlefield Publishers, ISBN 9780742567498.

Kwong, Peter. 1996. *The New Chinatown*. New York: Hill and Wang, ISBN 978-0809015856. First published 1987.

Lai, Rongdao. 2017. The Wuchang ideal: Buddhist education and identity production in Republican China. *Studies in Chinese Religions* 3: 55–70. [CrossRef]

Li, Wei. 2011. *Ethnoburb: The New Ethnic Community in Urban America*. Honolulu: University of Hawai'i Press, ISBN 978-0-8248-3671-9.

Li, Peter S., and Eva X. Li. 2013. The Chinese Overseas Population. In *Routledge Handbook of the Chinese Diaspora*. Edited by Chee-Beng Tan. London and New York: Routledge, pp. 31–41. ISBN 978-0-415-60056-9.

Lin, Jan. 1998. *Reconstructing Chinatown: Ethnic Enclaves and Global Change*. Minneapolis: University of Minnesota Press, ISBN 978-0816629053.

Long, Darui. 2000. Humanistic Buddhism from Venerable Tai Xu to Grand Master Hsing Yun. *Hsi Lai Journal of Humanistic Buddhism* 1: 53–84.

Madsen, Richard. 2008. Religious Renaissance and Taiwan's Modern Middle Classes. In *Chinese Religiosities: Afflictions of Modernity and State Formation*. Edited by Yang Mayfair Mei-hui. Berkeley and London: University of California Press, pp. 295–322. ISBN 978-0520098640.

Main, Jessica Lynn, and Rongdao Lai. 2013. Reformulating "Socially Engaged Buddhism" as an Analytical Category. *The Eastern Buddhist* 44: 1–34.

Pittman, Don Alvin. 2001. *Toward a Modern Chinese Buddhism: Taixu's Reforms*. Honolulu: University of Hawai'i Press, ISBN 978-0824822316.

Ritzinger, Justin. 2017. *Anarchy in the pure land: Reinventing the cult of Maitreya in modern Chinese Buddhism*. New York: Oxford University Press, ISBN 978-0190491161.

Shi, Yongdong 釋永東. 2016. *Renjian fojiao shijie zhanwang* 人間佛教世界展望. Taibei 台北: Lan tai 蘭臺, ISBN 9789865633226.

Taixu. 1998. *Taixu Dashi Quanshu* 太虛大師全書. Taipei: Shandao Si Fojing Liutong Chu, Available online: https://katalog.ub.uni-leipzig.de/Collection/0001141909 (accessed on 31 October 2018).

Taylor, Charles. 2007. *A Secular Age*. Cambridge: The Belknap Press of Harvard University Press, ISBN 978-0674986916.

Wang, Gungwu. 1998. Upgrading the Migrant: Neither Huaqiao nor Huaren. In *The LAST Half Century of Chinese Overseas*. Edited by Elizabeth Sinn. Hong Kong: Hong Kong University Press, pp. 15–34. ISBN 978-9622094468.

Werbner, Pnina. 2010. Complex Diasporas. In *Diasporas: Concepts, Intersections, Identities*. Edited by Kim Knott and Seán McLoughlin. London: Zed, pp. 74–78. ISBN 978-1-84277-948-4.

Xue, Yu. 2013. Re-Creation of Rituals in Humanistic Buddhism: A Case Study of Fo Guang Shan. *Asian Philosophy* 23: 350–64.

Yang, Huinan 楊惠南. 2006. Cong rensheng fojiao dao renjian fojiao 從人生佛教到人間佛教. In *Dangdai Fojiao Sixiang Zhanwang* 當代佛教思想展望. Taibei 台北: Dongda 東大, pp. 75–125. ISBN 9571928275.

Yang, Fenggang. 2018. Afterword. In *Encyclopedia of Christianity in the Global South*. Edited by Mark A. Lamport. Lanham: Rowman & Littlefield, pp. 957–58. ISBN 978-1442271562.

Yao, Yu-Shuang, and Richard Gombrich. 2018. Christianity as Model and Analogue in the Formation of the 'Humanistic' Buddhism of Tài Xū and Hsīng Yún. *Buddhist Studies Review* 34: 205–37. [CrossRef]

Zhou, Min. 2010. *Chinatown: The Socioeconomic Potential of an Urban Enclave*. Philadelphia: Temple University Press, ISBN 978-1566393379.

MDPI
St. Alban-Anlage 66
4052 Basel
Switzerland
Tel. +41 61 683 77 34
Fax +41 61 302 89 18
www.mdpi.com

Religions Editorial Office
E-mail: religions@mdpi.com
www.mdpi.com/journal/religions

www.ingramcontent.com/pod-product-compliance
Lightning Source LLC
Chambersburg PA
CBHW051315020426
42333CB00028B/3347